BOXING
Unseen Archives

BOXING
Unseen Archives

Photographs by the
Daily Mail

Tim Hill

p

This is a Parragon Book
First published in 2002

Parragon
Queen Street House
4 Queen Street
Bath, BA1 1HE, UK

All photographs
©Associated Newspapers archive

Text ©Parragon

Produced by Atlantic Publishing Ltd

Designed by John Dunne
Origination by Croxons PrePress

A catalogue record for this book is
available from the British Library.
ISBN 0-75258-516-9

Printed in China

Contents

Acknowledgements 7

Introduction 9

John L. Sullivan	10	Joe Louis	106	Larry Holmes	290
James J. Corbett	12	Ezzard Charles	130	Michael Spinks	298
Bob Fitzsimmons	15	Jersey Joe Walcott	143	Mike Tyson	302
James J Jeffries	20	Rocky Marciano	150	James Douglas	306
Tommy Burns	24	Floyd Patterson	160	Evander Holyfield	324
Jack Johnson	28	Ingemar Johansson	173	Riddick Bowe	340
Jess Willard	34	Floyd Patterson	174	Evander Holyfield	344
Jack Dempsey	40	Sonny Liston	186	Michael Moorer	350
Gene Tunney	62	Cassius Clay (Muhammad Ali)	202	George Foreman	355
Max Schmeling	69	Joe Frazier	252	Evander Holyfield	362
Jack Sharkey	72	George Foreman	266	Lennox Lewis	368
Primo Carnera	77	Muhammad Ali	274	Hasim Rahman	373
Max Baer	80	Leon Spinks	282	Lennox Lewis	374
James J Braddock	88	Muhammad Ali	286		

Acknowledgements

The photographs in this book are from the archives of the Daily Mail. They have been carefully maintained by the dedicated staff in the Picture Library without whose help this book would not have been possible.

Particular thanks to Steve Torrington, Dave Sheppard, Brian Jackson, Alan Pinnock, Paul Rossiter, Richard Jones and all the staff.

Thanks also to Cliff Salter, Richard Betts, Peter Wright, Trevor Bunting and Simon Taylor.

Design by John Dunne.

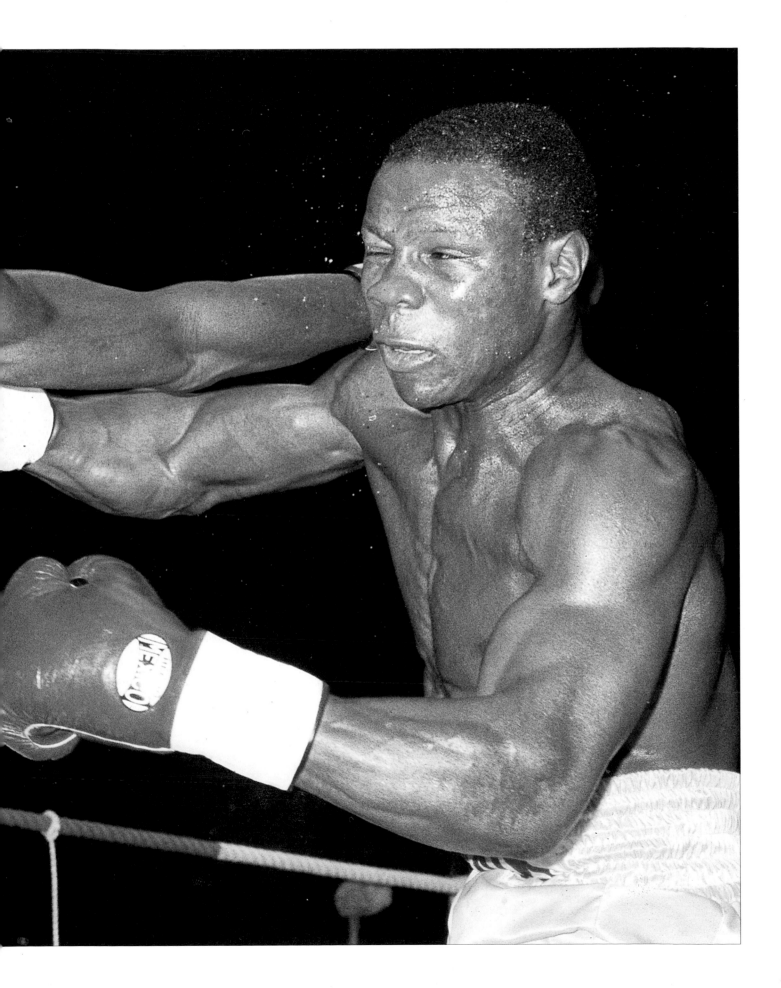

Introduction
The greatest prize in sport

The heavyweight championship of the world is universally regarded as the greatest prize in sport. Even when boxers fought for a tiny fraction of the sums that Lennox Lewis currently commands, there was always the glory of the title to spur them on. Men have gone to extraordinary lengths to win the crown, and equally extraordinary lengths to hang onto it. The Daily Mail's Boxing: Unseen Archives tells the story of how each achieved membership of this most exclusive of clubs.

To say that the book chronicles the history of the heavyweight championship is to provoke two further questions: Which fighter do you take as the historical benchmark? And how do you deal with the problem of multiple pretenders to the crown, one which has dogged boxing for so many years?

The answer to the first question is easy: John L. Sullivan. By the mid-19th century, polite society on both sides of the Atlantic frowned on boxing, regarding it as an undesirable, morally corrupting pursuit. Banned in Britain and most American states, prize-fighting was pushed to the margins. John L. Sullivan changed all that. The "Boston Strong Boy" popularised boxing almost single-handedly, and in the process became its first superstar. Crucially, he also gave the sport mainstream respectability. Finally, he ruled the fistic world at a time when bare-knuckle prize-fights gradually gave way to glove contests under Marquis of Queensberry rules. In short, boxing's modern era began with John L. Sullivan, and so does this book.

The second question, which is all about the integrity of the heavyweight title, is a thorny one. When James J. Jeffries retired undefeated in 1905, he nominated which two boxers should fight for the right to succeed him. Jeffries was an unabashed racist, and it was no surprise that he named two indifferent white fighters, Marvin Hart and Jack Root, overlooking the claims of the crop of brilliant black heavyweights that was around at the time. The greatest of these, Jack Johnson, got a second chance three years later. Others, such as Sam Langford - a boxer thought by some to be on a par with Johnson - weren't so lucky.

60 years later, a different kind of travesty took place, one sanctioned by the sport's governing body itself. The World Boxing Association stripped Muhammad Ali of the title for the heinous crime of agreeing to a rematch with Sonny Liston. The WBA conducted its own tournament and duly installed the winner, Ernie Terrell, as champion. This was the first egregious decision on the part of the boxing authorities; it wasn't to be the last. Since the 1970s, there have been long periods - farcical periods - in which rival organisations have trumpeted their own champions. Vested interests have made unification fights all too rare a sighting in the sporting calendar.

The underlying principle of this book can be expressed in the words that Riddick Bowe used in 1992, when he became the latest champion to have the title taken from him by a bureaucrat, not an opponent. Bowe said: "Boxing titles are won and lost in the ring. In order to be a champion you must fight a champion and beat a champion. "Wherever a fork in the championship road has occurred, this book has sought to apply the Bowe test in determining which path to follow.

Woven into the thread of the heavyweight championship over the past 120 years are some of the greats of the lower divisions. Boxers of the stature up of Georges Carpentier, the glamorous French light-heavyweight who brought women flocking to the ring in the post-World War One era; Sugar Ray Robinson, the welterweight and middleweight champion of the 1940s and 1950s who is still widely regarded as the best pound-for-pound fighter of all time; and Robinson's namesake, Sugar Ray Leonard, who in the 1980s joined Thomas "The Hit Man" Hearns as the only two fighters in history to have held world titles at five different weights.

But the main focal point of the book remains the heavyweight crown, and the circuitous route by which it has passed from John L. Sullivan to Lennox Lewis. Accompanying the detailed commentary are more than 600 stunning photographs from the Daily Mail archives, many reproduced for the first time. Together they describe a 120-year journey, one which is punctuated with triumph and heartbreak. It makes for unremittingly compelling theatre. The dramatis personae are men of enormous courage and skill. The ring is their stage. The stories are of men prepared to risk all for the ultimate sporting prize.

John L. Sullivan

John L. Sullivan was boxing's first superstar. He dominated the heavyweight scene for 10 years, during the time when it emerged from the seedy world of bare-knuckle prizefights to become a mainstream sport under Marquis of Queensberry rules.

John Lawrence Sullivan was born in Boston, Massachusetts, on 15 October 1858. His Irish father was small of stature but very handy with his fists. John L. inherited those skills in abundance. He scrapped his way through the best Boston had to offer, then became the state champion when he beat Dan Dwyer, the recognised holder of that title. It wasn't long before this KO specialist from New England, nicknamed the "Boston Strong Boy", was the talk of fight fans everywhere. He raised his profile even more when he met John Flood in 1881. Flood, who was known as the "Bull's Head Terror", was thought to be the man who could bring Sullivan's inexorable progress to a halt. The two met on a barge anchored in the Hudson River. The contest was conducted under London Prize Ring Rules, which also allowed wrestling holds. Such contests were of unlimited duration, each round continuing until one man went down. A floored fighter had 30 seconds to "come up to scratch". Failure to reach the mark within the specified time meant defeat. The Sullivan-Flood fight lasted 16 minutes, during which time the "Bull's Head Terror" had been put down on eight occasions. Flood's seconds had seen enough and threw in the sponge.

After taking a few more scalps, Sullivan earned himself a crack at America's recognised champion, Paddy Ryan. Ryan, a New Yorker who hailed from Tipperary, had won the title from Joe Goss in May 1880. The championship lineage of the previous 30 years hadn't always been totally pure. Some of the title claims in that time had been questionable. Sullivan was about to change all that.

Greatest weapon

On 7 February 1882, he took the crown from Ryan, needing just 10 minutes to finish the job. Having put Ryan down a number of times already, Sullivan ended proceedings with a trip-hammer right, his greatest weapon. The title, and the $5,000 purse, were his. A new boxing era was born. Sullivan proceeded to milk his newly acquired status for all it was worth. An extrovert and a braggart, he toured the country, throwing down the gauntlet to anyone who fancied his chances of going four rounds with the champion. Some 50 men tried their hand. Only one is said to have claimed the $1,000 prize on offer, and he was a rugged pro who used his experience and every trick in the book simply to survive the allotted time.

Those vanquished by Sullivan during his travelling circus days do not feature in the record books. While his victims doubtless included many complete no-hopers, Sullivan must have faced the roughest, toughest bar-room brawlers each town had to offer. He can't be accused of being a sleeping champion, not in the early stages of his reign, at least. John L. was soon the idol of the masses. His exciting, all-action fighting style, together with his charismatic personality, endeared him to a population only too keen to embrace a new sporting hero. By 1887, Sullivan's popularity was at its height. Boxing was the number one sport, with Sullivan its undisputed champion and star attraction.

Battle of the belts

To coincide with his latest national tour, some of Boston's prominent citizens and sports fans decided to honour their city's favourite son with a trophy: a jewel-encrusted gold belt. It was inscribed with the words: "Presented to the Champion of Champions, John L. Sullivan, by the citizens of the United States, July 4, 1887". This was not the only belt in circulation, however. Richard K. Fox, publisher of the *Police Gazette*, had also commissioned a belt to be made. This was awarded to his own heavyweight protégé, a man named Jake Kilrain. Kilrain was a veteran prizefighter, one of the best men of his era, and Fox had issued a challenge to Sullivan to fight his man. When John L. turned him down, Fox responded by declaring Kilrain the champion, complete with new "championship" belt. Understandably, there was considerable needle between the two camps. When Sullivan was awarded his belt, he praised its superior craftsmanship and beauty compared with Kilrain's, which he disparagingly described as "a dog collar".

The ill-feeling would rumble on for two more years before Sullivan and Kilrain could settle the issue inside the ring. First, there was an extended tour to Europe, where Sullivan had one man in particular in his sights: England's Charley Mitchell. Sullivan and Mitchell had met before, at Madison Square Garden in May 1883. England's top fighter had crossed the Atlantic, making it known that he had come with the express purpose of knocking Sullivan out. He couldn't back up his words on that occasion, however. Mitchell had been knocked out of the ring in the second round, and floored again in the third, at which point the police intervened to prevent the challenger from taking further punishment.

The bad blood between the two men was still in evidence five years later, when they met for a second time. The rematch took place near Chantilly, France, on the estate of Baron Rothschild. Their first encounter had been a glove fight; this time it was a bare-knuckle contest.

Underhand tactics

Mitchell did much better on this occasion, taking Sullivan 39 rounds before the contest was declared a draw. Both men claimed to have had the better of things, with Sullivan probably having the stronger claim. Mitchell had certainly avoided the champion's heaviest punches, but his survival also involved underhand tactics. He had repeatedly gone to ground without being hit, frustrating Sullivan's efforts to finish him off.

Back in the USA, Sullivan finally agreed to a showdown with his other big rival, Jake Kilrain. It took place in Mississippi, on a baking July day in 1889. It was a bare-knuckle contest fought under London Prize Ring Rules. It would be the last heavyweight championship fight conducted under such rules, and the two men made it a contest to remember. Two hours and 16 minutes after the protagonists squared up to each other, Kilrain's seconds threw in the sponge. Their man was out on his feet at the end of the 75 rounds that the fight had lasted. The battle of the two belts had been decided in the champion's favour, but it had been a bruising, attritional battle. It would be three years before Sullivan put his title on the line again. In that time, the champion lived life to the full, and also set a precedent that many of his successors would follow by taking to the stage. Apart from the boxing that was incorporated into his theatrical role, Sullivan fought only exhibition bouts during this three-year period. One of these matched him against James Corbett, the two men sparring for four rounds in full dress suits in May 1891. The following year, on 7 September 1892, they met again, this time for real. Despite being a month short of his 34th birthday, unfit and grossly overweight, Sullivan went into the fight as hot favourite. But his 10-year, vice-like hold on the championship was about to be broken by a man who was younger, fitter and who elevated ringcraft to a completely new level.

John L. Sullivan

Nickname:	"Boston Strong Boy"
Born:	Roxbury, Boston USA October 15 1858
Died:	February 2 1918
Height:	5' 10$\frac{1}{4}$"
Weight:	190-229lbs.
Heavyweight Champion of America:	1882-1892
Record:	Won 45 (31 KOs) Lost 1 Drawn 1

Boxing's first superstar

John L. Sullivan became a national hero in the ten years that he dominated heavyweight boxing. A notorious reveller in his youth, Sullivan mended his dissolute ways in later life. He went on lecture tours of America, warning of the evils of the demon drink.

James J. Corbett World Heavyweight Champion: 1892-1897

James J. Corbett secured his place in boxing history by becoming the first world heavyweight champion under Marquis of Queensberry rules. Perhaps more importantly, he assured himself a place in the pantheon of boxing greats by elevating pugilism from the preserve of the bar-room brawler to a "noble art" founded on science. Corbett's analytical approach to the sport led him to appreciate that technique was as important as brute strength, and superior ringcraft could compensate for lack of inches, pounds and power.

Corbett was born in San Francisco on 1 September 1866, of Irish-American stock. His talent for boxing manifested itself early, schoolboy skirmishes causing him to be expelled from two schools. He started work as a bank clerk, but he was bitten by the fight bug and yearned for a career in the ring. It was his white-collar background, impeccable manners and immaculate dress sense that earned him the soubriquet "Gentleman Jim". In fact, there were many instances of anything but gentlemanly conduct. Corbett's two wives had to put up with his serial womanising. He was also a racist, a trait which came to the fore when Jack Johnson became champion in 1908.

Left hook is born

It was in one of Corbett's early professional fights, in May 1889, that he is credited with inventing the left hook. The left jab was a favourite weapon in his armoury, but on this occasion - a bruising, attritional encounter with Joe Choynski - Corbett injured his hand. He improvised by throwing the punch in an arc and striking with the inside of the glove. In protecting his fingers Corbett showed off the left hook for the first time. However, it was a raking left to Choynski's chin which ended the contest, in the 27th round.

Corbett's battle with Australia's foremost prizefighter, Peter Jackson, two years later made the Choynski bout seem a sprint in comparison. This epic contest, held at the famous California Athletic Club on 21 May 1891, lasted 61 gruelling rounds. Jackson, nicknamed "The Black Prince", was a formidable fighter. American heavyweights, including the reigning champion John L. Sullivan, had avoided climbing into the ring with the man widely regarded as the black heavyweight champion of the world. Corbett needed all his celebrated fleetness of foot to keep out of range of Jackson's murderous right hand. The Australian did eventually connect with some mighty blows, which made Corbett wince. Gentleman Jim also came close to winning. A flurry of punches in the 28th round saw Jackson out on his feet, only for the bell to come to his rescue. Finally, more than four hours after the two men stepped into the ring, the referee declared a no-contest. By that time, Corbett and Jackson had slowed to a walk and could barely lift their arms.

The Corbett-Jackson fight has gone down as one of the greatest in the sport's history. For the two protagonists, however, the aftermath was very different. Corbett enjoyed international acclaim and an enhanced reputation. More importantly, the fight was a springboard which earned him a tilt at Sullivan's world crown the following year. Jackson, whom Corbett later described as the greatest fighter he'd ever seen, was less fortunate. He died from tuberculosis nine years later, disillusioned and penniless.

Sparring in evening dress

Corbett first stepped into the ring with Sullivan barely a month after the Jackson fight. It was an exhibition match, however, the two men sparring for four rounds in full evening dress. On 7 September the following year, the two met in New Orleans, this time for real, with the world title at stake.

The Boston Strong Boy was almost 34 when he met Gentleman Jim, and had been champion for 10 years. He was undoubtedly past his prime, and a tendency to overindulge in food and booze didn't exactly help to keep him in peak condition. Indeed, he preferred to make good money by appearing on stage. He lived quite well off his fearsome reputation and world title, and didn't want to risk losing his crown. He delayed meeting Corbett for some time, but eventually the lure of a $10,000 winner-take-all fight proved irresistible.

Despite the fact that a fair amount of Sullivan's 212lb bulk was excess fat, he was nevertheless a strong favourite to put Corbett away. What followed was a masterclass from the challenger as he took boxing into a new dimension. He easily evaded Sullivan's big swinging punches, then picked the champion off at will with incisive, stinging jabs. Sullivan fought gamely for 20 rounds, though he cut a sorry figure by that time. The end came in round 21, when Corbett caught his man with a right which put him down for the count.

Cashing in on title

Among those who witnessed the birth of the new era was world middleweight champion Bob Fitzsimmons, who lost little time in throwing down the gauntlet to Gentleman Jim. Like Sullivan in the latter years of his reign, Corbett was in no hurry to rush into a defence of his crown. First he wanted to cash in on his title. He too turned to the stage, and later appeared in a number of films. Apart from a lucrative income from acting, Corbett was also among the first sportsmen to boost his earnings through endorsements.

Over the next four years, Corbett fought a number of exhibition bouts, but defended his title only once, a brutal demolition of Englishman Charley Mitchell. He then considered retiring from the sport, even going so far as to nominate the man he believed should succeed him, Ireland's Peter Maher. He had no authority to make such a decision, and Fitzsimmons undermined it even further by dispatching Maher inside a round. Gentleman Jim had little choice now but to accept Fitzsimmons's challenge.

The fight took place in Carson City, on 17 March 1897. Apart from the title, there was a $15,000 purse at stake, with a $5,000 side bet. It was a winner-take-all deal.

Jim Corbett

Nickname:	"Gentleman"
Born:	San Francisco, California, USA September 1, 1866
Died:	February 18, 1933
Height:	6' 1½"
Weight:	173-190lbs
World Heavyweight Champion:	1892-1897
Record:	Won 11 (7 KOs), Lost 4, Drawn 2

Corbett sunk by "solar plexus" punch

Bob Fitzsimmons (left) on his way to winning the world title from "Gentleman" Jim Corbett in Carson City, 1897. Ruby Robert's famous "solar plexus" punch ended Corbett's 5-year reign.

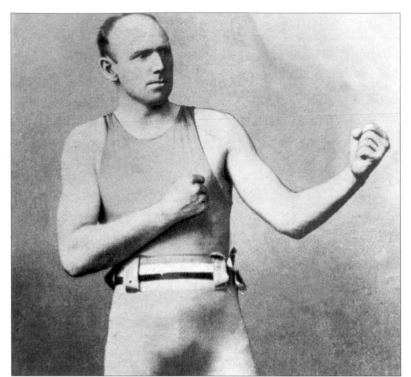

"The Fighting Blacksmith"

Left: Bob Fitzsimmons had spindly, featherweight's legs, but from the waist up he was a true heavyweight. His enormous upper body strength was developed during his days as a blacksmith.

Below left: A rare early photograph of John L. Sullivan, in classic ring pose. Sullivan could have been a professional baseball player, but chose to seek fame and fortune in the ring.

Below: Sullivan's tenure as champion spanned the era of bare-knuckle prize-fights and glove contests under Queensberry Rules. He preferred the latter, since he only had to put his opponents down for 10 seconds to secure victory.

Bob Fitzsimmons

World Heavyweight Champion: 1897-1899

Bob Fitzsimmons cut a strange, almost comical figure in the ring. He was variously described as "grotesque" and "a cartoonist's caricature". He had a powerful, heavyweight's torso - a legacy of his years working as a blacksmith in New Zealand - but his legs were spindly and he was knock-kneed. Facially, he looked older than his years. He had receding red hair and was covered with freckles. His colouring gave him his politest nickname, Ruby Robert. He was also known as The Fighting Blacksmith and, less kindly, The Freckled Freak. Fitzsimmons was born in Helston, Cornwall on the 26 May, 1863. His family emigrated to New Zealand when he was a child, and it was in the antipodes that he carved a reputation as a formidable fighter. He served his boxing apprenticeship under the tutelage of the Norfolk gypsy, Jem Mace, and then in the Sydney gym-saloon of Mace's protege, Larry Folcy. Fitzsimmons learned his lessons well. In eight years he suffered only one defeat. When he was 28, Fitzsimmons headed for the United States to further his career. In an age before global media, he was an unknown quantity to the American boxing scene. Opponents and fans alike must have raised an eyebrow at this odd-looking figure, weighing in at just 11st 4lb, who was prepared to take on all-comers from middleweight to heavyweight. They quickly learned that Fitzsimmons packed a mighty punch for one so light. Having taken the middleweight title by beating "Nonpareil" Jack Dempsey in 1891, Fitzsimmons set his sights on the heavyweight crown. He was present at the Sullivan-Corbett fight a year later, and wasted no time issuing a challenge to the new champion. It would be five years before Corbett's hand was forced. In the intervening period one of Fitzsimmons's victims was Peter Maher, the man Corbett nominated as heir to his crown when he flirted with retirement. The pressure on the champion was growing. Even the public joined in the fun, regularly taunting Corbett for avoiding Fitzsimmons.

"Movin' pitcher"

Ruby Robert raised the stakes by taking on Maher yet again. This time he beat the big Irishman even more easily. Annoyed that the fight was to be filmed on the new Edison Kinetoscope and that he was to receive no percentage of the money the "movin' pitcher" would make, Fitzsimmons responded by knocking Maher out barely a minute into the contest, and before the Kinetoscope operators had got their machines working. The clash between Corbett and Fitzsimmons was now inevitable. In the run-up to the contest, which took place in Carson City, Nevada, the ill-feeling between the two men was much in evidence. On one occasion, Corbett violently tweaked Fitzsimmons's nose in

a hotel lobby. The champion then added insult to injury by asking his brother to sign the register on Fitzsimmons's behalf. Fitzsimmons, who was semi-literate, had to be restrained, otherwise the big fight would have been staged there and then. It is little wonder that there was no handshake when the two stepped into the ring just before noon on 17 March, 1897. Taller, 15lb heavier, faster and with a glorious array of punches, the champion toyed with Ruby Robert for the first five rounds. Strutting and grinning, Corbett picked his man off at will and made him look like a novice. In round 6 a vicious uppercut from Corbett lifted Fitzsimmons clean off his feet. The challenger slumped to the ground and lay like a rag doll. Corbett stood by menacingly, ready to go in for the kill. Referee George Siler insisted that Corbett retire before he began the count. That, and the fact that Corbett berated Siler for counting too slowly, gave Fitzsimmons time to recover.

Burning desire

Corbett continued to mete out a lot of punishment but couldn't put Fitzsimmons away. The challenger was tough as teak; he also had a burning desire to win. By the 10th round, Corbett was beginning to tire and the tide began to turn. In round 14 Corbett rocked backwards to avoid a scything right from Fitzsimmons. Previously he had danced his way out of trouble; now he wanted to stay in close so that he could counter. It proved a fatal mistake. He left his body exposed momentarily and Fitzsimmons drove a sickening left into the pit of the champion's stomach. Fitzsimmons's wife Ruby, who was in her husband's corner, had been yelling "hit him in the slats!"; Ruby Robert finally got the chance to heed her advice in the 14th round, to decisive effect. The body blow dropped Corbett to his knees, his face contorted with agony. He tried to get up at eight and reached for the ropes, only to fall ignominiously flat on his face. When he did recover, an incandescent Corbett railed at his opponent that it was just a lucky punch. It was certainly a punch that Fitzsimmons had used to good effect before.

Wyatt Earp betting ring

The previous year he had sent Tom Sharkey writhing to the canvas with an identical blow, in a contest refereed by the legendary Wyatt Earp. The "solar plexus punch", as it came to be known, was devastating and perfectly legal. Against Sharkey, Earp had ruled it a low blow and disqualified Fitzsimmons, but that was because he was involved in a betting ring which had invested heavily on Sharkey. There were no such underhand shenanigans this time; the solar plexus punch won Bob Fitzsimmons the heavyweight championship of the world at the age of 33. Corbett could hardly complain when Fitzsimmons ignored all pleas for a rematch, the new champion also preferring to cash in on his celebrity status by taking to the stage. It would be two years before he was tempted into a title defence, and then only to satisfy the clamours of the boxing fraternity and to replenish his own coffers. Instead of a return with Corbett, Fitzsimmons lined up James J. Jeffries, a mountain of a man whom Gentlemen Jim had sparred with and used as a punchbag. On the eve of the fight, which took place at Coney Island Athletic Club on 9 June, 1899, the supremely confident champion went out with friends, carousing late into the night. He believed that Jeffries' 50lb weight advantage would simply mean he would hit the canvas that much harder. But it was Fitzsimmons who was to come down to earth with a bump.

Bob Fitzsimmons

World Heavyweight Champion:	1897-1899
World Light-Heavyweight Champion:	1903-1905
World Middleweight Champion:	1891-1897
Record: Won 46 (39 KOs) Lost 8 Drawn 10	

Below: "Sailor" Tom Sharkey, pictured when he was about 50 years old. In 1896, Sharkey won a controversial fight against Bob Fitzsimmons when the latter was disqualified for a low blow. The following year, Fitzsimmons won the world title with an identical punch.

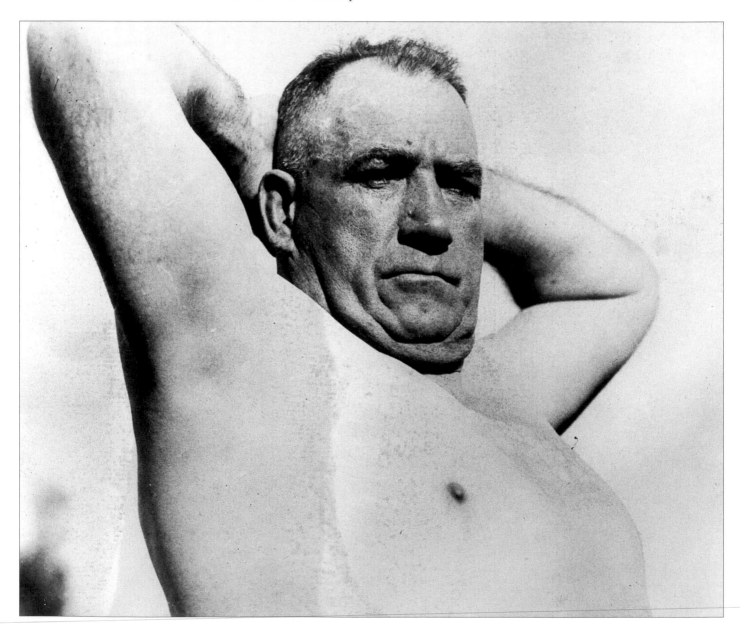

Jeffries the powerhouse fighting machine

Above: Jim Jeffries was no great stylist, but he was immensely strong. His power and durability brought him the title, which he held for five years before retiring undefeated.

Johnson the first black champion

Left: Jack Johnson honed his skills by fighting groups of other young black hopefuls for nickels and dimes to entertain white boxing fans. It was an experience which shaped his attitude to whites when he became champion.

Below: In 1910, Jim Jeffries (left) responded to the clamour for him to come out of retirement and wrest the title from the reviled Jack Johnson.

Right: Not content with handing Jeffries a terrible beating in the "Fight of the Century", Johnson taunted the former champion throughout the contest.

James J. Jeffries

Born:	Carroll, Ohio, USA April 15, 1875
Died:	March 3, 1953
Height:	6' 2"
Weight:	206-227lbs.
World Heavyweight Champion:	1899-1904
Record:	Won 18 (15 KOs) Lost 1 Drawn 2

Standing 6ft 2in tall and weighing 220lb, James J. Jeffries was regarded as the most formidable fighting machine of his era.

James J. Jeffries
World Heavyweight Champion: 1899-1904

Had it not been for an ill-advised return to the ring when he was 35, James J. Jeffries would have joined an elite group of boxers who retired from the ring undefeated. Public pressure, born of racial prejudice, brought Jeffries out of retirement to face reigning champion Jack Johnson in 1910. It was a decision which brought him a big payday, but cost him a place in the record books and diminished his reputation.

A decade earlier it was a very different story. Jeffries was an unsophisticated but destructive champion. He had a seemingly limitless capacity to absorb punishment, often using his body as a means of wearing down his opponents. And when they had punched themselves out and began to tire, Jeffries, who weighed in at 220lb, didn't need to catch his adversaries too many times to put them away for good.

Jeffries was born in Ohio, on 15 April 1875, his family moving to Los Angeles when he was a child. Powerfully built and 6ft 2in tall, Jeffries sought to supplement his meagre income by stepping into the ring. He became known as the Fighting Boilermaker, after one of his early jobs.

Corbett's sparring partner

Jeffries sparred with Corbett when the latter was heavyweight champion. He took all the punishment that the mercurial Corbett doled out to him, then set about forging a professional career in his own right. By the time Fitzsimmons became champion, in March 1897, Jeffries was confident that he could lift the greatest prize. He had to wait two years for his opportunity, Fitzsimmons preferring the limelight of vaudeville to the risk of a title defence. When the champion could no longer resist the pressure to climb back into the ring, he chose Jeffries, firmly believing that the Fighting Boilermaker would be a slow, lumbering target for his heavy punches.

Impervious

The fight took place at Coney Island, on 9 June 1899. Fitzsimmons hit the 24-year-old challenger hard and often, but to little effect. Most worrying of all for the champion, Jeffries appeared impervious to the crushing solar plexus punch that had had Corbett, Sharkey and others doubled up in agony. Jeffries kept coming forward. Fitzsimmons's numerous scoring punches had put him comfortably ahead on points, but he didn't look like finishing Jeffries off. The challenger continued to bear down on his man, looking for the opening he needed. It came in the 11th round, Jeffries nailing the champion with a left hook followed by a right uppercut.

After outpointing Tom Sharkey, Jeffries' second defence of the title saw him matched against former champion, Gentleman Jim Corbett. Corbett had been frustrated by Fitzsimmons's refusal to fight him; now, his interest was renewed, especially since the new champion was his old sparring partner, whom he had always handled with consummate ease.

The two met at Coney Island on 11 May 1900, in a 25-round contest. The 35-year-old Corbett gave the younger, heavier man a boxing lesson that day. Jeffries had been coached to abandon his upright, open stance in favour of a crouching position. It hardly made any difference. Corbett punched and connected; Jeffries chased shadows. The champion had not prepared well for the fight, and it looked like costing him dearly. But in the 23rd round Jeffries had his one chance, and took it. He caught Corbett on the ropes, feinted with his right, then crashed home a big left hook.

Momentary lapse

The next thing Corbett knew someone was bringing him round with smelling salts. His momentary lapse had snatched defeat from the jaws of victory. Jeffries had retained his title, but Corbett was feted for the boxing masterclass he gave that day.

Next up for Jeffries was a rematch against Bob Fitzsimmons. Ruby Robert had scored some notable victories against some of the top contenders of the day, and they rightly earned him another crack at the title in 1902. Once again, Fitzsimmons threw everything at the title holder and did plenty of damage. But Jeffries shrugged off the extensive cuts and bruises - not to mention the broken nose and cheekbone - and retained his title with an eighth-round knockout.

After five more comfortable defences, 30-year-old Jeffries announced that he was giving up the ring and returning to his farm in California. Although it was true that there were no other white contenders left for him to take on, there were certainly some top-quality black heavyweights around. But Jeffries, like Sullivan before him, refused to step into the ring with black opponents. The man who suffered most from this crass attitude was Jack Johnson, who was deemed to be the black heavyweight champion of the world.

Jeffries retires undefeated

Jeffries did indeed retire with his hundred per cent record intact, nominating two white boxers, Jack Root and Marvin Hart, to battle it out for the vacant title. Jeffries officiated at the contest, and it seemed that boxing fans had seen the last of him with the gloves on. But five years later, with the first black heavyweight ensconced on the throne, Jeffries was lured back into the ring. A huge purse was one reason; the other was the deafening clamour from white America to put Jack Johnson in his place.

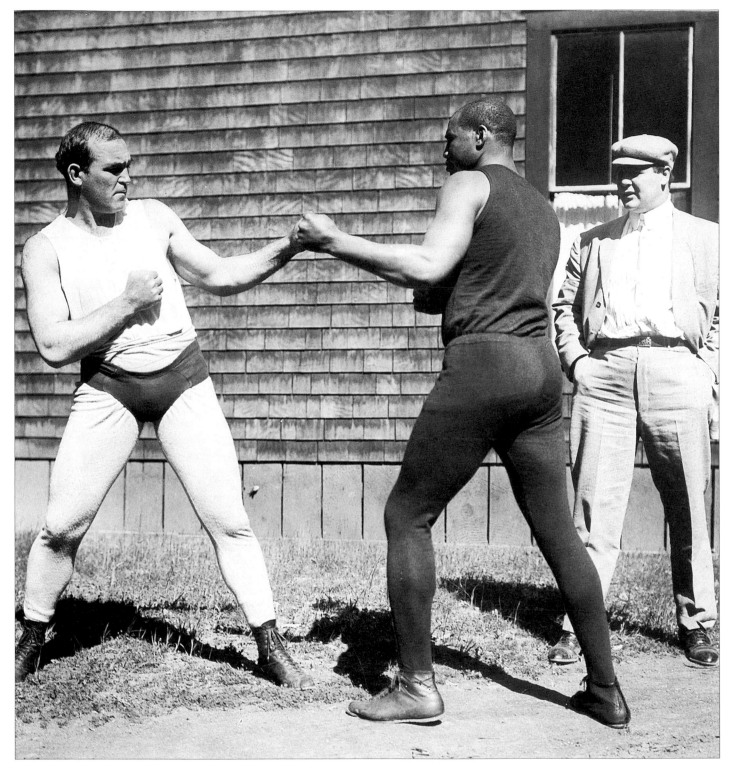

Johnson provokes national outrage

Left: As world champion, Jack Johnson played the part of the dandy to the full. His taste for fine clothes, motor cars - and in particular beautiful white women - outraged the American establishment.

Above: Jim Jeffries (left) spars with Bob Armstrong in preparation for his comeback fight against Jack Johnson. Observers soon realised that the 6-year lay-off had dented the former champion's aura of invincibility.

Tommy Burns
World Heavyweight Champion: 1906-1908

If Gentleman Jim Corbett was the first scientist of the ring, Tommy Burns has been described as its first dictator. He was a shrewd operator. He knew as much about finance as he did about fighting; and when it came to laying down the terms of a contest, Burns proved himself to be an extremely smart promoter.

Burns also stands in the record books as the least impressive physical specimen to hold the heavyweight crown. He stood just 5ft 7in tall, and weighed a mere twelve-and-a-half stones. Far from making the most of his inches, Burns accentuated his diminutive frame by adopting a crouching, panther-like stance. His greatest assets were his speed - he was exceptionally quick on his feet - and enormous upper body strength. His huge shoulders gave him a 74-inch reach, greater than many men six inches taller.

Burns was born Noah Brusso on 17 June 1881. The tough French-Canadian battled his way through the middleweight ranks, then showed his hallmark astuteness by eyeing up the more lucrative heavyweight division. His timing was impeccable. When Jeffries announced his retirement, white contenders were thin on the ground. Corbett, Fitzsimmons and Tom Sharkey were too old. The best heavyweights around were black, with Jack Johnson the pick of them. But America wasn't about to accept a black champion. Tommy Burns saw his opportunity and grabbed it with both fists.

He took on champion Marvin Hart over 20 rounds in Los Angeles on 23 February 1906. It was Hart's first defence after beating Jack Root for the title vacated by James J. Jeffries. Using his legendary speed, Burns comfortably picked off the champion - who was much the bigger man - while dexterously avoiding the blows coming the other way. Burns won on points and walked away with the title, while Hart was left to take his place as probably the least known and least impressive of all heavyweight champions.

String of defences

Unlike some of his predecessors, who sat on the crown for long periods, Burns's title defences came thick and fast. In less than three years he had 13 title fights. Of the first 12 contests, the only blot on his record was a draw with light-heavyweight champion Jack O'Brien. Burns won the rematch in a fight that also went the 20-round distance.

Burns was the first man to see the commercial potential of taking championship fights on the road. After knocking out the Australian heavyweight Bill Squires in two minutes 15 seconds to win the shortest title bout on record, Burns travelled to Britain to take on the British champion, the tough, tattooed "Gunner" James Moir. Moir was as tough as they come, but without the mental sharpness needed to step up to championship class. Against the cunning, polished, fleet-footed Burns, the bigger, heavier man came up short. Moir didn't lay a glove on the champion during the fight, which ended when Burns floored his opponent with a crushing right to the jaw in the 10th round.

After a brief interlude in Dublin, where Burns disposed of that country's top man, Jem Roche, in double-quick time, the champion moved on to Paris. There he faced a novice named Jewcy Smith. The result was never in doubt, but Burns agreed to let the contest go a few rounds to give the crowd their money's worth. The champion was as good as his word, until a photographer's magnesium flash set fire to some of the streamers with which the hall was festooned in honour of his appearance. As panic began to spread, Burns laid out Smith with a right to the chin, then made a swift retreat to the safety of his hotel room.

From France it was on to Australia, where the pattern continued. Burns took on Bill Squires for the third time, and knocked him out for the third time. He then disposed of Bill Lang, who had claimed the Australian title in Squires's absence.

Pursued by Johnson

On all his travels Burns was pursued by Jack Johnson. Like Burns, Johnson realised that the heavyweight crown was all that mattered if a boxer wanted the greatest prestige and, more importantly, the serious money. Burns didn't discount the match on principle, as Sullivan and Jeffries had done. He would fight the top black heavyweight, providing the terms were favourable. Finally, the money was right. Burns was offered $25,000 to meet Johnson, the largest purse ever guaranteed to a heavyweight champion.

The two met at Rushcutters Bay, Sydney; fittingly enough, it was Boxing Day, 1908. Burns' 13th title fight would be his last. He finally came up against a man several classes above any other heavyweight he'd met during his reign. He also bore the brunt of Johnson's seething resentment at the way he'd been treated for so many years. It was a bloodbath.

Tommy Burns

Nickname:	Noah Brusso
Born:	Chesley, Ontario Canada June 17 1881
Died:	May 10 1955
Height:	5' 7"
Weight:	175lbs.
World Heavyweight Champion:	1906-1908
British Empire Heavyweight Champion:	1910-1911
Record:	Won 47 (39 KO's) Lost 1 Drawn 4

Opposite: Tommy Burns was an unlikely and underrated champion. However, he notched eight straight KO victories, an achievement that none of his more illustrious successors could match.

Johnson in England

Above: June 1911: Jack Johnson and his wife arrive in Plymouth for the coronation of George V.

Right: Johnson shares a joke with a serviceman and boxing fan during his trip to England. At home it was a very different story. Johnson was a hate figure for white America.

Jack Johnson
World Heavyweight Champion: 1908-1915

There are boxing aficionados who put Jack Johnson above Joe Louis and Muhammad Ali in the all-time list of heavyweight greats. The first black champion reigned for seven years, and it certainly would have been a lot longer had the likes of Jeffries and Burns avoided meeting him for so long. As it was, Johnson had to wait until he was 30 for his chance. It was only after six successful defences and one draw that he relinquished the title, and then it has to be remembered that "L'il Arthur" had turned 37.

Johnson was born in Galveston, Texas, on 31 March 1878. His early experience of boxing came in the infamous "Battles Royal". In this brutal activity, between six and a dozen black youngsters were thrown into a ring together for the entertainment of a white crowd. The sole survivor scooped the pool, which might consist of nickels and dimes tossed disdainfully by the spectators. It was an experience which burned deep into the aspiring heavyweight, and when he fought his way to the top, he showed that he had a long memory.

Uncanny defence

Ironically, it was probably at least in part because of the Battles Royal that Johnson developed a defence which verged on the uncanny. At a shade over 6 ft and 13st 10lb when he fought for the title, Johnson was no giant by modern standards. But he was a master of his craft, and the fact that the boxing fraternity rates him so highly nearly a hundred years on speaks volumes for his contribution to the sport.

By 1903 he had beaten all the top contenders and was regarded as the best black heavyweight in the world. He openly challenged Jeffries for the title, but the latter made it clear that he wouldn't step into the ring with a negro. Several years later, he was to change his mind as far as Johnson was concerned, and take a terrible beating as a result.

When Tommy Burns became champion in 1906, Johnson embarked on a pursuit that lasted two long years. One of the greatest chases in sporting history saw Johnson follow Burns from America to Britain, France and Australia. He finally pinned his man down to a contest in Sydney, on 26 December 1908.

Police intervene

Ever the shrewd businessman, Burns negotiated himself a guaranteed fee of $25,000, win, lose or draw. It was just as well. Johnson received just $5,000, but the coveted title at last was within his grasp. He knocked Burns down in the first round, and again in the seventh. It was clear that he could have finished off the champion at any time he liked. Johnson didn't like, however. After all the years of racial abuse, all the years of being humiliatingly marginalised by the white boxing establishment, Johnson wanted to savour the moment. The fight was eventually stopped in the 14th round, the police intervening to prevent the game French-Canadian from taking further punishment.

After such a long struggle to get to the top, Johnson intended to enjoy the fruits of being the heavyweight champion. He played the part of the dandy to the full. He enjoyed flashy cars, fine clothes, cigars and champagne. When he smiled he showed off a mouthful of gold teeth. He had a weakness for gambling, and for white women. White America was outraged at the thought of a negro boxing champion in general, and a dissolute, debauched champion such as Johnson in particular. The search for a contender to wipe the gold-toothed smile off Johnson's face began in earnest.

High living

Johnson continued to enjoy the high life. He interrupted his hedonistic pursuits for the absolute minimum time necessary to remain on top of the boxing world. He often looked as if he'd come into the ring straight from a bar instead of a gym, yet no one came close to making him pay for his lack of preparation.

The clamour for Jeffries to come out of retirement was now greater than ever, and the former champion finally relented. After six years out of the ring, he agreed to fight Johnson. The match - or mismatch as it transpired - took place in Reno, on 4 July 1910. Johnson did to Jeffries what he'd done to Burns. He cut him, taunted him, toyed with him, humiliated him. He finally smashed the previously unbeaten Jeffries to the canvas in the 15th round.

Unable to get the better of Johnson in the ring, his enemies turned to the law. The champion was charged under a new piece of legislation which made it illegal to transport white women across state lines for immoral purposes. It didn't matter matter whether - as in Johnson's case - the women were willing participants. Many were liable to prosecution under this ridiculous new law. Unsurprisingly, Johnson was targeted. His guilt was never in doubt and he was sentenced to a year and a day's imprisonment. Released on bail, he managed to skip the country by joining a Canadian baseball team on tour in the USA. Johnson took the place of a lookalike in the team when it returned home.

From Canada he headed for Europe. After two defences of his title in Paris, and another in Buenos Aires, Johnson agreed to fight the latest Great White Hope, a 6ft 6in cowboy named Jess Willard. Johnson had turned 37 by the time they met, in Havana, Cuba, on 5 April 1915. Not only was Johnson at a disadvantage in terms of age, height and weight, his dissolute lifestyle was finally catching up with him. It was a fight too far for L'il Arthur.

Jack Johnson

Born:	Galveston, Texas USA March 31, 1878
Died:	June 10, 1946
World Heavyweight Champion:	1908-1915
Record:	Won 68 (49 KOs) Lost 10 Drawn 10

Above: The finest cigars and clothes, gold teeth and first-class travel; only the best was good enough for Jack Johnson when he ruled the boxing world. With him is Etta Duryea, the first of his several white wives.

Carpentier KOs Wells in one

Left: 19-year-old Georges Carpentier delivers a first-round knockout to Bombardier Billy Wells. The fight took place on December 8, 1913, at the National Sporting Club.

Below: Carpentier stands over Wells after the 73-second KO. A natural light-heavyweight, Carpentier would follow a well-trodden path in attempting to step up in class and win the ultimate prize.

Right: Jack Johnson overcame blatant racism as well as his opponents in the ring to become the first black heavyweight champion, in 1908. He held the title for seven years.

Johnson avoids Langford

Left: Jack Johnson, pictured at the wheel of his racing car in London, 1914. He had come to England to discuss arrangements for a fight with the superb black heavyweight Sam Langford. The match never materialised; Johnson preferred to make easy money knocking over the Great White Hopes of the day.

Below left: Folk-hero Georges Carpentier dons the gloves to entertain French soldiers during the First World War.

Right: Johnson believed that even at the age of 37 and carrying excess flab, he would be good enough to withstand the challenge of Jess Willard.

Below: Johnson made all the early running in his fight with Willard. He couldn't put the giant Texan away, however, and after the 20th round his lack of training began to exact its toll.

Jess Willard

World Heavyweight Champion: 1915-1919

The contest between Jack Johnson and Jess Willard was scheduled for 45 rounds, effectively making it a fight to the finish. It was the last championship bout that would be fought under such terms. It was actually settled in the 26th round, and boxing had a new heavyweight champion. It was far from a cut and dried affair, however. The end of the Johnson-Willard fight has sparked more comment, claim and counter-claim than any in the sport's history. It is a controversy that continues to engage boxing fans, though inevitably a present-day debate over a fight that took place in 1915 is bound to generate more heat than light.

The eighth man to attempt to wrest the title from Jack Johnson was a 6ft 6in cowboy and a somewhat reluctant fighter. Jess Willard was born in Kansas, on 29 December 1881. He had Welsh blood in him on both his father's and mother's side, but his mid-west upbringing was in the great American outdoors tradition. The sometime ranch-hand and horse-dealer turned to labouring when his business was adversely affected by the burgeoning motor car industry. It was while wielding a pickaxe as if it were a matchstick that a fellow worker suggested that he ought to consider boxing. "I have never had a glove on in my life," replied Willard. "I have no inclination to punch others around."

Fairground fights

His companion undertook to teach him the rudiments of the noble art, and Willard found that he could knock men off their feet with consummate ease. He won a number of fairground fights, despite having turned 30, and slowly built a reputation as the man who might reclaim the heavyweight crown from the reviled negro incumbent.

Although he was ponderously slow, Willard's right hand could do a lot of damage. It was a punch that cost a boxer named Bill Young his life in 1913. Young got caught with a right from Willard in the 11th round, and died the following day. His neck had been broken. Willard was cleared of blame but vowed never to fight again. In fact, the guilt-ridden lay-off lasted just a few months. He had a few minor bouts where he took things easy, then drifted off the boxing scene for almost a year.

Confident challenger

When promoter Jack Curley offered Johnson $30,000 to fight Willard, the champion laughed. He was 37 and out of condition, but saw no danger in meeting a man who had only been boxing for four years, and hadn't stepped into the ring at all for the past 12 months.

Willard was tempted by the prospect of fighting for the world title. The fact that the contest was set for 45 rounds convinced him that he could beat Johnson, who was as ring-rusty as himself. The odds were 8-5 on Johnson, but it was Willard's analysis which proved correct. For 25 rounds he withstood all Johnson's efforts to knock him out. The champion was streets ahead on points, but that was never going to be a factor. In the 26th round, after more than an hour and 40 minutes under a broiling sun, Willard's famed right hand caught the champion square on the chin and put him on the canvas.

The picture of Johnson being counted out has been reproduced many times, and has become one of the most celebrated and controversial stills in sporting history.

Conspiracy theory

The photo shows Johnson holding his hands over his face, apparently shielding his eyes from the sun. This is a perfectly natural reaction under normal circumstances - but not for a man who had just been laid out and was not supposed to know what day it was. Conspiracy theorists have used this to support the view that Johnson threw the fight. Why would he do such a thing? Years later, Johnson himself fanned the flames by saying that he took a dive in exchange for his freedom to return to the United States, with the charges hanging over his head dropped. In short, he cut a deal.

This is by no means universally accepted as a true account of what happened on that April day in Havana. Testimony from impartial ringside observers said that the unfit champion had simply been battered to exhaustion by the 26th round. Any limb movements from the beaten man were totally involuntary.

The new champion made just one successful defence of his title, against Frank Moran, on 25 March 1916. Moran had been outpointed by Johnson over 20 rounds two years earlier and was no pushover. Willard cannily insisted on a 10-round, no-decision contest. He knew he was far too durable for Moran to knock him out over such a distance, and it proved a comfortable, if tedious, defence.

The Moran fight was the only time Willard put his title on the line in four years. He preferred to make easy money with the touring circus he'd formed. When he was finally lured back into the ring, it was against a man 5$1/4$ in shorter and 4$1/2$ stone lighter. Willard was confident that he could make short work of Jack Dempsey.

Johnson era ends in controversy

Above: End of an era. Johnson is knocked out by Willard in the 26th round. He would later claim that he threw the fight as part of a deal with the US authorities.

Right: A huge crowd gathered in Havana, Cuba, for the Johnson-Willard encounter. The fact that it was a 45-round contest fought under a broiling sun stacked the odds in Willard's favour.

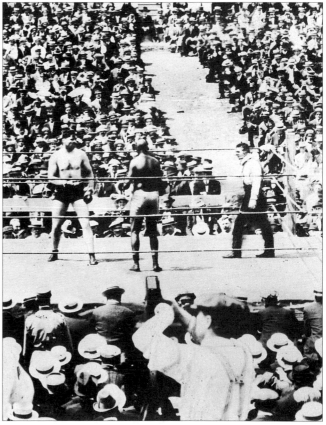

Jess Willard

Nickname:	"Pottawatomie Giant"
Born:	St.Clere, Kansas, USA. Dec 29, 1881
Died:	Dec 15, 1968
Height:	6' 6" Weight: 225-250lbs.
World Heavyweight Champion:	1915-1919
Record:	Won 32 (20 KOs) Lost 8 Drawn 5

Carpentier not ready to challenge for heavyweight crown

Left: Georges Carpentier was touted as a possible challenger to Jack Johnson towards the end of the latter's reign as champion. Carpentier could get the better of most heavyweights but decided against stepping into the ring with the best in the business.

Right: Carpentier (left) was an airman in the First World War. Here, he steps into a makeshift ring to put on a show for some of his comrades.

Below: Carpentier knocks out England's Joe Beckett to become European heavyweight champion in December 1919.

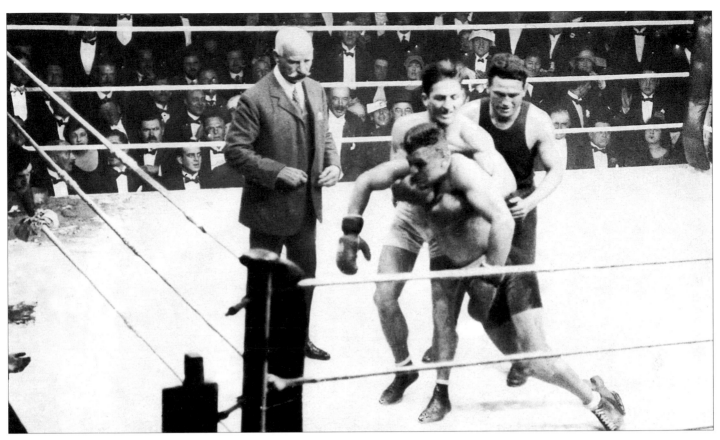

Old adversaries reunited

Opposite: July 1919: Two ex-champions reflect on the best of the current heavyweight crop. Jim Jeffries (right) returned to his California farm after retiring from boxing. "Gentleman" Jim Corbett spends a vacation with his old friend and adversary, and the two take the opportunity to discuss Jack Dempsey's recent demolition of Jess Willard.

Above: Georges Carpentier helps England's Joe Beckett to his feet after knocking him out in their 1919 encounter. Beckett had been promised a shot at Jack Dempsey if he won the fight. Now it was the Frenchman who had the world title in his sights.

Left: Carpentier stuns Beckett in the early exchanges of the fight. The Frenchman had been the scourge of British champions from welterweight through to heavyweight for a number of years.

Above: September 6, 1920.
Jack Dempsey retains his title by knocking out Billy Miske in the third round of their encounter at Benton Harbor, Michigan. Dempsey agonised over the fight. Miske was a good friend who was suffering from a terminal illness. Dempsey agreed to the match to give him one last big payday.

'Jack' Dempsey William Harrison Dempsey

Nickname:	"Manassa Mauler"
Born:	Manassa, Colorado, USA. 24 June 1895
Died:	New York, 31 May, 1983
Height:	6' Weight: 190lbs.
World Heavyweight Champion:	1919-1926
Record:	64 wins (49 KOs) Professional boxer: 1914-1940

Jack Dempsey

World Heavyweight Champion: 1919-1926

William Harrison Dempsey was the ninth of 11 children born to a poor Mormon schoolteacher and his wife in the Colorado town of Manassa. He had a harsh upbringing, and by his mid-teens was living virtually as a hobo. He did anything to make money: washing dishes, shining shoes, breaking horses. He was also a hustler and saloon brawler. It was in the bars of the mining towns that he made a name for himself with his fists. Fights would be put on to entertain the customers, and a hat would be passed round to reward the winner. Dempsey travelled from town to town by jumping on freight cars at night. It was a meagre, uncertain existence. But the experience toughened him up and made him hungry for success when he decided to make his living in the ring.

By 1914, when he was 19 years old, he was fighting regularly as a professional. At first he boxed under the name of Kid Blackie, but soon changed it to Jack, after one of his brothers who was also a fighter.

Early defeats

His rise to the top was not without its setbacks. He lost two and drew one of his first three fights, and in 1917 he suffered a first-round knockout at the hands of Jim Flynn. Flynn had had a tilt at the title in 1912, losing to Johnson in nine rounds. In 1918, Dempsey avenged this defeat by putting Flynn away in one.

Although he became known primarily as a very destructive puncher, he combined sheer power with the ringcraft of a Corbett or Johnson. Such was the impression he made on the boxing world that he was given a shot at the title on 4 July 1919.

Jess Willard undertrained for their showdown, in Toledo, Ohio, but at almost five stones heavier and five inches taller, he was confident of putting the challenger in his place. The punters agreed and the champion was a firm favourite. In the event, Willard found himself on the receiving end of one of the worst beatings ever witnessed in the ring. Crouching low, his head bobbing and darting like a cobra about to strike, Dempsey tore into his man from the start. A bone-crunching right to the heart, followed by a fast left hook put Willard on the canvas early in the first round.

Severe punishment

By the end of that three minutes, the champion - who had never before been put down - was floored another six times. At the seventh knockdown, the referee counted Willard out and raised the hand of the new champion, only to find that amid the tumult he had failed to hear the bell. Dempsey, who was already on his way to the dressing room, had to be recalled to continue the demolition job.

Willard gamely stayed on his feet throughout round two, though he took further severe punishment. He also somehow survived the onslaught in the third round, but that was the end. He summoned his last ounce of strength to throw in the towel himself. In the nine minutes of the fight's duration Willard landed 11 punches. Dempsey had found his mark 62 times.

Dempsey's first defence was against a friend who was dying and needed a big payday. Billy Miske was suffering from Bright's disease when he faced Dempsey at Benton Harbor, on 6 September 1920. The champion agonised about whether to put his friend through an attritional battle or dispatch him quickly. In the end he opted for the latter, knocking Miske out in three.

Fans' hostility

After another successful defence inside the distance, against Bill Brennan, Dempsey faced Europe's premier fighter, world light-heavyweight champion Georges Carpentier. When the two stepped into the ring, in New Jersey, on 2 July 1921, it was the Frenchman who was received as the hero, while there was considerable hostility shown towards the home-grown champion. The reason was that Dempsey had been the subject of a vitriolic media campaign on the subject of draft-dodging. Carpentier, by contrast, was presented as a war hero. He was also handsome, flamboyant and charming - qualities that brought women flocking to a boxing match for the first time. Financially, it was by some distance the biggest fight ever staged. More than 80,000 spectators crammed into the specially built stadium in Jersey City. At one stage the police and fire department chiefs feared that the arena was in danger of collapsing. The fight grossed $1,75 million.

The shrewd promoter Tex Rickard took one look at the crowd and realised it was the biggest day in boxing history. "Don't kill him, Jack," he exhorted Dempsey before the fight. "If you kill him, you kill boxing. I just want you to knock him out. And not with one punch, or in the first round. Give them a run for their money."

To the delight of the crowd, Carpentier caught Dempsey with a terrific right to the cheek in the second round, and followed it up with a flurry of punches without reply. In the fourth, a left hook put Carpentier down for a count of nine. Another left sent him reeling again, and this time the champion nailed "Gorgeous" Georges with a right as he was falling. It was all over.

Brutal encounter

After a tedious points win over Tom Gibbons, Dempsey signed to fight Argentina's Luis Firpo, the Pampas Bull.

Firpo was a toe-to-toe slugger out of the Dempsey mould. Their short, brutal encounter has gone down in boxing's annals as one of the classic rough-house battles.

It lasted just three minutes 57 seconds. During that time Firpo was floored nine times, Dempsey twice. The second time the Pampas Bull caught the champion, he put him clean out of the ring. Dempsey landed on the typewriter of sports journalist Jack Lawrence, who pushed him back into the ring. Dempsey later said he remembered nothing from that moment on. Purely by instinct he continued trading blows with Firpo, neither man making any effort at defence at any stage. The champion finally put Firpo down for good after 237 seconds; it was the most

extraordinary exhibition of unalloyed savagery in the history of glove fighting. Dempsey's fee worked out at £415 per second.

It was three years before Dempsey laid his title on the line again. When he did so, it was against an opponent at the very opposite end of the spectrum to Firpo. Gene Tunney was no bar-room brawler. Intelligent and cultured, Tunney firmly believed that brains would triumph over brawn every time. Although he was a natural light-heavyweight - the US champion in that division - he was convinced he had the ammunition to beat the great Jack Dempsey.

The canny Canadian

Above: Tommy Burns was a shrewd operator, both in and out of the ring. He managed himself, cut some lucrative deals and walked away from the sport with a lot more money than many of his contemporaries.
Opposite: Tommy Burns, pictured during a visit to England in 1920.

Burns makes unwise comeback

Right: In 1920, after some 10 years out of the ring, Burns attempted a comeback against British champion Joe Beckett. Despite the advice of trainer Pat O'Keefe, Burns, who was nearly 40 at the time, couldn't roll back the years. Beckett knocked him out.

Left: Far from making the most of his inches, Tommy Burns adopted a crouching style. With his low centre of gravity and exceptional speed, he specialised in lightning attacks which often left bigger, heavier men in a heap on the canvas.

Below: Tommy Burns (left) in training for his fight with Joe Beckett.

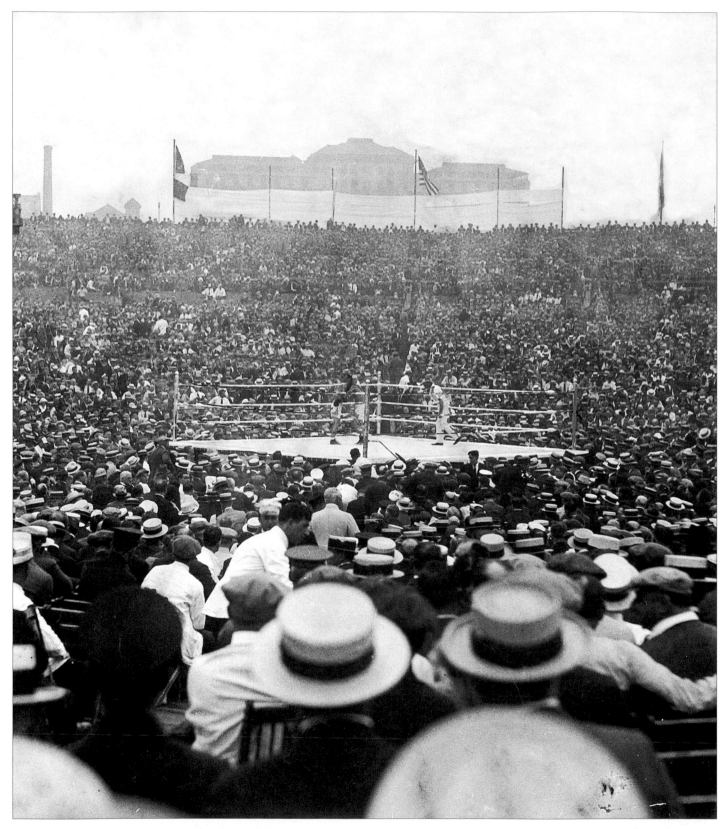

The stadium at Boyle's Thirty Acres, New Jersey, was purpose built for the Dempsey-
Carpentier fight. More than 80,000 fans packed the venue, with receipts exceeding
$1.75million
The tumultuous scene in New Jersey, as the eagerly awaited clash between Dempsey
and Carpentier gets under way.

Dempsey pulverises Carpentier in four

Above left: The end is nigh for Carpentier. Having stunned Dempsey in the second round, the Frenchman took a lot of punishment to the body in the third. It was all over in round four.

Left: Carpentier beats the count this time, but Dempsey waits to deliver the knockout blow.

Above: The Gallic charm and good looks of "Gorgeous" Georges Carpentier (left) attracted many female fans to boxing.

Georges Carpentier

Nickname:	"Orchid Man"
Born:	Lens France January 12 1884
Died:	October 28 1975
Height:	5' 11½" Weight: 126-175lbs.
World Light Heavyweight Champion: 1920-1921, 1922	
White Heavyweight Championship of the World: 1914-1920	
Heavyweight Champion of Europe: 1914, 1914-1920 1922	
Record:	Won 85 Lost 12 Drawn 5 (49 KOs)

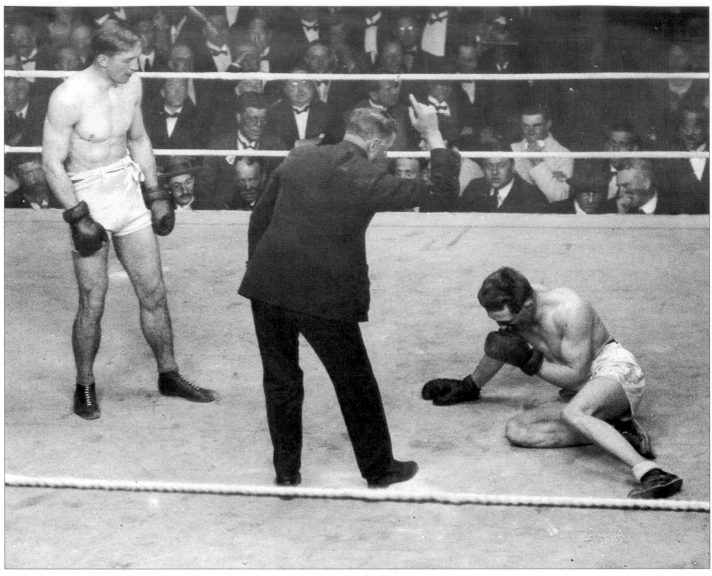

Ted Kid Lewis
KOd by Carpentier

Above: Ted Kid Lewis was a top welterweight whose career extended from 1910 to 1929. He came off second-best on this occasion, an encounter with Georges Carpentier in May 1922.

Below: The referee holds Carpentier at bay after a lightning right drops Lewis to the canvas.

Opposite: Carpentier digs into Lewis's midriff in their 1922 clash. The Frenchman won by a knockout.

Siki captures light-heavyweight crown

Opposite top: September 1922: Senegalese light-heavyweight Battling Siki rocks back to evade a rapier left from Georges Carpentier. Siki sprang a surprise by knocking Carpentier out in the sixth, much to the chagrin of the Parisian crowd.

Opposite bottom: Siki upsets the odds by taking Carpentier's world light-heavyweight crown. A round-arm punch ended the fight in the sixth.

Right: Siki helps the defeated champion to his feet.

Below: Carpentier took severe punishment from the fourth round until the end of the fight in the sixth. 30 years later, the Frenchman would claim that the result had been pre-arranged.

French fans stunned

Right: The fans are stunned as their idol, Georges Carpentier, loses his world light-heavyweight crown to Battling Siki.

Opposite: Carpentier still hasn't come round as he is helped back to his corner.

Below: The new champion is carried aloft by his jubilant seconds.

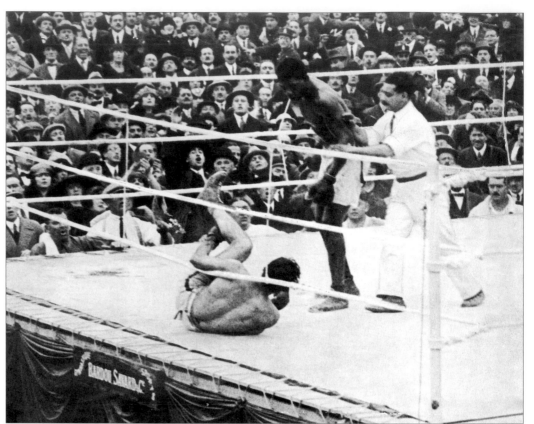

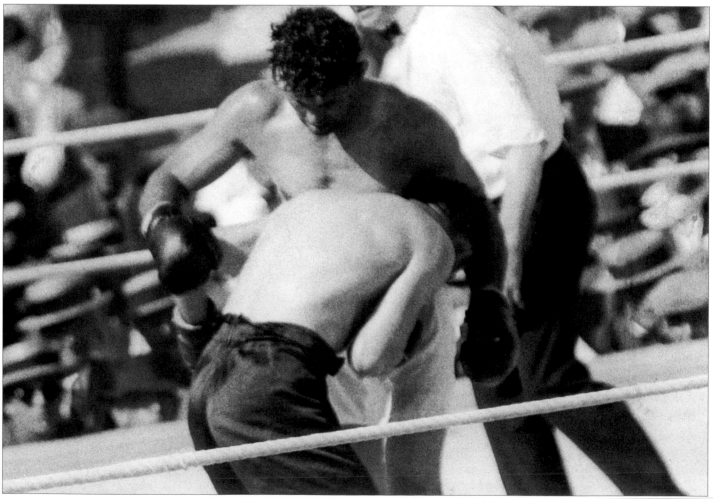

Dempsey cleans out Shelby

Below left: Jack Dempsey's fourth title defence matched him against wily old campaigner Tom Gibbons, who used all his experience to survive the full 15 rounds. The result was never in doubt, but it was a drab affair. It was also a financial disaster for Shelby, Montana, where the fight was staged. Barely 7,000 fans paid $66,000 to see the contest. Dempsey's guaranteed fee of $300,000 caused several local banks to go broke.

Left: After his defeat by Dempsey in 1921 and the loss of his light-heavyweight crown the following year, Carpentier bounced back to win France's heavyweight title in 1923. His victim was Marcel Nilles, who was knocked out in the 8th round by one of the best punches Carpentier ever threw.

Right: October 1923: Carpentier knocks out British heavyweight Joe Beckett.

Below: Carpentier and his camp look well pleased with their night's work after the win over Beckett.

Dempsey wins fans over

Above: Fight fans didn't take Jack Dempsey to their hearts immediately. There was a suspicion of draft-dodging, and in the ring some thought he was a raw slugger lacking in finesse. By the end of his reign, the Manassa Mauler's all-action style had made him a living legend.

Left: A disappointed Georges Carpentier leaves the ring following his points defeat by Tom Gibbons.

Tunney survives "long count" to retain title

Right: Jack Dempsey hadn't fought for three years when he came up against Gene Tunney in September 1926. A bruised and battered Dempsey (right) had no answer as Tunney picked him off at will.

Below: The famous "Long Count". Dempsey hovers menacingly after putting Tunney down in the seventh round of their rematch. A vital few seconds elapsed before Dempsey retired to a neutral corner, giving Tunney valuable extra recovery time.

Opposite: Was this the moment that cost Dempsey a place in the history books as the first man to regain the heavyweight crown? Referee Dave Barry had made it clear before the fight that a man scoring a knockdown should go to the farthest neutral corner before the count could begin.

Opposite below: Tunney later claimed that the "Long Count" hadn't saved him and that he could have beaten a count of ten. The glazed expression on his face suggests that the extra seconds were vital to his recovery.

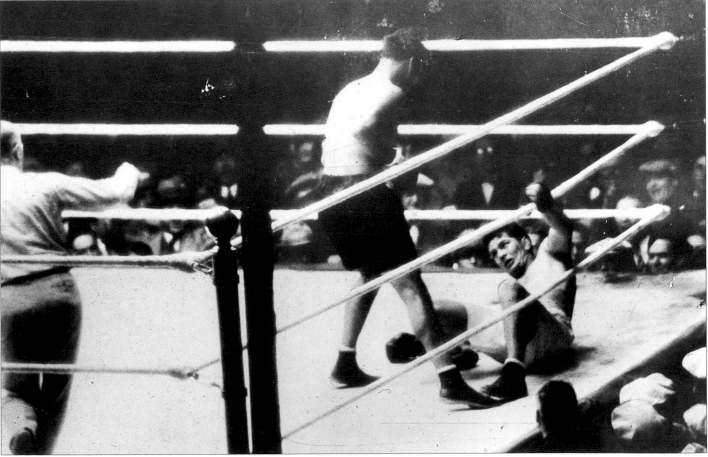

Gene Tunney

Born:	New York, USA. May 25, 1898	
Died:	November 7, 1978	
Height:	6' 0¹/₂" Weight:	155-192lbs.
World Heavyweight Boxing Champion:	1926-28	
Record:	Won 65 (47 KOs) Lost 1 Drawn 19	

The fighting marine

Gene Tunney was cultured and intelligent, qualities he took into the ring. He didn't endear himself to the fans, who preferred Dempsey's rugged style. Some also took exception to the fact that "Gentleman Gene" walked away from the sport after just two defences, very rich and totally unmarked.

Gene Tunney
World Heavyweight Champion: 1926-1928

Few people gave Gene Tunney much of a chance when he came up against the Manassa Mauler in Philadelphia on 23 September 1926. It was widely expected that Dempsey would reproduce his usual devastating form and see off a challenger who was a natural light-heavyweight. The supremely confident Tunney had other ideas.

James Joseph Tunney was born on 25 May 1898, in Greenwich Village, New York. The son of poor Irish-Catholic parents, Tunney worked as a clerk for the Ocean Steamship Company after leaving school. It was during this period that he began boxing. In 1917, the year the United States entered the First World War, Tunney joined the Marines and went to Europe with the American Expeditionary Force. He continued to box, and in Paris in 1919 he won the AEF championship. Demobbed and back in New York, he notched up a string of victories which eventually made him light-heavyweight champion of America. He took that title from Battling Levinsky in January 1922.

Dirty fighter

In May of the same year, Tunney suffered his only defeat, and the loss of his cruiser title. His victor was Harry Greb, a formidable fighter - and a dirty one. Tunney took a terrible 15-round beating, then promptly vowed to avenge the defeat and regain his title from the same man. He studied Greb's unseemly tactics, learned how to counter them and made good his promise in 1923. The following year he knocked out Georges Carpentier and set his sights on going one better than the Frenchman: relieving Dempsey of the heavyweight crown.

Dempsey, at 31, wasn't in peak condition for what was his sixth title defence. He was also preoccupied by legal and business concerns. Even so, the boxing world was unprepared for what transpired. Tunney astonished everyone by deftly sidestepping and riding whatever Dempsey threw at him, while he himself gave a virtuoso display of incisive counterpunching. By the 10th and final round, one of Dempsey's eyes was closed, he was bleeding profusely and virtually out on his feet. Tunney was picking him off at will. An emphatic points victory brought Dempsey's seven-year reign to an end.

Dempsey congratulates victor

At the end of the fight, Dempsey's sight was so badly impaired that he asked one of his seconds to point him in Tunney's direction so that he could shake the new champion's hand. It wasn't a popular victory. The fans loved Dempsey's all-action style. Tunney's chief passion was for the arts. He read Shakespeare and counted George

Bernard Shaw among his friends. His cultured ways didn't endear him overmuch to the fight fans of the day. It was a fitter Dempsey who entered the ring in Chicago, on 22 September 1927, for the rematch. The first few rounds began in the same vein as the previous encounter, Tunney weaving and counterpunching to good effect. By the seventh round, he was comfortably ahead on points, when Dempsey finally caught him with a devastating flurry of combination punches. Tunney hit the canvas and the referee ordered Dempsey to a neutral corner, as agreed before the fight.

The "Long Count"

A vital few seconds elapsed before Dempsey consented and the referee began the count. Tunney rose at nine. He repaid the compliment by putting Dempsey down in the following round, and went on to record another comfortable points victory. The Long Count has gone down in boxing history as one of the great imponderables. Some maintain that those extra seconds saved Tunney. Dempsey himself graciously accepted the champion's version of events: that he could have risen earlier, but sensibly made the most of the time available to him.

Tunney defended his title only once more, against New Zealander Tom Heeney. Heeney was strong and brave, but no match for the immaculate Tunney, who toyed with him for 11 rounds. Heeney was bleeding so badly from one eye that Tunney dropped his hands and pleaded with the referee to end the contest. The referee refused and the fight continued, but Tunney didn't lay a serious glove on his man until the referee finally did call a halt to proceedings. Gentlemen Gene later said he wasn't prepared to risk a blow which might have cost an opponent his sight.

Tunney retired from the ring after the Heeney fight. He married Josephine Lauder, heiress to the Carnegie Steel fortune, and became a successful businessman in his own right. His decision to walk away from the sport after making in the region of $1.75 million from his three title fights once again didn't play well with the fans. He may not have ranked high in the popularity stakes, but his superb ringcraft had twice got the better of one of the most feared fighters in boxing history.

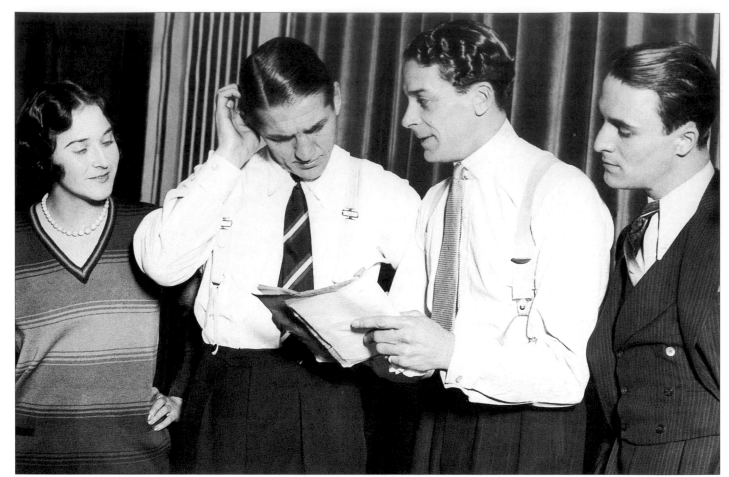

Mobsters back Carnera

Right: October 1929: Primo Carnera (right) greets Dick Smith at his hotel in Walworth. Carnera was an awesome physical specimen but is widely regarded as one of the poorest heavyweight champions.

Opposite: Carnera (right) spars with "Smiling" George Smith at the London Alhambra, October 1929. His mobster backers took him across the Atlantic to "conquer" America at the end of that year.

Above: Georges Carpentier (second left) follows a well-trodden path for boxers in taking to the stage. Here, he takes direction from celebrated actor Jack Buchanan.

Carnera-Stribling fight ends on foul

Above left: The Albert Hall, London, October 1929. Primo Carnera rolls on the canvas in agony after being felled by a low blow from Billy "Young" Stribling. Stribling was disqualified, giving the Ambling Alp another uninspiring victory.
Left: December 1930: Carnera takes on the giant Basque heavyweight Paulino Uzcudun. Three years later, Carnera would outpoint the same man in his first title defence.
Above: Although Carnera's rise to the top was carefully managed, there were some notable victories. Here, he is pictured on his way to an impressive two-round KO of Vittorio Campolo. The fight took place at Madison Square Garden, November 27, 1931

Schmeling's hopes dented by Baer

Opposite: June 8, 1933: Clown Prince of the ring Max Baer decides to take a fight seriously for once. Ex-champion Max Schmeling is floored by a right in the tenth; the fight is stopped in the same round.

Left: Gene Tunney rocks Jack Dempsey with a terrific right to the head in their 1927 clash in Chicago.

Below: Tunney survives the famous "Long Count" of round seven and repays the compliment by dropping Dempsey to the canvas in the eighth.

Max Schmeling

World Heavyweight Champion: 1930-1932

The scramble for the title vacated by Gene Tunney in 1928 lasted two years. Many eliminators featuring all the top contenders were fought during that time. The two men to emerge from this lengthy process and fight for the crown were tough American Jack Sharkey and the European heavyweight champion Max Schmeling.

Schmeling incurred the displeasure of his family when he eschewed a business career and took up boxing. He also probably surprised them, for he had lost two fingers of his right hand, the result of a childhood accident. He was nevertheless a stylish boxer, a good technician and a damaging puncher.

Shunned by promoters

His rise to the top was by no means meteoric. There were some solid victories, including wins over the rugged Spaniard Paulino Uzcudun and Johnny "Rubber Man" Risko. But there were reverses too. Defeat inside one round to moderate British cruiserweight Gypsy Daniels did nothing to enhance his reputation. In fact, when he travelled to Britain in search of engagements, no promoter would look at him. His fortunes improved when he arrived in America. A string of victories took Schmeling to a showdown with Sharkey at the Yankee Stadium on 12 June 1930.

There was probably less interest in this contest than any heavyweight title fight of the post-war era. Schmeling wasn't a well-known figure as far as American boxing fans were concerned, while their compatriot, Sharkey, had a reputation for inconsistency. He could be brilliant one day and fight like a novice the next, and as a result the fans didn't take him too seriously.

Low blow

It was, in fact, a short and controversial encounter. Sharkey had the better of the early exchanges, including a terrific right hook to Schmeling's jaw in the third round, a blow which sent the German reeling onto the ropes. The fight ended in the next round when Schmeling went down in agony after an undoubted low blow from his opponent. The bell sounded when the count reached six. Schmeling's manager, Jim Jacobs, was incandescent. His cries of "Foul!" were taken up by large sections of the 80,000-strong crowd; others disagreed vehemently. After a considerable delay in which the referee consulted the judges, Schmeling was declared the winner. He became the only German to win the title, and the only man to take the crown on a foul. The decision reverberated through the boxing world and precipitated a rule change: in future, a boxer guilty of a low blow would be cautioned, but not disqualified.

Schmeling successfully defended his title the following year, against Young Stribling, the referee intervening in the 15th and final round to save the American from further punishment. Schmeling then agreed to a return match against Sharkey. It was to prove another controversial affair. Schmeling had profited from a contentious decision in 1930; this time he found himself on the receiving end of what was widely regarded as an injustice.

Max Schmeling	
Born:	Klien-Luckow Germany September 28 1905
Height:	6' 1"
Weight:	189lbs
World Heavyweight Champion:	1930-1932
Record:	Won 56 (37 KOs) Lost 10 Drawn 4

Carnera sent into the ring every two weeks

Right: January 1932. Primo Carnera in training at the Palais des Sports, Paris, for his fight with Moise Bouquillon. The Italian's backers put him through a gruelling schedule of 28 contests in a 14-month period. He won 25 of them, lost twice and fought one no-decision contest.

Above: Carnera cradles world flyweight champion Young Perez as if he were a baby. The Ambling Alp didn't have the fighting mentality to match his physical attributes.

Jack Sharkey

World Heavyweight Champion: 1932-1933

Jack Sharkey was a veteran four months short of his 30th birthday when he got his second crack at the world title. Many thought he would have gone on to beat Schmeling in their first meeting had it not been for that infamous low blow. The tough Bostonian's Achilles' heel was undoubtedly the erratic nature of his performances. He could look a world-beater one day and a second-rater the next. Fans wondered which Sharkey would turn up for his rematch with Schmeling, at Long Island, on 21 June 1932.

Jack Sharkey was born Joseph Paul Zukaushaus on 26 October 1902, the son of immigrant Lithuanian parents. He grew up in Binghamton, New York. His first taste of boxing came when he joined the US Navy in 1920. When he left the service four years later, he had done well enough as an amateur to persuade a manager that he could make the step up to the professional ranks.

Sharkey takes name from heroes

The name under which he rose to become a top contender was derived from two of his boxing heroes: current champion Jack Dempsey and Sailor Tom Sharkey, who had lost to Jeffries on points in 1899. Although his record wasn't unblemished, Sharkey took a lot of scalps. He was skilful, a good puncher and light on his feet. In 1927 he came up against the man whose Christian name he'd appropriated. Jack Dempsey had lost his title to Tunney and was looking for a tough warm-up before an attempt to regain the crown. Sharkey had the former champion reeling early on, and later said he was just one punch short of putting his hero away. He couldn't find that knockout blow, however, and Dempsey recovered to win in the seventh. The ex-champion put in a succession of pulverising body punches which Sharkey thought were low. He turned to the referee to remonstrate, leaving his jaw temporarily unguarded. Dempsey needed no second invitation and ended proceedings with a huge left hook. Despite the result, many regard those early rounds against Dempsey as Sharkey's finest display in the ring.

Bounces back against Carnera

Tunney retained his title with the famous Long Count victory over Dempsey. Sharkey was in the frame to meet Gentlemen Gene but could only draw with Tom Heeney in the eliminator, and it was the latter who got the opportunity instead. When he lost to Schmeling two years later in such controversial circumstances, Sharkey must have thought that his chance had passed him by. Yet he bounced back with a destructive performance against the man-mountain from Venice, Primo Carnera. The ex-circus performer did well to survive the 15-round duration of the

fight, for Sharkey's tutored fists had rendered him a sorry sight by the end.

New York was keen to proclaim Sharkey as the heavyweight champion of the world. He was hardly that, but he had done more than enough to earn a rematch with Schmeling. It was to be as controversial as their first encounter, though for very different reasons. The fight went the full 15 rounds, but neither the reporters nor the crowd had much doubt that Schmeling had retained his title.

Fortunate decision

The former group included Gene Tunney, who put aside patriotism to make Schmeling "a comfortable winner". The referee, former contender Gunboat Smith, and one of the judges saw it differently. Sharkey was undoubtedly fortunate to take the crown on a split decision. Schmeling hid his obvious disappointment and went over to congratulate a stunned Sharkey. The German's manager, Joe Jacobs, was less sanguine, yelling: "We were robbed!"

A year later, Sharkey's first defence saw him matched against Carnera, the man he had beaten so convincingly between the two Schmeling fights. His pre-fight comments suggested that he didn't rate Carnera's boxing ability and that the contest would go the same way as the first. The Ambling Alp gave two reasons why it would be different this time. Firstly, he was better developed, both physically and in terms of boxing ability. Secondly, he revealed that two days before his first meeting with Sharkey he had been involved in a car crash which left him unconscious for an hour. The 26-year-old thought he could beat Sharkey and go on to hold the title for several years, for he couldn't see anyone coming through the ranks who would pose a serious threat. He was half right.

Jack Sharkey

Born: October 26 1902	**Died:** August 17 1994
World Heavyweight Champion:	1932-1933
American Heavyweight Champion:	1929-1936
Record: Won 38 (14 KOs) Lost 13 Drawn 3	

Opposite: Georges Carpentier works out at Holborn Stadium, London, April 1934. He had long since retired from competitive boxing but kept himself in superb condition.

Carnera prepares to take on Clown Prince

Left: Primo Carnera throws his 260lb weight into pummelling a sandbag as he warms up for his title defence against Max Baer.

Above: Max Baer stars in *The Prizefighter and the Lady*, a romantic melodrama in which a boxer falls for a gangster's moll. Primo Carnera and Jack Dempsey also featured in the movie, giving it an authenticity which proved popular at the box office.

Primo Carnera | World Heavyweight Champion: 1933-1934

An overactive pituitary gland was responsible for turning Primo Carnera into a 6ft 6in, 280lb man-mountain. Despite his intimidating physical presence, Carnera was a simple soul, a true gentle giant. At 13 he left his alpine village to join a travelling circus. He might have stayed there, taking on all-comers in wrestling and boxing bouts had it not been for Leon See, a Frenchman who realised that Carnera's physical prowess could be deployed more profitably on the bigger stage.

See had his work cut out to turn Carnera into a fighting machine. He couldn't punch anywhere near his weight; he couldn't take a punch, either. But with his sheer bulk and strength Carnera had natural assets which would make him a dangerous customer when he learned the tricks of the boxing trade.

Exploited by mobsters

Carnera was indeed tutored in the noble art, although that hardly mattered in the early days. See wasn't about to risk any opponent making contact with his man's glass jaw, and duly paid them off to ensure the desired outcome. After "conquering" Europe in this manner in the late 1920s, the pair headed off to the United States. The sham continued, with some of the era's infamous mobsters getting in on the act. A veritable production-line of fighters was set up for Carnera. He disposed of most of them in double-quick time, earning himself a big reputation, and the dubious figures behind him a healthy amount in prize money. Carnera was almost certainly unaware of the underhand dealings which were propelling him to the forefront of the heavyweight boxing scene.

On 29 June 1933, Carnera faced Jack Sharkey at Long Island, in the latter's first defence of his crown. The champion scored heavily in the opening five rounds, beating Carnera's defences on numerous occasions with head and body shots.

Terrific uppercut

In the sixth round, however, Carnera caught Sharkey with a terrific right uppercut. Sharkey was sent reeling to the canvas and was counted out. There was suspicion as to whether this was yet another stage-managed affair. Sharkey ought to have been too cute to lose to the likes of Carnera. On the other hand, the blow which ended the contest is widely regarded as the best the Ambling Alp ever landed.

Carnera won two unedifying contests in his year-long tenure as heavyweight champion. His first opponent was the giant Basque Paulino Uzcudun. What ought to have been a clash of the titans was in fact a tedious affair, won on points by Carnera. His second defence matched him against former light-heavyweight champion Tommy Loughran. Despite a weight advantage of more than six stones, Carnera couldn't put Loughran away. Instead, he had to settle for yet another uninspiring points decision.

Three months later, on 14 June 1934, Carnera came up against a man who was more than a match for him, and someone from whom his gangster managers couldn't protect him. That man was Max Baer. It was a fight which finally put Carnera's nominally impressive record into true context.

Ambling Alp toppled

The Italian had risen to the top in an era which was indifferent as far as heavyweights were concerned, and then only on the back of some blatantly corrupt contests. None of which was the fault of Carnera, who was a victim of the most egregious exploitation. But on that June day in 1934, the Ambling Alp was felled and humbled in dramatic style. He would also soon be discarded by the unsavoury characters who now saw him as a liability instead of a cash cow. Only then would Italy's sole heavyweight champion begin to realise the extent to which he had been manipulated and exploited, and, worse still, that his place in boxing history was forever tainted.

Carnera down eleven times as he loses title

Opposite top: Baer sends Carnera crashing to the canvas, one of eleven knockdowns on his way to winning the world crown. The referee delighted the crowd but offended good taste by allowing the contest to go as far as the eleventh round.
Opposite bottom: Baer loses his balance after putting Carnera down in the second round, and both men end up on the canvas.

Primo Carnera

Nickname:	"The Ambling Alp"
Born:	Sequals, Italy. October 26, 1906
Died:	June 29, 1967
Height:	6' 6"
World Heavyweight Champion: 1933-34	
Record:	Won 88 (69 KOs) Lost 14

Comedy fight has brutal ending

Right and below: The Carnera-Baer fight was dubbed "The Comedy Battle" for its many tumbles and slips. Carnera hit the deck eleven times, and Baer himself went down on six occasions. When both men found themselves on the canvas at the same time, Madcap Maxie couldn't help but see the funny side, declaring: "Last one up's a rotten egg."

Opposite: Carnera survived this early knockdown, but by the eleventh round, when the fight was stopped, he was in a terrible state. When he had recovered from the physical injuries, the Italian had to contend with the extent to which he had been manipulated and exploited by his unsavoury backers.

Max Baer
World Heavyweight Champion: 1934-1935

In an era widely regarded as undistinguished as far as heavyweight champions were concerned, Max Baer stood out on two counts. Firstly, he was the Clown Prince of the ring, an ebullient showman who always had a smile on his face. Secondly, he was thought to possess the hardest right-hand punch the sport had ever seen.

Maximilian Adelbert Baer was born on 11 February 1909, in Omaha, Nebraska. His family moved to California when Max was a child, and it was here that he began making a name for himself as a boxer. The sheer power for which he was known came from the heavy work he did on his father's ranch, including wielding the axe which dispatched pigs in the family-run abattoir.

Baer came to the attention of no less a figure than Jack Dempsey, who obviously saw shades of himself in his powerhouse if unrefined performance. Other boxing aficionados were unconvinced, but Dempsey predicted that Baer would win the heavyweight crown and, equally importantly with the top division in the doldrums, pull in the kind of crowds that Dempsey himself had attracted a decade earlier.

Haunted by ring death

Baer's main weapon, that big right hand, had killed a boxer named Frankie Campbell in a fight in San Francisco in 1930. Some maintain that he always held something back after that tragic incident, and that it prevented him from scaling even greater heights in the boxing world. Others said that if he had spent as much time training and honing his skills as he did clowning around, he would have enjoyed a more dominant reign as heavyweight champion.

Even so, he rose to become a top contender, particularly after his meeting with Max Schmeling in 1933. The ex-champion made his superior technique tell in the early rounds. By the eighth, Baer seemed to be tiring and the result appeared in little doubt. The Californian was then galvanised by his manager, who yelled that the result of the fight would determine whether he would sink into obscurity or be given a shot at the title. It did the trick. Baer tore into Schmeling in the ninth, raining down a barrage of blows on his man. In the next round he hit Schmeling with a mighty right to the chin. The German did beat the count - just - but the referee stopped the fight seconds later.

Playing to gallery

Even when the world title was at stake a year later, Baer's casual and lighthearted approach remained the same. It was still more than enough for a demolition job on Primo Carnera. In the 11 rounds that the fight lasted, Baer put Carnera down 11 times. By the end, the Italian giant's face and body had been battered to a pulp. Baer couldn't resist playing to the gallery, which included thousands of smitten female fans. He added insult to injury by weighing in with plenty of verbal taunts. The crowd loved it; few had any sympathy for the badly beaten and soon-to-be ex-champion.

Talk of a rematch quickly subsided; Carnera's time at the top was up. He later turned to wrestling, and opened a store. He eventually returned to the Alpine village of his birth, where he died in relative obscurity on 29 June 1967.

Pleasure seeker

Baer was the breath of fresh air that heavyweight boxing had long needed. He was charismatic, popular with women as well as men, and on his day a destructive boxer out of the Dempsey mould. Unfortunately, he preferred socialising and womanising to fighting. And once crowned champion he set about his hedonistic pursuits with abandon. When he could defer a title defence no longer, he signed to fight a man few people thought would pose him many problems. James J. Braddock had had an unspectacular boxing career, so much so that in 1934 - the year before he faced Baer - he had been forced to apply for unemployment relief. They met at Long Island on 13 June 1935. Braddock had put in a lot of solid training to prepare for a fight no one gave him a chance of winning. Baer did what he always did: caroused and enjoyed himself when he should have been getting into peak condition. The consequence was that the title he had held for a day short of a year went to the biggest underdog in heavyweight history.

Max Baer

Born:	Omaha, Nebraska, USA. February 11 1909
Died:	November 21 1959
World Heavyweight Champion: 1934-1935	
Record:	Won 72 (52 KOs) Lost 11

Madcap Maxie celebrates

Opposite above: A forlorn and battered Primo Carnera looks on as Max Baer celebrates winning the world title.
Opposite below: Carnera (left) and Baer square up in a scene from the film *The Prizefighter and the Lady*, in which the two heavyweights starred. Jack Dempsey looks on in the role of referee.

Baer and Carnera clash in the ring and on film

Above: A smiling, relaxed Max Baer is passed fit to take on champion Primo Carnera. It was to be the crowning moment of Baer's ring career.

Opposite: A scene from *The Prizefighter and the Lady*. Carnera was the film's hero, but Baer gave the better performance, just as he did when the two met for real.

Baer KOs Levinsky, then it's downhill all the way

Opposite: A six-frame series of pictures showing Max Baer's KO of King Levinsky in the second round of their no-decision fight in Chicago, 9 January 1935.

Above: Baer pictured in his dressing room, following the defeat by Joe Louis in September 1935. Baer tries to explain his abysmal performance to his corner men, which included Jack Dempsey

Champions in decline

Above: Primo Carnera jolts Ray Impelletiere with a wicked right during their fight at Madison Square Garden, March 1935. After losing his title, Carnera became a liability for his mobster managers, who quickly lost interest in him.

Left: Max Baer carried on boxing for six years after losing his crown to Jim Braddock, but never scaled the heights again. He remained the great carouser and showman of his era.

James J. Braddock

James J. Braddock earned himself the nickname of "Cinderella Man" when he overturned odds of 10-1 against him and beat Max Baer to win the heavyweight crown. His was a classic rags-to-riches story, the kind that has always tempted hungry young men in deprived circumstances to chance their arm in the ring. It was a tale almost of "Rocky" proportions. Braddock was a journeyman boxer who had had his moments in the spotlight, including an unsuccessful challenge for Tommy Loughran's light-heavyweight title in 1929. By 1934, however, he was on his uppers claiming unemployment relief.

In June of that year, Braddock was drafted in as a late replacement to fight a top contender, Corn Griffin. Braddock was nearly 29, considered well past his best and not expected to give Griffin much trouble. To the amazement of everyone in the boxing world, Braddock knocked Griffin out in the third round.

Braddock had always been a solid puncher, game and durable. Now he had the added advantage of being in the right place at the right time. After grinding out two more points victories against quality opponents, Braddock justifiably earned himself a crack at the world title.

Longest odds

When he stepped into the ring against Max Baer on 13 June 1935, few gave him any chance at all. The bookies confidently offered 10-1 against the challenger, probably the longest odds ever offered in a title fight. Yet Braddock caused the greatest upset in the championship's history, partly due to his own cautious approach and partly to Baer's predilection for playing to the gallery.

Braddock had trained hard for the fight; Baer hadn't. The champion, like everyone else, was confident that he could clown around and still win the fight at a canter. It wasn't much of a spectacle; certainly no toe-to-toe slugging match. Baer didn't reproduce the kind of demolition job that he had done on Carnera 364 days earlier.

Champion leaves it too late

Braddock was cautious, yet did enough to rack up a healthy points lead. Baer belatedly realised what was at stake but left his move too late. Braddock absorbed everything the champion threw at him in the latter stages and was declared a unanimous points winner at the end of the 15-round contest.

Baer was beaten convincingly by rising star Joe Louis three months later and never scaled the heights again. Many purists had found his attitude in the ring hard to take and believed he threw away the title. Baer wasn't about to

change, despite that unexpected defeat by Braddock. The man who once quipped "I buy the Ziegfeld girls furs to keep them warm - and quiet!" finally retired from boxing at 41 and died from a heart attack nine years later, in 1959.

The new champion sat on his title for two years before agreeing to a defence. Joe Gould, Braddock's manager, studied the options carefully before making a match against the sport's new sensation, Joe Louis. Braddock had just turned 30 when the two met, in Chicago on 22 June 1937. Louis was 21.

Shrewd deal

Gould must have realised that there wouldn't be many more big paydays for his man, and had at least half an eye on the financial side of the deal. Under the terms of the contract, Braddock would get 10 per cent of Louis's earnings over the next decade, irrespective of the result of the fight. The fact that Louis not only won the contest but spent the whole of that 10-year period as heavyweight champion made it an inspired piece of negotiation on the part of Gould, who was himself to profit handsomely from his cut of the moneys due to Braddock.

The choice of Louis was by no means obvious. True, the 21-year-old had bludgeoned Max Baer to a four-round defeat in September 1935, just three months after Braddock's title fight against the same man. He had also beaten two other former champions, Sharkey and Carnera. But Louis's seemingly unstoppable rise to the top received a huge reversal when Max Schmeling knocked him out in 12 rounds. It ought to have earned Schmeling a crack at the title he had lost to Sharkey. Indeed, most pundits are convinced the German would have got the better of Braddock. Politics cost Schmeling the chance of regaining the title, however. The Nazi propaganda machine made much capital from Schmeling's defeat of Louis. Schmeling was no Nazi apologist, but in the prevailing climate in his home country there was little he could do. He was unfortunate to be tainted by association, and this manifested itself when it came to the next world title fight. In short, Schmeling was overlooked, and the man he had beaten so comprehensively, Joe Louis, was installed as the first challenger to James J. Braddock.

Opposite: Jim Braddock takes a few tips from past-master Jack Dempsey as he prepares for his showdown with Max Baer.

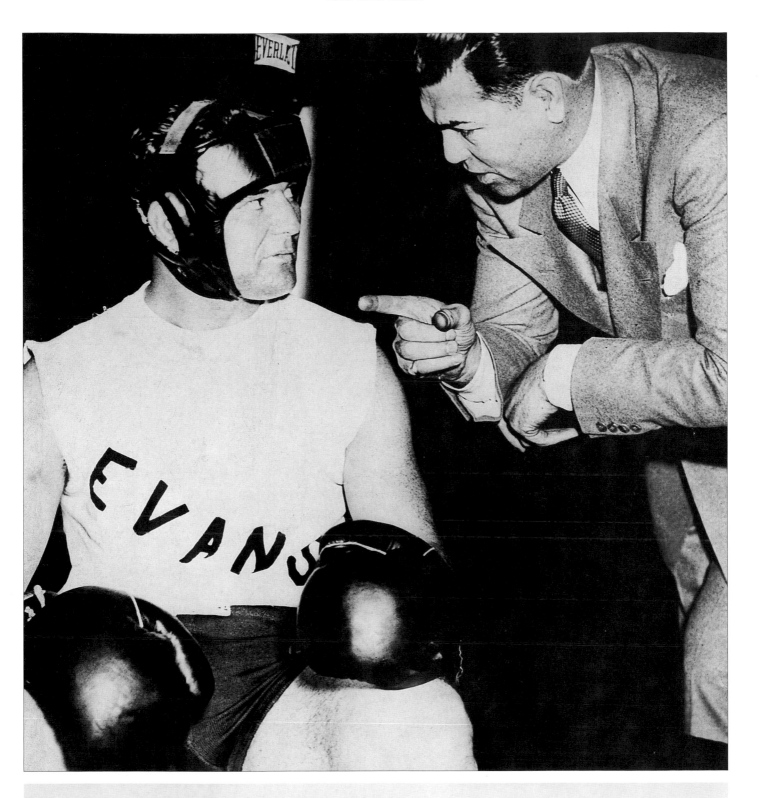

James J. Braddock

Nickname:	"Cinderella Man"	**Born:**	New York City, New York, USA. June 7 1906	
Died:	November 29 1974	**Height:**	6' 3"	**Weight:** 197 lbs
World Heavyweight Champion:	1935-1937	**Record:**	Won 45 (26 KOs) Lost 23 Drawn 17	

Braddock in shock victory over Baer

Above: Jim Braddock (right) was responsible for one of the biggest upsets in boxing history when he outpointed Max Baer in June 1935.

Opposite: After a lacklustre performance in the early stages of his fight with Braddock, Max Baer desperately tried to retrieve the situation. Here, he fails to connect with his famed right. Braddock stayed clear of trouble and won comfortably on points.

Battling performances from former champions

Above: Primo Carnera rocks back to avoid a jab from Spanish heavyweight Isadora Gastanaga. A cut over Gastanaga's left eye gave Carnera a TKO in the fifth, but the Italian's career was on a downward path in March 1936, when the fight took place.

Opposite: Max Baer (right) shakes hands with South African heavyweight Ben Foord at the weigh-in prior to their clash at Harringay Arena, May 1937.

Right: Baer is clearly enjoying himself in his victory over Foord, which included three knockdowns. On the other hand, the South African was hardly a top-drawer opponent.

Louis era ushered in with a KO

June 22, 1937. One brief, undistinguished reign comes to an end, and a long, glorious era is ushered in as Joe Louis knocks Jim Braddock out in the eighth round of their title fight in Chicago.

Left: Jim Braddock was a solid pro who seized his chance of winning the title with both fists. While Baer clowned, Braddock racked up the points which won him the heavyweight crown.

Baer the man about town

Left: Max Baer pictured at Elstree for a read-through of the script for *Over She Goes*, his first British film. His co-star is Gina Malo.

Above: May 1937. Following his victory over South Africa's Ben Foord, Max Baer enjoys a night out in London with actress June Knight.

Tunney conquers business world

Above: Gene Tunney pictured during a visit to England in 1936. "Gentleman" Gene enjoyed a successful business career after shocking the boxing world with his decision to quit the ring at the age of 31.

Right: Max Baer shows off his magnificent physique. His physical attributes and devastating right hand should have brought him greater success, but boxing always came second to hedonistic pursuits in Baer's scale of priorities.

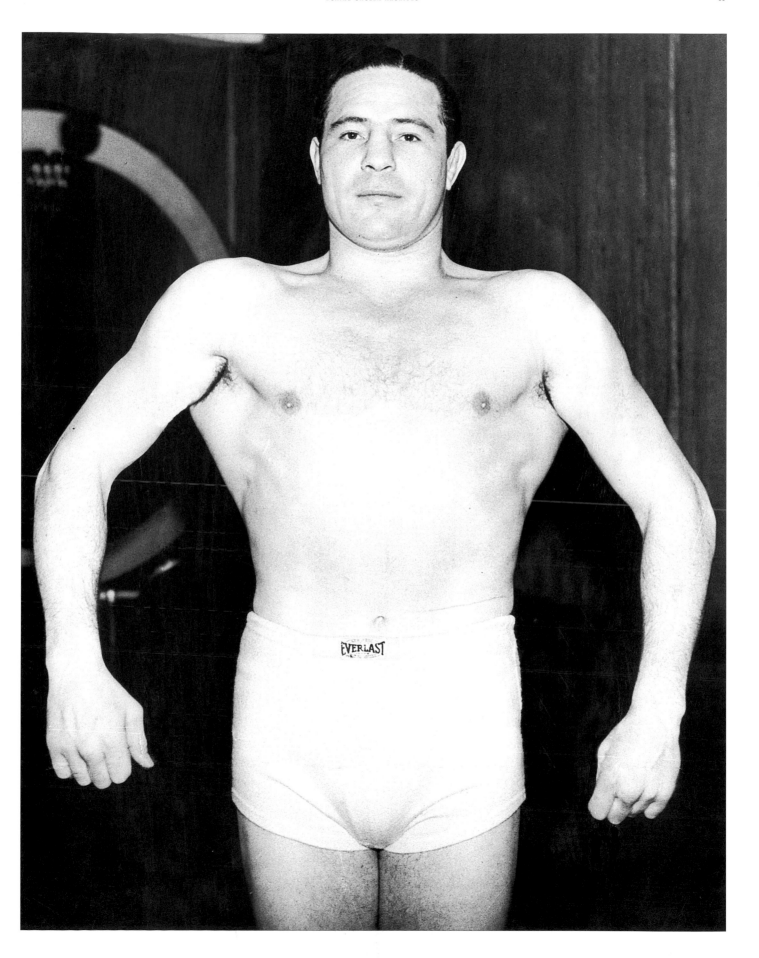

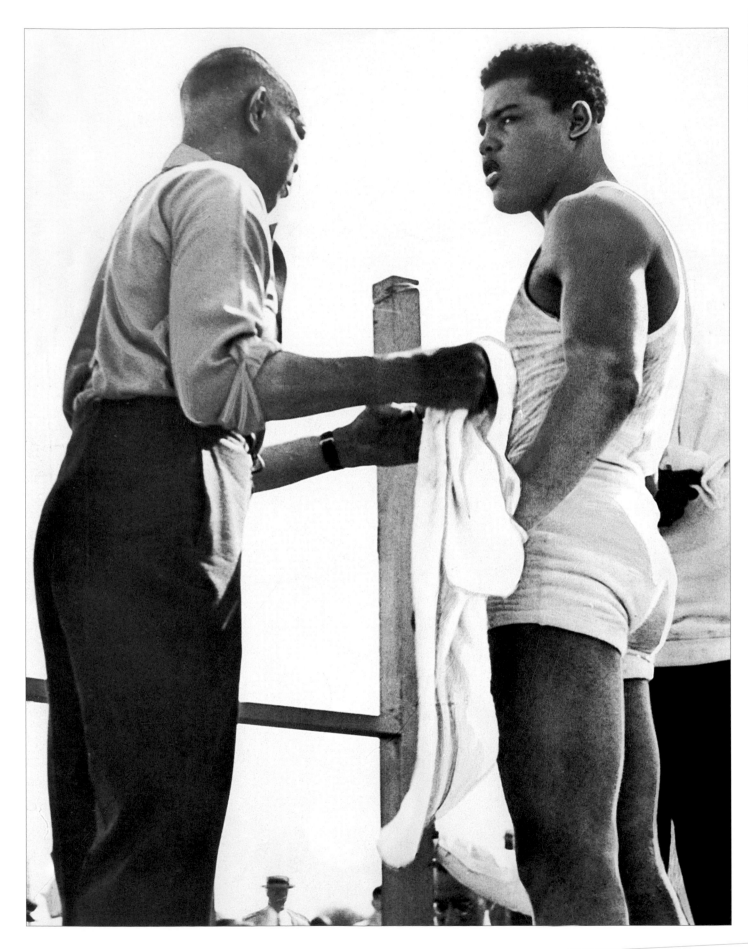

Brown bomber beats fourth champion on his way to the title

Left: Joe Louis in training for the Braddock fight. The Brown Bomber had already taken the scalps of three former heavyweight champions: Sharkey, Carnera and Baer.
Above: Jim Braddock leaves his dressing room after receiving first-aid for the terrible injuries sustained during his eight-round defeat by Joe Louis. Reports varied as to the number of facial stitches Braddock received; some put it as high as 50.
Right: Braddock (right) wins on points against England's Tommy Farr, his last fight before quitting the ring for good.

Cinderella man bows out with a victory

Above: Jim Braddock (right) on his way to a points win over Tommy Farr. The former champion could have walked away from boxing after the Louis fight, having cut a very lucrative deal, but he wanted to bow out on a winning note.

Opposite: Max Baer puts Tommy Farr down during their encounter in March 1938.

Godoy pays for taking Louis the distance

Above: Joe Louis (left) and Chile's Arturo Godoy eyeball each other as they sign for their Madison Square Garden clash on February 9, 1940. Louis won the fight on points, while Godoy joined Tommy Farr as the only men to take the champion the distance.

Left: June 20, 1940. Louis takes on Godoy for the second time in four months. The Chilean frustrated Louis in their first encounter, and the champion had been dissatisfied with his points win. The rematch was far more decisive, Louis inflicting severe punishment on his opponent. The referee stopped the fight in the eighth.

Opposite: Sgt Joe Louis (right), photographed during a visit to London in May 1944.

Joe Louis

World Heavyweight Champion: 1937-1949

Joe Louis's victory over James J. Braddock in Chicago, on 22 June 1937, ushered in an era of supremacy the like of which had never been seen. He would remain the champion for the next 12 years, during which time he defended his title 25 times. His victims would doubtless have numbered many more had it not been for the Second World War, which meant a lay-off of more than four years. He beat all the top contenders of the day, including five former champions and one future title-holder. He retired undefeated at the age of 35. There followed an ill-judged comeback, largely for financial reasons. Louis suffered two defeats, against Ezzard Charles and Rocky Marciano, the men who dominated heavyweight boxing in the early 1950s. These reverses shouldn't be allowed to taint the reputation of a man who is widely regarded as being among the top five heavyweights of all time. There are even those who put him at the top of the pile.

Grinding poverty

Louis grew up in Detroit, in straitened circumstances. His rise to the top is an archetypal story of a youngster who used boxing - for which he showed a remarkable natural aptitude - as a means of escaping grinding poverty. Louis's chief weapons were speed and awesome punching power. To make matters even worse for his opponents, his defence was also technically excellent. Louis was confident that he could take on anybody and beat them, and he had every reason to be.

But there was a problem. The rising star of the boxing world faced an obstacle that was potentially far trickier than any fighter in the opposite corner. He was black. Memories of the Johnson era came flooding back. The thought of a black heavyweight champion was still anathema to a lot of people, including many in the boxing establishment. Over the years, several very talented black boxers had been denied a shot at the title, passed over in favour of less talented fighters who were politically more acceptable.

Louis simply let his fists do the talking. Boxers of the stature of Primo Carnera and Max Baer were dispatched, and Louis was already being dubbed the champion-in-waiting.

Setback against Schmeling

His rise was halted in dramatic fashion in June 1936, when he met another former titleholder, Max Schmeling. Schmeling was given no chance, but arguably had his greatest fight ever in handing Louis his first defeat. Two of the German's trademark rights did the damage: one floored Louis in the fourth, the other finished him in the 12th.

Louis was soon back on track, putting away his opponents with monotonous regularity. But when a first challenger to reigning champion James J. Braddock was

being lined up, Louis could not have argued at being behind Schmeling in the pecking order. However, on this occasion, prejudice worked in Louis's favour, not against him. Schmeling abhorred Adolf Hitler and the Nazi regime, but his roots cost him what most pundits believed would have been a second stint as champion. Schmeling was passed over, and Louis was given a crack at the title.

He and Braddock met in Chicago, on 22 June 1937. Braddock fought magnificently for six rounds. In the first he actually dropped Louis to the boards with a right to the jaw. The challenger cut loose in the sixth with a series of pulverising rights to the head. A bloodied Braddock gamely came out for the seventh, swinging wildly in the hope of landing a lucky punch. He didn't connect, and Louis did even more damage. It was all over in the next round. One swing too many left Braddock exposed and off balance. Louis put him down - and out - with yet another terrific right.

Two of Louis's first three defences were routine early knockouts; the third was anything but. It pitted him against Tommy Farr, whom Braddock had outpointed after losing his title. Farr took Louis all the way, too, becoming one of only three fighters to go the distance with the champion.

Unfinished business

Louis's fourth defence was all about settling unfinished business. His defeat by Schmeling still rankled, and the way the German had been so cynically overlooked as number one challenger to Braddock also gnawed away at him. The issue was decided in the most dramatic fashion, on 22 June 1938. The fight took place against a backdrop of personal rancour and political propaganda. There was little love lost between the two men, and before the contest Louis had ominously declared: "It's revenge I'm after." On an ideological level, Schmeling was lauded as the symbol of Aryan supremacy. A thoroughly decent man, Schmeling was horrified at such talk. He was a victim of circumstance.

It was one of the most brutal contests ever seen, and lasted barely two minutes. In that time Louis unleashed a ferocious attack on his opponent. One body blow brought a cry of pain from Schmeling that was heard all round the arena. It later transpired that the punch had broken one of his lumbar vertebrae and driven it into a kidney. Schmeling would need weeks of hospital treatment to make a full recovery.

Broadcast halted

German radio was covering the fight live, anticipating a famous victory. Mysteriously, the plug was pulled on the broadcast before the referee called a halt to proceedings and allowed Schmeling to be stretchered out of the ring.

This was seen by many as Louis's finest hour, a

remarkable combination of raw power and artistry. The man himself later said that Schmeling was the only fighter he ever really got mad at.

Louis had a six-month lay-off after the Schmeling fight, returning to the ring in January 1939. In just over three years, he proceeded to see off no less than 17 challengers. The highlights, for very different reasons, were wins over Tony Galento, Arturo Godoy and Billy Conn.

"Two Ton" Tony Galento was a hulk of a man, who famously trained on beer, cigars and steaks. He refused to be intimidated by the champion. Galento took the fight to Louis, and even managed to put him down in the third round. But superior skill told in the end, and the end wasn't far away. Louis cut loose in the fourth, and Galento was a bloodied mess when the referee finished it.

Chile's Arturo Godoy was an unconventional boxer and an awkward customer. He frustrated Louis when they met in New York on 9 February 1940, and joined a very select club who would take the champion the distance. Louis had Godoy worked out when the two met again four months later; the fight was stopped in the fourth.

Conn's costly mistake

The last great bout before the Second World War caused a four-year hiatus saw Louis take on light-heavyweight champion Billy Conn. Conn was lightning fast, very skilful and ultra-confident. He matched Louis for 12 rounds, and Louis later said he came perilously close to losing his title on that June day in 1941. Conn only had to stay clear of trouble for the last three minutes and victory was assured. But he made the mistake of trying to slug it out with Louis in the 13th round, and a grateful champion put him out for the count.

A rematch with Conn was Louis's first fight after the war, on 19 June 1946. As usual, Louis didn't make the same mistake twice and this time Conn was knocked out in the eighth.

Time had taken its toll on Louis, and he was now a declining force. He still had too much punching power for most challengers, though. There were three more wins after the Conn fight, two of them against Jersey Joe Walcott. Walcott was already a veteran, even older than Louis. The two men met for the first time in New York, on 5 December 1947. Walcott became the third boxer to take Louis all the way. Unlike the Farr and Godoy fights, however, many thought Louis fortunate to get the decision this time.

One last hurrah

The two met again in June 1948. Louis was still the favourite, but nowhere near the 10-1 on odds which had once been the norm. His training displays were described as lazy and lacklustre; in sparring he looked ponderous and vulnerable. Stung by the criticism and worried that he might be outboxed, Louis broke his own rule and taunted

Walcott to come forward and make a fight of it. For nine rounds Walcott had much the better of things. The next six minutes witnessed one last hurrah for a great champion. In rounds 10 and 11 he rolled back the years, fighting like a man rejuvenated if not possessed. Observers said that Louis hit Walcott with every punch in the book. It was all over in the 11th, and it would have been a perfect way to bow out of the sport. After the fight, Louis said that even after Uncle Sam had taken his cut, the $250,000 purse would help him to enjoy life as an ex-champion and help support his business ventures. It was to prove an ominous remark, for crippling tax bills would force Louis back into the ring just two years later. It was to prove an unedifying spectacle.

Joe Louis

Nickname:	"The Brown Bomber"		
Born:	Lafayette, Alabama USA May 13 1914		
Died:	April 12 1981		
Height:	over 6'	Weight:	196 lbs.
World Heavyweight Champion: 1937-1949			
Record:	Won 63 (49 KOs) Lost 3		

Left: Joe Louis enlisted in the US Army as a private soldier, but the heavyweight champion was naturally the focus of attention wherever he went.

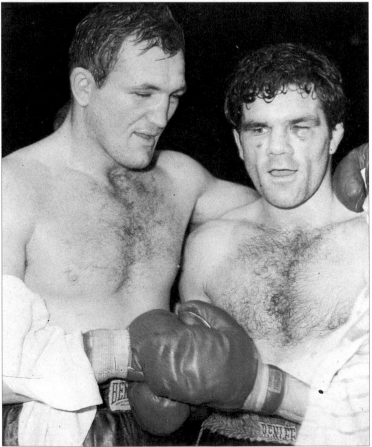

Louis entertains the troops

Above: May 1944. Joe Louis spars with Sergeant George Robinson for the entertainment of the officers and men of the Ninth Air Force Squadron.

Louis showed his patriotism by donating the purses of two title defences to the Army and Navy Relief Fund.

Right: England's Bruce Woodcock (right) shakes hands with France's heavyweight champion Georges Martin, prior to their meeting at Belle Vue in November 1946.

Left: Freddie Mills and Joe Baksi embrace at the end of their fight at Harringay, November 1946.

Louis picks up where he left off

Left: September 18, 1946. In his second fight following his discharge from the army, Joe Louis showed he had lost none of his sharpness. After knocking out Billy Conn in the eighth round on June 19, the champion followed it up with a comprehensive win over New Yorker Tami Mauriello, who was dispatched inside a round.

Above: Bruce Woodcock (back to camera) makes short work of France's heavyweight champion Georges Martin, knocking him out in the third round of their November 1946 encounter.

Lesnevich beats Mills
to win light-heavyweight crown

Opposite: America's top light-heavyweight Gus Lesnevich bears the scars of his vicious battle with British Empire champion Freddie Mills in London, May 1946. Lesnevich knocked Mills out in the tenth round to become the undisputed world champion.

Above: Lesnevich holds an ice-pack to his badly damaged eye as he commiserates with the defeated Mills. Mills would get his revenge in a return bout two years later.

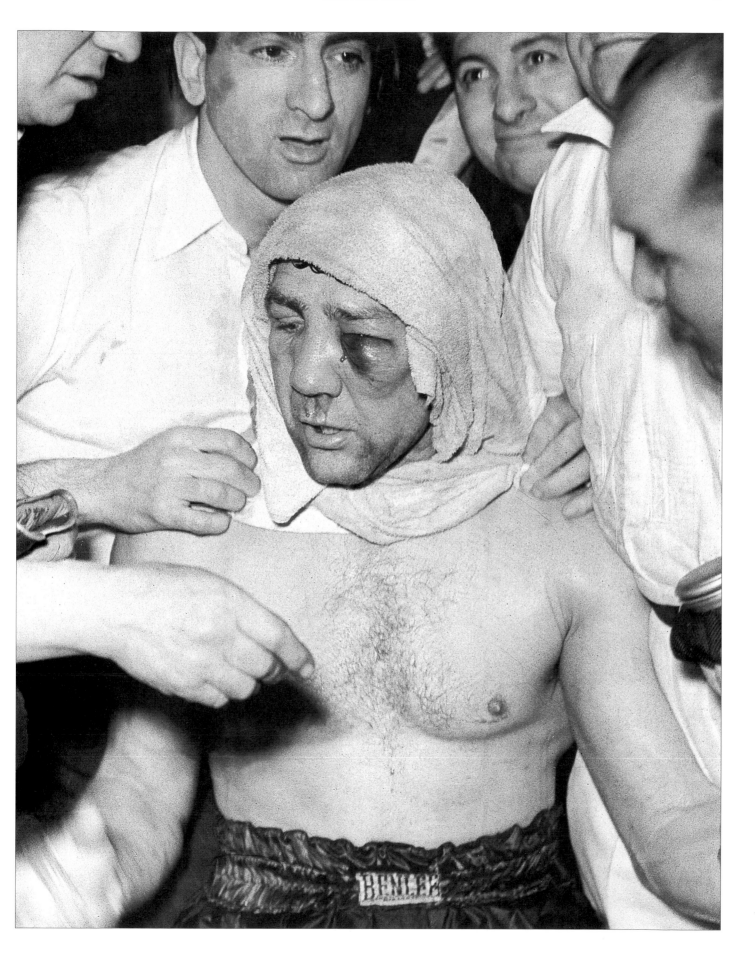

Woodcock wins battle of British giants

Left: Despite taking heavy punishment himself, Bruce Woodcock comes out on top against Freddie Mills in the clash between Britain's two premier fighters. The contest took place in London, June 1946.

Above: Al Phillips and Cliff Anderson in action at Olympia, July 1947. Phillips won the fight on a foul in round eight.

Right: Max Schmeling (left), making a comeback, in action against Werner Vollmer, one of Germany's leading heavyweights. A crowd of 30,000 saw Schmeling knock out Vollmer in the seventh round.

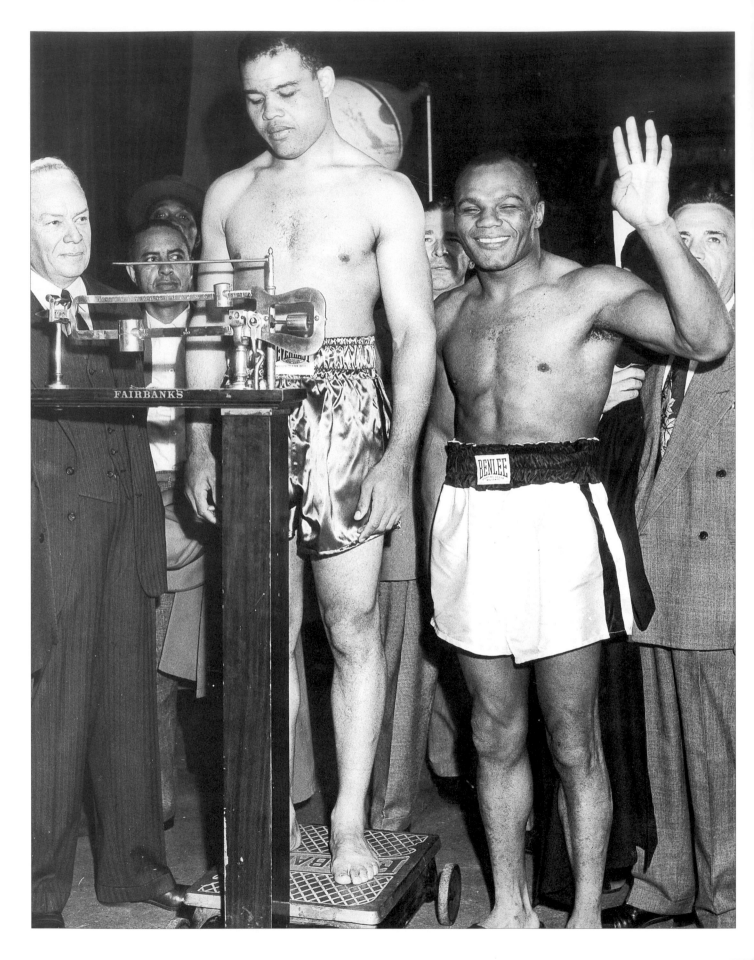

Unlucky Walcott runs Louis close

Opposite: 25 June 1948. A relaxed Jersey Joe Walcott acknowledges the fans at the weigh-in before his second fight with Joe Louis. The two had met the previous December, when most observers felt Louis had been lucky to get the decision. Walcott again made all the running, before succumbing to a Louis onslaught in the eleventh.

Right: 21 September 1948. British champion Bruce Woodcock makes a sensational return to the ring after a 17-month lay-off. America's Lee Oma, seen here taking a rapier straight left to the chin, lasts just four rounds.

Above: Bruce Woodcock is down but not out in his December 1948 encounter with Lee Savold. The Minnesota heavyweight was disqualified in the fourth round.

"25th and final defence," says Joe

Opposite: May 1948. Joe Louis sports a beard as he heads off to his New Jersey training camp to prepare for the rematch with Jersey Joe Walcott.

Above: Eleven years at the top means that the Brown Bomber can draw sizeable crowds just to watch him train. The 34-year-old managed to sharpen himself up for one final moment of glory against Walcott, but the signs of his decline were there for all to see.

Right: Double take. Joe Louis (left) adjusts the gloves of his sparring partner, "Shadow" Coley Wallace, prior to a charity exhibition bout at Washington's Griffith Stadium, September 1948. Wallace was given his nickname because of his uncanny resemblance to the champion.

Louis and Farr meet 11 years on

Opposite and above: March 1948. Joe Louis renews his acquaintance with former British heavyweight champion Tommy Farr. Louis, who was in London to appear in a "Health and Holiday Exhibition" at Earls Court, took the opportunity to relive his first defence of the title, eleven years earlier, when the Welshman gave him a stern test over 15 rounds. Some die-hard British fans actually thought Farr should have got the decision, but every impartial observer had Louis the clear winner.

Right: Cuban welterweight Kid Gavilan's face is distorted as Sugar Ray Robinson connects with a terrific left to the jaw. Many aficionados think Robinson is the best pound-for-pound fighter of all time. Even Muhammad Ali believes Sugar Ray was the greatest.

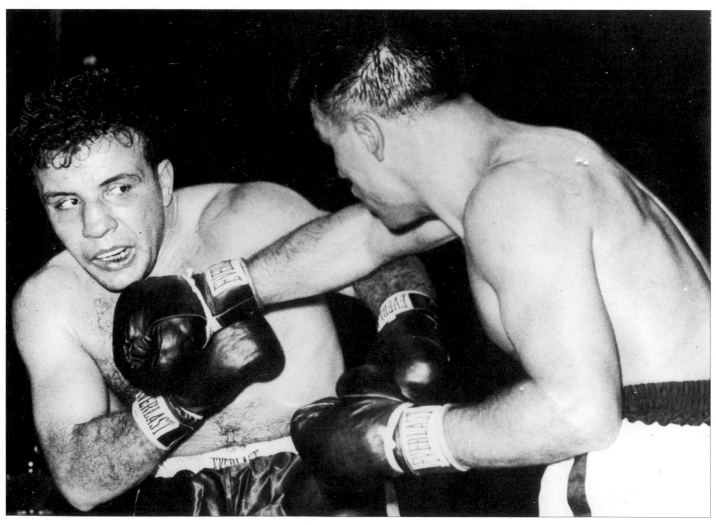

Money troubles force Louis back into the ring

Above: November 1949. Financial pressures force Joe Louis back into the ring, just eight months after announcing his retirement. He is still good enough to put the likes of Johnny Shkor down - something he managed three times in this exhibition bout - but Shkor survived the ten rounds.

Opposite, above left: Jersey Joe Walcott takes a right from Sweden's Olle Tandberg in his stride during the third round of their heavyweight clash in Stockholm, August 1949.

Opposite, above right: To the dismay of 45,000 Swedish fans, Walcott ends Tandberg's hopes of challenging for the world crown by knocking him out in the fifth round.

Opposite, below: World middleweight champion Jake La Motta is beaten on points by France's Robert Villemain in December 1949. Fortunately for the Bronx Bull, it was a non-title fight.

Walcott makes it a double defeat for Johnson family

Opposite: Philadelphia light-heavyweight Harold Johnson winces as he is examined following his defeat by Jersey Joe Walcott in February 1950. Not only was this a particularly impressive performance from Walcott, it also gave rise to a perennially popular quiz question. Fourteen years earlier, Jersey Joe had knocked out Phil Johnson, Harold's father. To make the symmetry complete, both contests took place in Philadelphia and both ended in third-round KOs.

Above: December 10, 1949. Pat Valentino goes down under the full force of a Joe Louis right in the eighth round of their exhibition bout in Chicago. Those who believed that the 35-year-old ex-champion could still produce the goods at the top level would be disabused of that notion the following September, when Louis attempted to regain the crown from Ezzard Charles.

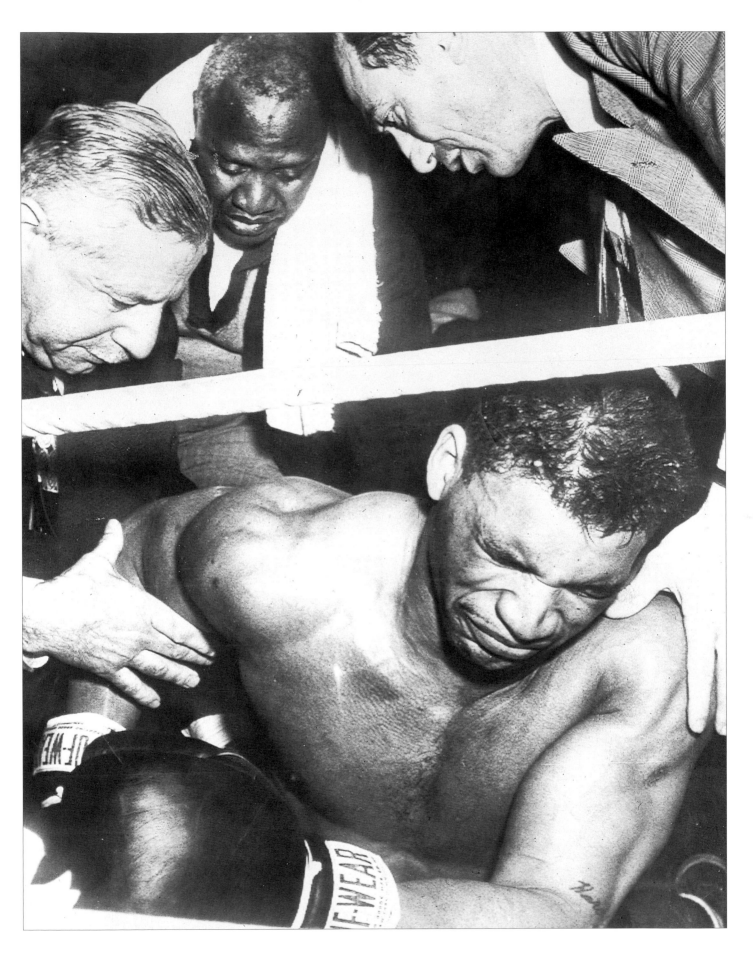

Walcott bids for fourth title shot

Right: Mannheim, 28 May 1950. Jersey Joe Walcott (left) stays in contention for a fourth tilt at the world title by winning a ten-round decision over Germany's heavyweight champion Hein Ten Hoff. After the contest, the 6ft 6in German paid tribute to his opponent's punching power, which broke his nose in the first round.

Opposite: Jake La Motta (left) shoots a left to the body of Tiberio Mitri during the early stages of their middleweight title fight at Madison Square Garden, 12 July 1950. It proved to be a comfortable first defence of his title for La Motta, who won on points.

Above: California's Manuel Ortiz (right) loses his Bantamweight boxing crown to Vic Toweel from South Africa.

Charles retains title with victory over his hero

Opposite, bottom: Champion Ezzard Charles (left) finds Joe Louis ponderously slow and an easy target in their title fight at New York's Yankee Stadium, on September 27, 1950.

Opposite, top: Charles grimaces as Louis connects with a solid punch in the tenth round. The fight went the distance, with Charles gaining a unanimous points decision. Many observers felt that the champion could have finished his hero inside the distance had he wanted.

Left: Louis smashes a left hook into Charles's face. In days gone by such a punch would have put an opponent out; Charles didn't even go down.

Above: Germany's heavyweight champion Hein Ten Hoff bounced back from his defeat at the hands of Jersey Joe Walcott by by knocking out Wilson Kohlbrecher in the first minute of the second round. The fight took place in Berlin, on August 1, 1950.

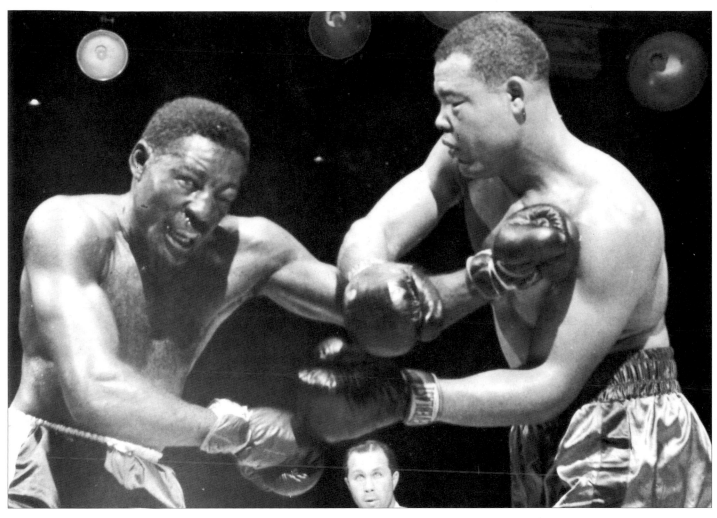

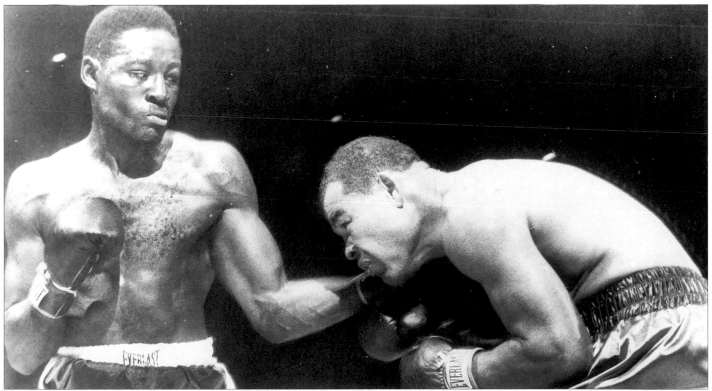

Ezzard Charles

World Heavyweight Champion: 1949-1951

After two fine performances against Joe Louis, one of which he should have won, Jersey Joe Walcott was one obvious contender for the title vacated by the Brown Bomber. The other was Ezzard Charles.

Charles was hardly an overnight sensation. He was a month short of his 28th birthday when he faced Walcott, and had served a long apprenticeship. He had 42 straight wins as an amateur, then continued to enhance his reputation in the professional ranks. Charles's career had to be put on hold after he was called up for military service in 1943. He did a three-year stint in the army. Joe Louis was similarly handicapped, of course, but perhaps it was rather more frustrating for someone trying to fight his way to the top than for an established champion.

Step up in class

After he was discharged, Charles picked up where he had left off. If the loss of three years wasn't bad enough, two more factors impinged on his progress. First, his best fighting weight was around 13 stones, and many of his bouts had been at light-heavyweight. The fact that there was little money to be made in that division forced Charles to step up and take on the bigger men. He didn't pack a particularly powerful punch; Charles's strengths were his lightning moves and scintillating combinations. Not for nothing was he called "The Cincinnati Cobra".

If Charles could compensate for his lack of power, he found a second handicap much more difficult to deal with. It was a psychological barrier, and stemmed from his fight against Sam Baroudi in 1948. Charles handed out a savage beating on the night, and his opponent died from the injuries sustained some hours later.

Haunted by ring death

Charles was devastated. His time as world champion was still ahead of him, but many observers said that he fought within himself after that. It seemed that he was not prepared to risk the possibility of an unfettered killer instinct having the same consequences. Even so, he was still good enough to keep notching up the victories. Two years later, Joe Louis had little hesitation in nominating the farmer's son from Lawrenceville, Georgia, as the man to face Jersey Joe Walcott for the vacant title.

The contest, which was held in Chicago on 22 June 1949, was a drab affair in which the 27-year-old Charles outpointed his 35-year-old opponent. Recognition that Charles was now world heavyweight champion was by no means universal, and the fact that Joe Louis was soon back in circulation confused matters even more.

After three successful "defences" of his crown, Charles found himself stepping into the ring against his hero: the Brown Bomber himself. Charles won on points against a man who was a mere shadow of his former self. Even though many observers felt that Charles deliberately held back, not wishing the great man to finish the contest on his back, the now undisputed champion was forever tainted in the eyes of some fight fans for making Louis look a sorry sight.

Within a year, Charles had seen off four more challenges, one of them a points victory over Jersey Joe Walcott, who was now 37. That was in March 1951. Four months later, on 18 July, Walcott and Charles squared up again. It was Charles's ninth title defence, and Walcott's fifth tilt at the crown. Charles's two-year reign came to a dramatic end that night.

Immortalised by Beatles

He was by no means finished, though. There would be three more title fights, one of them rated among the best contests of all time. More of that later. For now it is enough to point out that Charles didn't get the credit he deserved as champion. Only later, when multiple sclerosis had devastated him, did many come to regard him as probably the most underrated of all the heavyweight champions. If he was only belatedly elevated to boxing's Hall of Fame, he was immortalised in an unexpected way in 1967: he features on the cover of the Beatles' *Sergeant Pepper* album.

Ezzard Charles

Nickname:	"The Cincinnatti Flash"
Born:	Lawrenceville, Georgia USA July 7 1921
Died:	May 27 1975
Height:	6' 0"
Weight:	192lbs.
World Heavyweight Champion:	1949-1951
Record:	Won 96 (58 KOs) Lost 25 Drawn 1

Walcott's title hopes take a jolt

Opposite: Madison Square Garden, November 28, 1950. Jersey Joe Walcott (left) takes a hard right to the jaw from young American heavyweight Rex Layne. Layne went on to win the fight on points, a result which seemed to be a major setback to Walcott's hopes of a fourth shot at the title.

Below: Chicago Stadium, November 29, 1950. Joe Louis (left) grimaces as he engages in some in-fighting with Argentina's Cesar Brion. Louis won a unanimous points decision in what was his second comeback fight.

Left: The Sugar Ray Robinson bandwagon rolls on with a two-round win over France's Jean Stock, in Paris, November 1950. Having held the world welterweight title for four years, Robinson now set his sights on the middleweight crown.

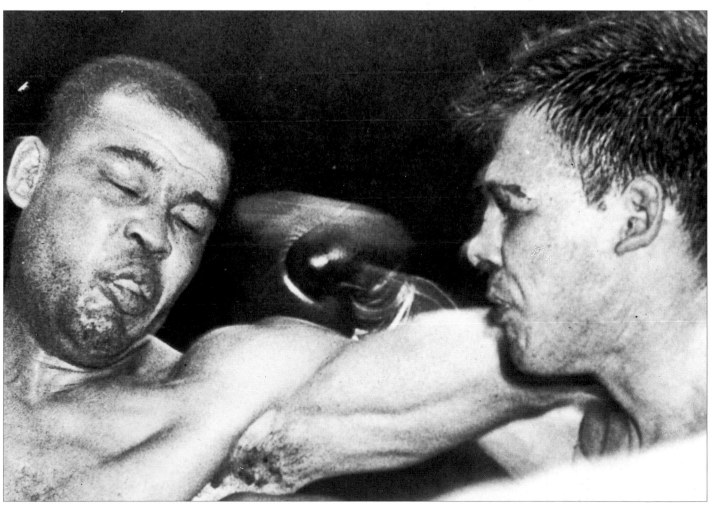

Walcott again takes Charles the distance

Opposite, top: Ezzard Charles rocks Jersey Joe Walcott on his way to retaining his title in March 1951. The fact that Walcott took the champion the full 15 rounds for the second time earned him another crack at the title four months later.

Below: Detroit, May 2, 1951. Joe Louis shows a glimpse of his former powers as he explodes a right to the jaw of Cuba's Omelio Agramonte. Louis won the fight on a unanimous decision.

Opposite, bottom: It's the battle of the veterans as 37-year-old Joe Louis (right) and 36-year-old Lee Savold weigh in for their Madison Square Garden clash in June 1951. Louis won by a knockout in what was the best performance of all his comeback fights.

Right: Carmarthen, December 1950. 13 years on from his glorious defeat at the hands of Joe Louis, Tommy Farr (right) is still battling on. On this occasion, he goes down on points against Lloyd Marshall.

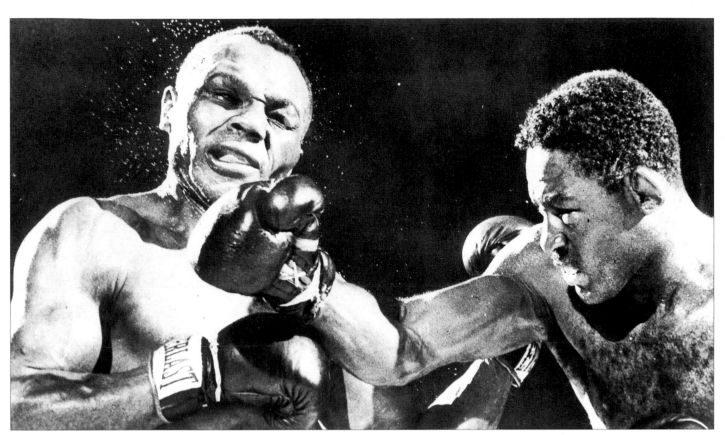

Turpin stuns boxing with victory over Sugar Ray

Above: Randolph Turpin ducks to avoid a left from middleweight champion Sugar Ray Robinson during their fight at Earls Court, July 10, 1951. Robinson had beaten Jake La Motta to win the title five months earlier. Having been on a whistle-stop tour of Europe, where he engaged in a series of non-title fights, Robinson chose to lay his crown on the line against Turpin, who was the British and European champion. Robinson was thought to be unbeatable, but Turpin stunned the boxing world with a clear points victory. He became only the second man to get the better of Sugar Ray in 132 fights. The other was La Motta himself, although the Bronx Bull lost to Robinson on five other occasions.

Opposite: Argentina's top contender Cesar Brion (left) on his way to a points win over Jack Gardner at the White City, June 1951.

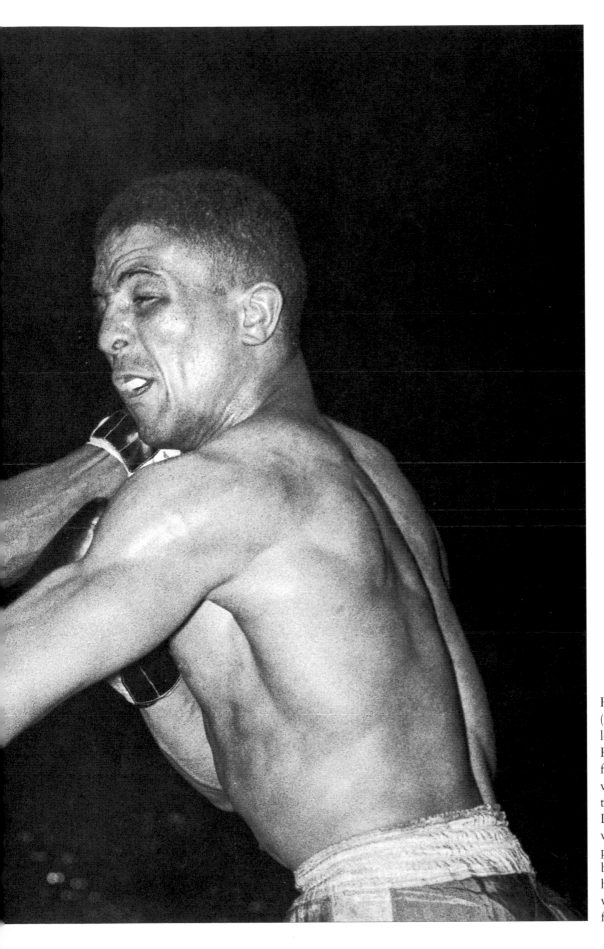

Randolph Turpin (right) survived this left from Sugar Ray Robinson in the fourth round and went on to become the pride of Leamington Spa by winning the fight on points. Robinson blamed the recent hectic European tour, which involved six fights in 52 days.

Turpin's reign lasts 64 days

Opposite: Sugar Ray Robinson ducks and holds on, while Randolph Turpin racks up the points that would bring him the world middleweight crown. The rematch was set for New York's Polo Grounds 64 days later.

Below: The Robinson-Turpin return clash, September 12, 1951. With a badly cut left eye threatening his ability to continue, Robinson launches a savage attack on Turpin in the tenth round. Turpin is laid out on the canvas, but gamely manages to beat the count.

Right: Still groggy from the knockdown, Turpin backs into the ropes and is caught by a barrage of blows from Robinson. Referee Ruby Goldstein intervenes to prevent Turpin from taking further punishment, and the title is Sugar Ray's once again.

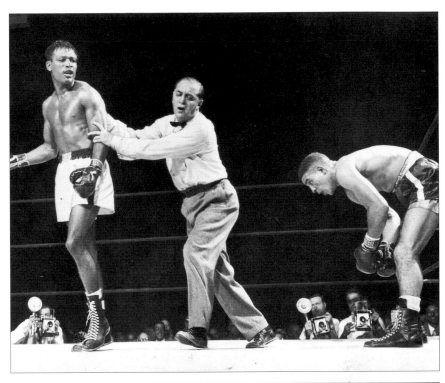

Opposite: Primo Carnera (centre), pictured at London Airport in the early 1950s. The Ambling Alp turned to wrestling after his boxing days were over. With no shadowy figures trying to exploit him, Carnera enjoyed a relatively prosperous career in the grappling ring. He certainly made enough money to enable him to return to Sequals, his home town in Italy, where he opened a liquor store. He died there on June 29, 1969.

Above: Philadelphia, September 23, 1952. Jersey Joe Walcott takes a hard left from Rocky Marciano, with a forearm follow-through for good measure. Walcott was comfortably ahead on points after 12 rounds, but Marciano delivered a knockout blow in the 13th to take the title.

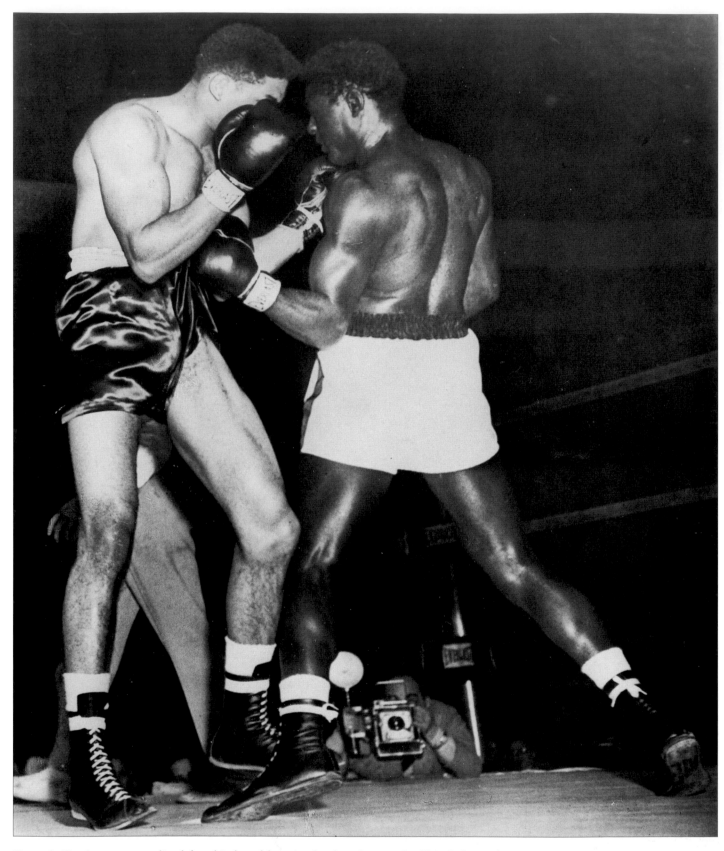

Ezzard Charles was penalised for this low blow in the fourth round of his fight with top contender Tommy Harrison in Detroit, February 1953. He was warned twice more, but still won the fight on a TKO in the ninth. A string of fine performances from the ex- champion set him up for two titanic battles with Rocky Marciano the following year.

Jersey Joe Walcott

World Heavyweight Champion: 1951-1952

Jersey Joe Walcott's place in the history books is secure, simply on the grounds of having won the heavyweight crown at the age of 37. He was also a master boxer, someone who survived prejudice, self-doubt and financial hardship to take his seat at boxing's top table.

Walcott was born Arnold Cream in Merchantville, New Jersey, on 31 January 1914. When he began boxing in 1930, his given name obviously wouldn't do. Joe Walcott was world welterweight champion at the turn of the century and a hero of the young aspiring fighter. He adopted it, and added "Jersey" in honour of his place of birth.

Fighting for peanuts

Like many excellent black boxers of his era, Walcott suffered from lack of opportunity. While Joe Louis carried all before him in the 1940s, Walcott often fought for peanuts. Promoters were very wary about the commercial implications of a title bout between two black fighters. When Louis took on John Henry Lewis in 1939, much was made of the fact that it was the first time two black men had contested the heavyweight title since Jack Johnson fought Jim Johnson 26 years earlier. The fact that the Louis-Lewis fight ended inside a round probably didn't help the cause of Walcott and the other good black heavyweights who were around at the time.

By 1944 Walcott had lost belief in himself. He decided to quit the ring and take a job to support his wife and family. That could easily have been the last anyone heard of him. But he was persuaded to come out of retirement and enjoyed a fine run of success. Then, in 1947, he was sensationally catapulted back into the limelight as the 24th challenger for Joe Louis's heavyweight crown. At 33 he was older than the champion and a rank outsider. It should have been a routine victory for Louis and a very nice payday for Walcott in the twilight of his career. In fact, he put Louis down twice in the early stages, and at the end of the 15 rounds most observers thought he was the clear winner. The referee agreed, but to everyone's amazement the judges scored it in Louis's favour. Even the champion thought that Walcott had been robbed.

Walcott showed this was no fluke in the early rounds of the return match. This time, however, he succumbed to a classic Louis battering in the 11th round. When Walcott also lost to Ezzard Charles for the vacant title, following Louis's decision to retire, it meant that over an 18-month period he had been beaten in three successive heavyweight championship fights. At the age of 35, Walcott could easily have shuffled off the stage with his head held high. Not a bit of it. There followed another points defeat by Charles, then the two met for the third time - Walcott's fifth attempt to win the title - on 18 July 1951.

Perfect left hook

Charles later recalled the night he lost his title. Of his seventh-round knockout he said: "Walcott drove a soft left jab to my belly. I fell for it. I dropped my hands and moved towards him. With the same motion he came through with as perfect a left hook as was ever thrown in the ring. It caught me on the button."

A rematch was inevitable. Walcott and Charles met for the fourth and final time for the heavyweight title in Philadelphia, on 5 June 1952. For the third time it went the distance, with Walcott getting the decision on this occasion.

Next up for Walcott, less than four months later, came a young slugger by the name of Rocky Marciano. After twice getting the better of a craftsman and technician of Charles's stature, Walcott was confident that skill would win out over the crude power that was Marciano's chief weapon. He was very nearly right.

Jersey Joe Walcott

Born:	Merchantville, New Jersey, USA. January 31 1914
Died:	February 25, 1994
Height: 6' 6"	**Weight:** 197lbs
World Heavyweight Champion:	1951-1952
Record: Won 53 (33 KOs) Lost 18 Drawn 1	

Ancient Archie makes it three in a row against Maxim

Opposite: World light-heavyweight champion Archie Moore pins Joey Maxim onto the ropes in the second round of their encounter in Miami, January 27, 1954. It was the third time the two men had met in thirteen months. Moore had taken the title from Maxim in December 1952, and retained his crown in a close points decision in January 1953. This fight also went the distance, with Ancient Archie a much more clear-cut winner.

Above: Britain's Don Cockell (right) takes on American heavyweight Harry Matthews at the White City, June 1954.

Different tactic, same result

Above: New York, September 17, 1954. Ezzard Charles spent much of his second title fight with Rocky Marciano trying to avoid the latter's bombs. His strategy worked well up to the eighth round, when the champion unleashed a ferocious bombardment which put Charles down for the count.

Opposite: Marciano covers up in the third round of his rematch with Ezzard Charles. Charles outboxed Marciano in the early rounds, and split the champion's nose so badly that the referee came close to stopping the contest at the end of the seventh. Marciano's camp pleaded for one more round, and Rocky made the most of his chance.

Charles within seconds of regaining title

This page: A five-frame sequence shows Ezzard Charles desperately trying to stave off a ferocious assault from Rocky Marciano in the fourth round of their September 1954 clash. In rapid succession he uses his elbow to block a right, then parries a booming left hook from the champion. By combining evasive action with some incisive counter-punching, Charles was actually ahead on points at this stage.

Opposite: Marciano stands over the vanquished Charles after bludgeoning him to the canvas 2 min. 36 sec. into the eighth round. Had Charles managed to stay on his feet for the remaining 24 seconds of the round, the terrible injury to Marciano's nose would almost certainly have ended the fight in a TKO.

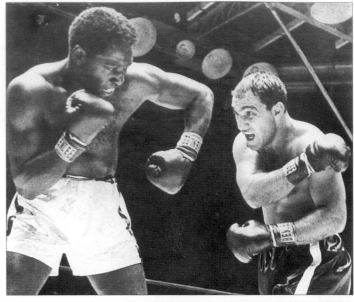

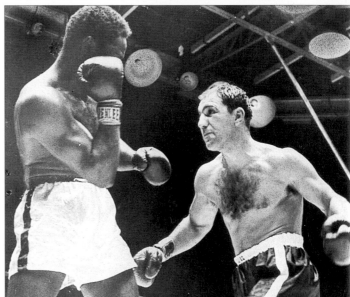

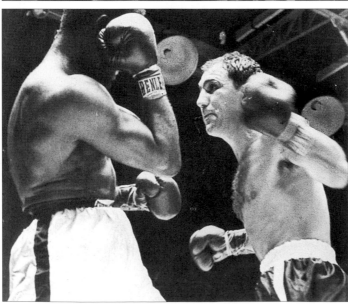

Rocky Marciano
World Heavyweight Champion: 1952-1956

Rocky Marciano was a fighting machine out of the Dempsey mould. He was no fistic stylist, but he had two huge assets: he was a destructive puncher, and he was incredibly resilient. This simple formula proved to be devastatingly effective. The record books don't lie: 49 fights, 49 wins, 43 of them inside the distance. Nobody else has achieved 100 per cent success rate. Maybe Marciano didn't either. It is said that he did suffer one defeat as a professional, early in his career, and that his manager deliberately erased it from the record books. Does this matter? To the sport's statisticians, certainly; but whatever the truth of the matter, it cannot detract from the fact that Marciano reigned supreme from 1952 to 1956.

Rocco Francis Marchegiano was born in Brockton, Massachusetts, on 1 September 1923. He excelled in many sports in his early years, but decided to concentrate on boxing after winning several competitions during the Second World War, when he was stationed in England. After he was discharged, he wrote to Madison Square Garden, hoping to be taken into the professional ranks.

Al Weill, who would later become his manager, was initially unconvinced. At 5ft 10½ in Marciano was small; he weighed in at just 13 St 2lb; his reach was woefully short; and his lack of technique made him an easy target. Weill slowly changed his mind when he saw that Marciano had extraordinary stamina, durability and punching power.

After turning professional in 1947, Marciano was nursed through his early fights. Weill wanted to keep his record intact; he also wanted to buy time for the trainers to get to work on his technical flaws.

Tears as Louis KO'd

A major step up the ladder came in 1951, when Marciano had to face one of his heroes, Joe Louis. Marciano took everything the former champion could throw at him, and knocked him out in the eighth round. Many onlookers - Marciano included - were said to have had a tear in their eye at the end of the fight.

Marciano had soon beaten all the top contenders as well as a string of has-beens. He was widely being talked about as the Great White Hope. A crack at Jersey Joe Walcott's title was now inevitable.

The champion was confident. "He can't fight. If I don't win, take my name out of the record books." It was, quite literally, fighting talk.

The contest took place on 23 September 1952, in Philadelphia. It was a bruising encounter. Marciano was down in the very first round, seeming to support the view of those who thought Walcott's superior ringcraft would win the day. But Marciano brushed aside Walcott's

superbly executed left hook with apparent disdain. As his corner screamed at him to take an eight-count, Marciano bounded to his feet at three. It must have been very demoralising for the champion.

Marciano kept going forward like a juggernaut, seemingly impervious to the punches Walcott landed. He even shrugged off the fact that he was having difficulty seeing. This had nothing to do with physical damage. Marciano's corner suspected that Walcott's gloves had been smeared with a substance which was causing their man's eyes to sting. Whatever the cause, Marciano wasn't about to let it stand in his way. He was a man on a mission. Round after round the two continued to pound each other.

"Suzy Q" wins title

By the 13th, Walcott was well ahead on points. Had he been able to stay out of trouble, victory was his. But that disappeared in one short pulverising right to Walcott's jaw in round 13. Marciano's right was a hammerblow affectionately named Suzy-Q; Walcott became the latest fighter to feel its awesome power. He crumpled to the canvas and didn't move until long after the count was over.

Almost inevitably, the new champion's first defence was a rematch. This was also brutal, but this time it was one-sided and short. Walcott was knocked out inside a round.

After stopping Roland La Starza, Marciano had two titanic battles with former champion Ezzard Charles. The first encounter was a classic. Charles took the champion the distance, and it was probably his finest hour in the ring, despite the fact that it ended in defeat. Both men handed out and took severe punishment; Marciano got the verdict.

All or nothing

In their second battle, Charles had the better of the early rounds, and also managed to split Marciano's nose wide open. The referee came perilously close to stopping the fight after seven rounds, but the stakes being what they were, he decided to allow the champion the latitude of another three minutes. Marciano knew it was all or nothing. He waded into Charles and hit him with everything, ignoring his opponent's shots as he did so. Charles didn't survive the onslaught.

Marciano's penultimate defence pitted him against England's Don Cockell. The champion was always savage and brutal in the ring; and on that May night in 1955 he was also positively dirty. He butted, elbowed and thumbed Cockell; he hit him low, and hit him when he was down. After the fight was stopped in the ninth round, Cockell was remarkably phlegmatic. He bore Marciano no ill will, and gave a very apt description of what had happened. "Rocky kept beating away at me like a demented butcher flattening a lump of veal."

Marciano's swansong came on 21 September 1955, with world light-heavyweight champion Archie Moore his opponent. The veteran challenger started very well, and put Marciano on the canvas in the second round. It was a beautiful punch, but as usual, Marciano shrugged it off and was up at two. Seven rounds later, Marciano ground his man down and battered him into submission. He had taken a lot of punishment, but he had given better than he had got.

Computer puts Marciano No.1

Under pressure from his family to quit, and with no other obvious contender in sight, Marciano chose to retire the following year, his reputation intact, his place in the history books secure.

Outside the ring Marciano was gentle, courteous and slow to anger. Inside it he was frightening. His raw power, ability to absorb punishment and sheer will to win gave him an air of invincibility. Would he have beaten Louis in his prime? Or Dempsey? Or Muhammad Ali? A computer thought so. In 1967, two years before his death in a plane crash, Marciano came out on top of the pile in a computerised contest between 16 of the greatest heavyweights of all time.

Rocky Marciano

Born:	Brockton, Massachusetts, USA. Sept 1 1923		
Died:	August 31 1969		
Height:	5' 10¼"	Weight:	189lbs
World Heavyweight Champion:	1952-1956		
Record:	Won 49 (43 KOs)		

Rocky Marciano's manager and mentor Al Weill embraces his man after a devastating performance against Britain's Don Cockell in May 1955. Weill had astutely seen beyond the young Marciano's lack of skill and style, focusing instead on the vast potential of his awesome punching power.

Marciano in vicious battle with Cockell

Rocky Marciano's fifth defence of the title matched him against British Empire champion Don Cockell. The fight took place in the Kezar Stadium, San Francisco, on 16 May 1955. It was an ugly, one-sided encounter, which Cockell bravely extended to the ninth round before the referee stepped in to save him from further punishment. Backed into a corner (opposite), the challenger survived an onslaught in the eighth. One round later and it's the beginning of the end when Marciano rocks Cockell with a wicked right (below). Marciano emerged with his title and record intact, but with very little credit. Many observers were incensed by his rough-house tactics, although Cockell himself said he had no complaints.

Disgraceful performance from Marciano

Above and right: A long right to the chin from Marciano in round eight leaves Cockell draped through the ropes. The champion holds off on this occasion, waiting to see if his opponent will recover. At other times during the fight Marciano wasn't quite so restrained; some observers went so far as to castigate him for flagrant breaches of the rules. He was certainly guilty of more than one low blow, and of hitting Cockell when he was going down. Marciano also butted, elbowed and thumbed his man, all with impunity.

Opposite: Don Cockell goes down for the final time after 54 seconds of the ninth round. The referee is about to step in to put an end to the savage beating. Many were of the opinion that he should have intervened much earlier to warn Marciano about his disgraceful performance. To his credit, the champion is said to have been ashen-faced when he saw a recording of the fight.

"Wanted: Marciano - by order of sheriff Archie"

Above: World light-heavyweight champion Archie Moore provided the fifth and final challenge to Rocky Marciano. Moore had been gunning for a showdown, even going so far as to put up spoof "Wanted" posters with Marciano's name on them. The fight took place in New York, on September 21 1955. The veteran Moore, who was said to be around 40 at the time, did well in the early rounds, but Marciano then started to find his range. Here he connects with a solid blow to "Ancient Archie's" temple.

Right: Marciano ducks a right thrown by Moore in the seventh round. The champion recovered from an early knockdown, and was now well on top. He knocked Moore out in the ninth.

Opposite: Referee Frankie Brown finally takes decisive action in the Marciano-Cockell fight, stepping in to end the bloodbath in the ninth.

Low point for Charles

Right: Following his two titanic battles with Rocky Marciano, Ezzard Charles's career went into freefall. Over the next five years he fought 23 times, losing on thirteen occasions. He is pictured (right) taking a bludgeoning right to the head on his way to a points defeat by Tommy "Hurricane" Jackson in New York, August 4 1955.

Above: Charles (left) takes on Newport's Dick Richardson in London, October 1956. This was the nadir for Charles, who was disqualified for repeated holding and booed from the arena. By the early 1960s, Charles was broke. He later developed multiple sclerosis and was confined to a wheelchair. He died in 1975, at the age of 54.

Opposite: Two of Britain's top heavyweights, Joe Erskine and Henry Cooper, clash in November 1955. Erskine (left) crouches as he prepares to launch an attack on Cooper's body.

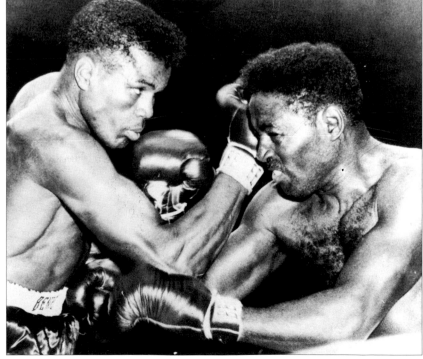

Floyd Patterson

World Heavyweight Champion: 1956-1959

When Rocky Marciano finally announced his decision to retire, in April 1956, one contender for his crown was Archie Moore, the light-heavyweight champion who had given him such a tough fight the previous September. The other was Floyd Patterson.

Patterson's manager Cus D'Amato had decided his man was ready to step up and challenge for the heavyweight title several months earlier. He told Patterson so at a party to celebrate the latter's 21st birthday, in January of that year. Events then took their course, and instead of challenging Marciano, Patterson found himself in an eliminator against Tommy "Hurricane" Jackson for the right to meet Moore. Jackson was rated second in the heavyweight ranks; it was the biggest test of Patterson's career and he came through on points. Now only Archie Moore stood between him and the greatest prize in sport.

"Budding delinquent"

Patterson was born in Waco, North Carolina, on 4 January 1935. In demeanour he was shy, reserved, humble and sensitive. Yet the young Patterson still came dangerously close to going off the rails. He later admitted that he was "a budding juvenile delinquent" and that boxing saved him from graduation to the fully-fledged article. At 12 he was carrying the boxing kitbags of his elder brothers. At 14 he met Cus D'Amato, the man who guided him through nine amateur championships at welterweight and middleweight. He turned professional after winning the middleweight title at the 1952 Olympic Games, when he was just 17.

Patterson's inexorable rise suffered a jolt in June 1954, when he was matched against veteran Joey Maxim, ex-light-heavyweight champion of the world. Maxim won on points, albeit controversially. Patterson was unhurt - except for his pride. He learned from the defeat and went on collecting cruiserweight scalps. It was a run of success which led to the final eliminator against Jackson, in June 1956, and then to the big one against Archie Moore.

Youngest champion

Youth and speed triumphed in Chicago on 30 November, 1956. Patterson knocked Moore out in the fifth with the sweetest of left hooks to become the youngest ever heavyweight champion. He was 21 years 11 months old, 14 months younger than Joe Louis had been when he took the title off James J. Braddock.

Patterson's first two defences were poor fare. "Hurricane" Jackson, the man Patterson had outpointed to earn a crack at the title, was dispatched far more readily in July 1957. The next defence matched the champion against Peter Rademacher. Rademacher had an Olympic gold medal

to his name, but he had never boxed professionally in his life. It was a total farce, ending in a sixth-round knockout.

Roy Harris was Patterson's only challenger in 1958. Harris was tough, but no match for Patterson's lightning speed and scintillating combination punching. This completed a hat-trick of indifferent contests. Was it simply that there was a paucity of good heavyweights around at the time? Not quite. D'Amato studiously ignored some of the more dangerous candidates, men such as Xora Folley, Eddie Machen and Sonny Liston. Patterson's manager was undoubtedly hand-picking opponents who best served the purpose - that being to keep the title exactly where it was. The picture was further confused by the fact that D'Amato had a long-running feud with the International Boxing Club, and wouldn't allow Patterson to fight anyone connected with that organization.

Patterson later said that he regretted being denied the opportunity to fight the men both the press and public were calling for.

London defies boxing board

The pattern continued with Patterson's next fight, against Brian London. London wasn't even the British champion, having lost his title to Henry Cooper in January 1959. When Cooper's manager turned down the chance of fighting Patterson, London jumped at the opportunity. The British Boxing Board of Control refused to sanction London's trip to America, feeling that the fight "wasn't in the interests of British boxing". London defied the ruling body and went anyway. He took a lot of punishment for 10 rounds and succumbed to a left hook in the 11th.

Even before the London fight, Patterson's next defence was being lined up. Sweden's Ingemar Johansson, the European heavyweight champion, had leapt into the frame by beating top contender Eddie Machen inside a round. The Patterson-Johansson fight took place on 26 June 1959, just eight weeks after the champion's demolition job on Brian London.

Floyd Patterson

Born:	Waco, North Carolina, USA. January 4 1952		
Height:	5' 11½"	Weight:	194lbs
World Heavyweight Champion:		1956-1961, 1961-1962	
Middleweight Olympic Gold medal:		1952	
Record:	Won 55 (40 KOs) Lost 8 Drawn 1		

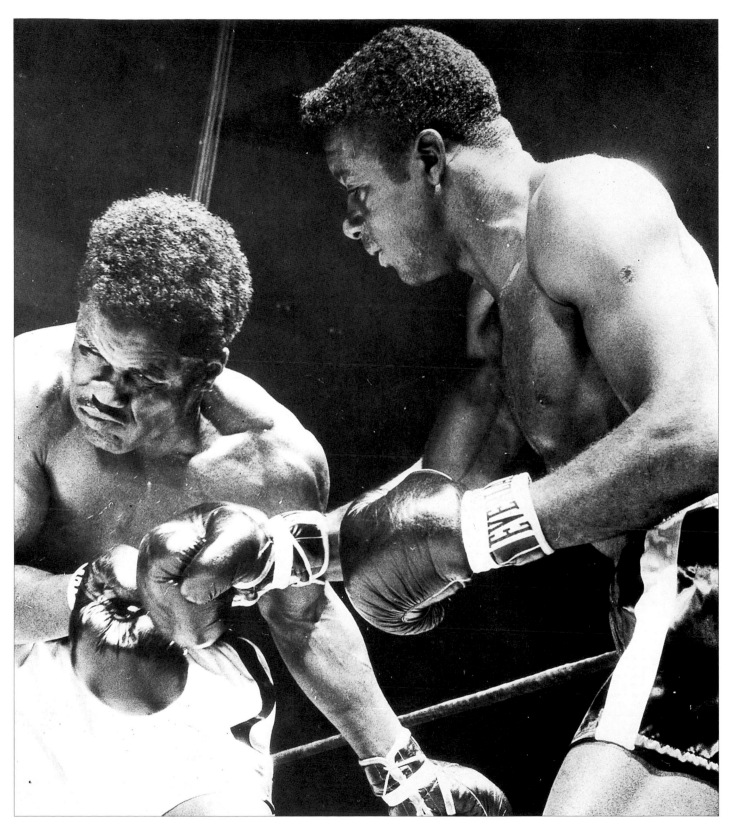

Patterson to meet Moore in title decider

Floyd Patterson lands a right to the jaw of Tommy "Hurricane" Jackson and goes on to win the fight on points. This match, which took place in June 1956, was a final eliminator to decide Rocky Marciano's successor. Patterson's victory earned him a meeting with Archie Moore to decide who was to be the new heavyweight champion.

Patterson becomes youngest champion

Opposite: Chicago, November 30, 1956. The lightning speed of the young Floyd Patterson gets the better of wily old campaigner Archie Moore in their fight for the vacant heavyweight crown. Moore had gone into the fight as warm favourite. He was the craftsman who had given Marciano such a tough fight the previous year. He was also the KO king, having knocked out more men than any other boxer. But it was Moore who was counted out, following a terrific left hook from Patterson in the fifth round. At 21 years 10 months, Patterson became the youngest-ever holder of the heavyweight crown.

Above: Earls Court, February 19, 1957: Henry Cooper (left) and Joe Bygraves battle it out at close quarters during their fight for the British Empire heavyweight title. Bygraves came out on top.

Sugar Ray defeated

Above: September 24, 1957. Sugar Ray Robinson, left, and challenger Carmen Basilio during their bout at Yankee Stadium. Basilio won the middleweight crown on a split 15 round decision.

Left: Joe Erskine plants a straight left smack on the nose of Henry Cooper during their British heavyweight championship clash at Harringay Arena, September 17, 1957. Erskine retained his title on points over 15 rounds.

Opposite: Brian London avoids a swinging right from giant American heavyweight Howie Turner. The Blackpool boxer scored an unexpected points win over the American in this December 1957 encounter in London.

London emulates father's achievement

Opposite: June 3, 1958. Brian London celebrates becoming the new British and Empire champion. He took both titles from Joe Erskine, whom he knocked out in round eight of their scheduled 15-round contest at the White City. Sharing the moment of glory is Brian's father, Jack, himself a former holder of the British heavyweight cown.

Right: September 30, 1958. Four months after taking the British heavyweight title, Brian London stops America's Willie Pastrano in the fifth round of their contest at Harringay, London. Pastrano would go on to take the world light-heavyweight title five years later.

Below: September 28, 1958. The scene at London Airport becomes a Who's Who of boxing as many former stars of the ring arrive for a parade of champions at Harringay.

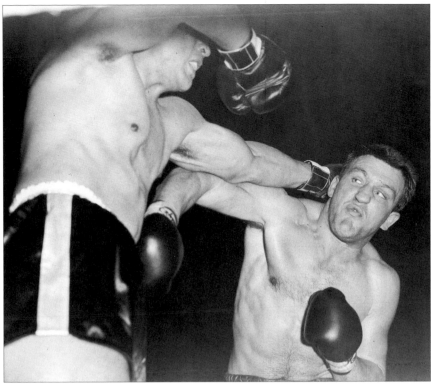

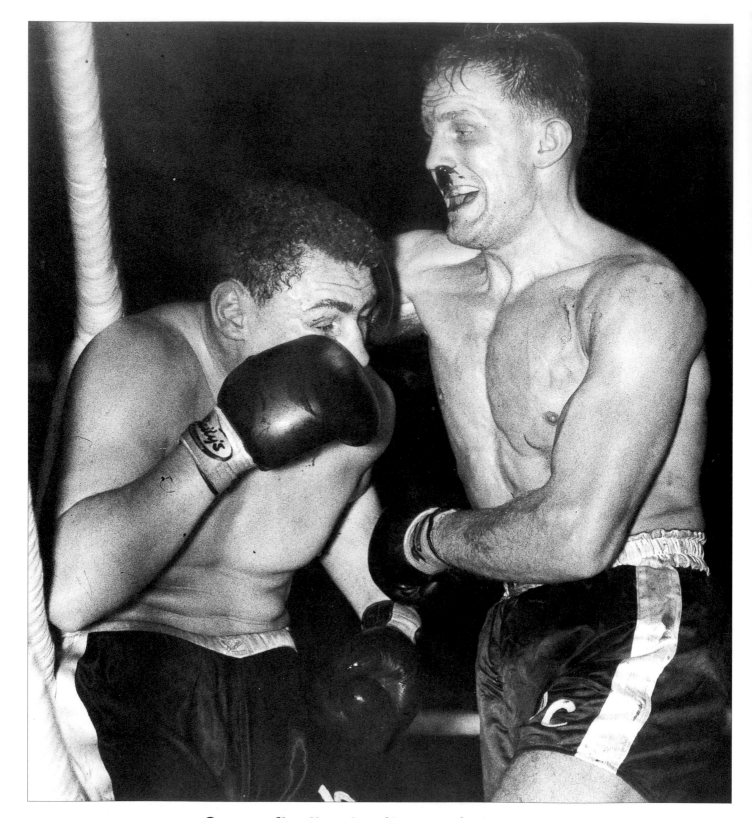

Cooper finally wins the coveted belt

Opposite: Battle-scarred Henry Cooper poses wearing the coveted Lonsdale Belt after wresting the British and Empire heavyweight titles from Brian London at Earls Court, January 12, 1959.

Above: Joe Erskine and Henry Cooper in action during their 15-round title fight at Harringay, September 17, 1957. Erskine won on points to retain his British crown.

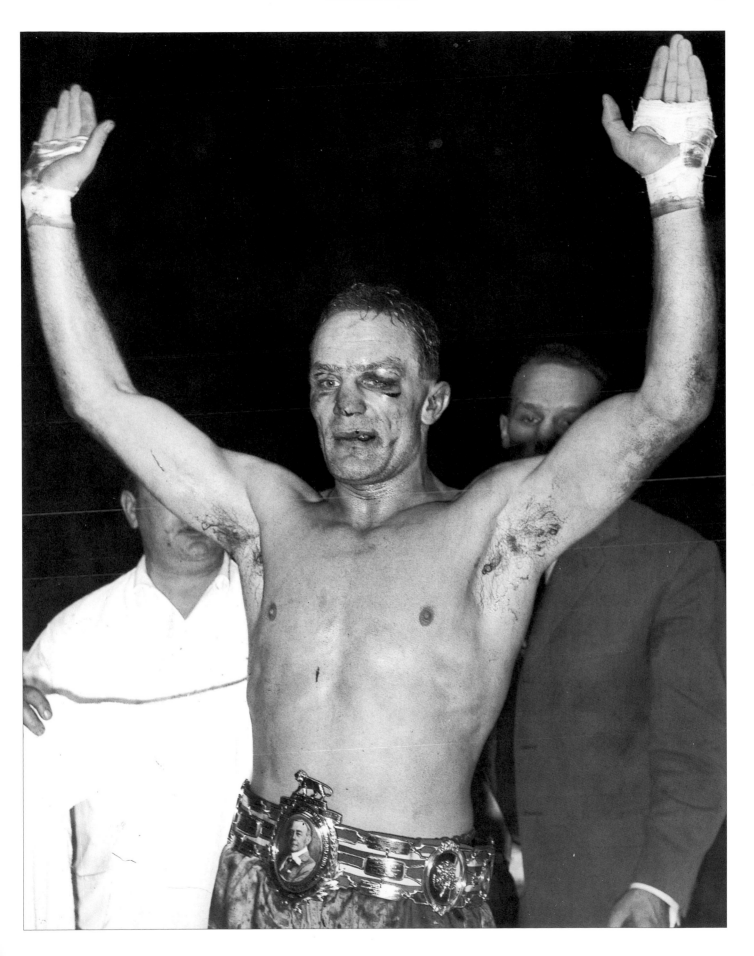

London challenges Patterson after Cooper declines

Opposite: It looks bad for Henry Cooper as he goes down in the fifth round of his title fight with Brian London, blood pouring from his nose and eye. London took even worse punishment over the 15 rounds, however, and 24-year-old Cooper was a convincing points winner of an epic contest. American promoters were at the fight, ready to sign the winner for a world title fight against Floyd Patterson.

Right: Indianapolis, May 1, 1959. Referee Frank Sikora counts Brian London out during the 11th round of his world title fight against Floyd Patterson. London had jumped at the chance of a tilt at the title, following Henry Cooper's decision not to take the fight.

Below: New York, June 26, 1959. Floyd Patterson listens to referee Ruby Goldstein's count as he tries to shake off the effects of the thunderous right which had put him down in the third round of his title fight against Ingemar Johansson. "Ingo's Bingo" put the champion down seven times in all, before Goldstein called a halt to proceedings.

Titanic battles between Patterson and Johansson

Above: New York, June 26, 1959. 4-1 underdog Ingemar Johansson becomes the new world champion 2 min. 3 sec. into the third round of his title fight with Floyd Patterson. The Swede had put Patterson down seven times before referee Ruby Goldstein intervened. This equalled Jack Dempsey's heavyweight championship record for the greatest number of knockdowns in a single round, the Manassa Mauler having put Luis Firpo on the canvas seven times in their famous encounter in 1923.

Right: Miami, March 13, 1961. Ingemar Johansson exhorts referee Billy Regan to allow him to continue in round six of his explosive third meeting with Floyd Patterson. Johansson had been floored by a left-right combination and just failed to beat the count. The former champion's protestations cut no ice with Regan. It meant that Patterson had won the rubber of the two men's personal battle, and more importantly, he had retained the heavyweight crown.

Ingemar Johansson

Ingemar Johansson's star flickered briefly at the top level. He had three world title fights in the space of the year - all against Floyd Patterson - winning once and losing twice. Thereafter he chose to shuffle off the biggest stage, with a lot of money in his pocket and his looks and faculties intact.

The 1952 Olympic Games in Helsinki was the launchpad for Johansson's professional career, just as it was for Patterson. However, the Swede joined the professional ranks in spite of his performance at the Games, not because of it. He was disqualified from the tournament for "not giving of his best" against a giant of a man named Eddie Sanders. Like the Olympic judges, Patterson noted how cautious and defensive Johansson was. He was a counterpuncher by instinct; he liked to draw his opponents onto him and hit them with his right, which he called "Thor's Hammer". Sanders didn't want to play ball on that occasion, however, and Johansson had no opportunity of unleashing his biggest weapon.

Patterson was not overly impressed. When the two men met for the world crown seven years later, he would underestimate his man badly.

Perfect record

In the interim period, Johansson made steady if unspectacular progress. He had a perfect record from his 21 fights, and 13 of his opponents had failed to go the distance. His manager carefully imported heavyweights to provide stepping stones for his man. It was his 22nd straight win, in September 1958, that made the boxing world sit up and take notice. His victim was Eddie Machen, who was rated second to Patterson at the time. The fact that Machen lasted less than a round meant that Johansson's stock rose dramatically. He now had Patterson in his sights, while the champion finally had a worthy opponent. Patterson was stung by the criticisms about the quality of his previous opponents. He believed his fifth defence would gain him the approval and credibility that he craved.

Johansson fools media

The two met in New York, on 26 June 1959. Johansson arrived with a glamorous girlfriend in tow, and didn't appear to take training too seriously. He put his faith in "Thor's Hammer". The fans were sceptical, and so was Patterson. There was plenty of kidology going on, though. For while Johansson looked and acted the part of the playboy, he knuckled down and put in the necessary work when he was out of the media spotlight.

Patterson later said that he trained hard for the fight, but didn't have his usual edginess going into it. He admitted not having the highest regard or respect for his opponent. That view didn't change after the first two rounds. In that time Johansson flicked his left out something like 200 times. Patterson said these punches were simply annoying; he never felt any of them. As others had done before him, Patterson was becoming frustrated that Johansson wasn't making much of a fight of it.

Johansson had thrown a half-power right in the first round. Understandably, Patterson wasn't overly impressed. He later realised that the Swede had just been testing the water, waiting for the right moment to unleash the real thing.

Thor's hammer unleashed

Going into the third round, Patterson decided to move in. Johansson again kept working his left, and that was where the champion concentrated his attention. He convinced himself that the right was either over-hyped or even non-existent. Within a few seconds he discovered that "Thor's Hammer" was no illusion. Johansson put Patterson down seven times before the round - and the fight - was over.

The two men met again 51 weeks later. In the interim period Johansson had enjoyed his new status as world champion. He had been in jovial mood on the *Ed Sullivan Show* just after his victory. In January 1960, he returned to the States to receive the Sportsman of the Year award. He was constantly interviewed, regularly quoted. He never tired of telling how Patterson hadn't known what hit him. The implication was clear: Johansson was confident that the second fight would go the same way as the first.

Patterson had other ideas. He was seething at the manner of his defeat. He realised that he had taken Johansson too lightly, just as the new champion was now underestimating him. Eschewing his wife Sandra's exhortations to call it a day, Patterson counted the hours until he could step back into the ring with the man who had robbed him of the title.

Ingemar Johansson

Born:	Gothenburg, Sweden September 22 1932		
Height:	6' 1"	Weight:	201lbs
World Heavyweight Champion:		1959-1960	
Olympic silver medal 1952 (awarded in 1982)			
Record:	Won 17 (17 KOs) Lost 2		

Floyd Patterson
World Heavyweight Champion: 1961-1962

For a long time following his defeat by Johansson, Patterson suffered from a crisis of confidence and plumbed the depths of despair. He then received a welcome fillip from an unlikely source: Archie Moore, the man he had beaten for the vacant title three years earlier. Moore told him that he had fought "a stupid battle", and that the Swede was no great shakes. If Patterson used his jab more and moved better, he would be the first man to regain the heavyweight crown. It was the boost Patterson needed. From that moment he was single-minded in his determination to wrest the title back from the Johansson.

The fight took place in New York on 20 June, 1960. It was to be Patterson's finest hour - or rather less, since he put his man away in the fifth round. He had comfortably won three of the first four. Johansson's one bright moment came in the second round, when he connected with "Thor's Hammer". Patterson saw it coming this time and it caught him high on the head. Instead of retaliating, Patterson stuck to his game plan, which was to clinch and move away while he recovered.

The end came courtesy of two glorious left hooks. The first connected square on the jaw and put Johansson down on one knee for a count of nine. Patterson was on his man as soon as he was up, smashing him all round the ring before finishing him off with a second left hook. Many said it was the best punch Patterson ever threw. Certainly Johansson

toppled like a tree and was out cold for several minutes. Patterson rushed to Johansson's side, concerned that he had done him serious damage. When the Swede finally came round, Patterson was able to celebrate his historic achievement, and assure the vanquished champion that that after one win apiece, there would have to be a rubber.

Patterson v Johansson 3 took place in Miami on 13 March, 1961. It started with a bang and ended in a whimper. Johansson had Patterson down twice in the opening three minutes, only for the champion to return the favour with a crashing left hook. The pair slugged it out for the next four rounds, with the champion getting the better of the exchanges. The end came after a terrific left- right combination from Patterson in round six. Johansson went down, seemed to be getting up, then pitched forward and was counted out. It had been one of the most thrilling contests of all time, yet there was booing from the crowd. The feeling was that this had been the least effective knockdown of the fight, and not worthy of ending it. Or were the spectators just disappointed that the excitement was all over?

Johansson continued to fight on the European stage for two more years, before retiring to his haulage business with a mountain of cash to show for his efforts. For Patterson, it was a question of who was next in line to challenge for the crown. The number one contender was Charles "Sonny" listen, a gorilla of a man and an ex-convict. D'Amato was suitably wary, but Patterson and his manager parted company, and the champion accepted Liston's challenge, after he had had one more fight. That was against Tom McNeely, in December 1961. It was an easy victory against a second-rate opponent. Ten months later, against Liston, it would be a very different story.

Opposite: Miami, March 13, 1961. The clock is running and Ingemar Johansson just fails to beat the 10 count in his third clash with Floyd Patterson. Johansson continued boxing for a couple of years but never challenged for the world crown again. He became a successful businessman, with $1,500,000 from the three Patterson fights helping to swell the coffers.

Left: Ingemar Johansson exhorts referee Billy Regan to allow him to continue in round six of his explosive third meeting with Floyd Patterson. Johansson had been floored by a left-right combination and just failed to beat the count. The former champion's protestations cut no ice with Regan. It meant that Patterson had won the rubber of the two men's personal battle, and more importantly, he had retained the heavyweight crown.

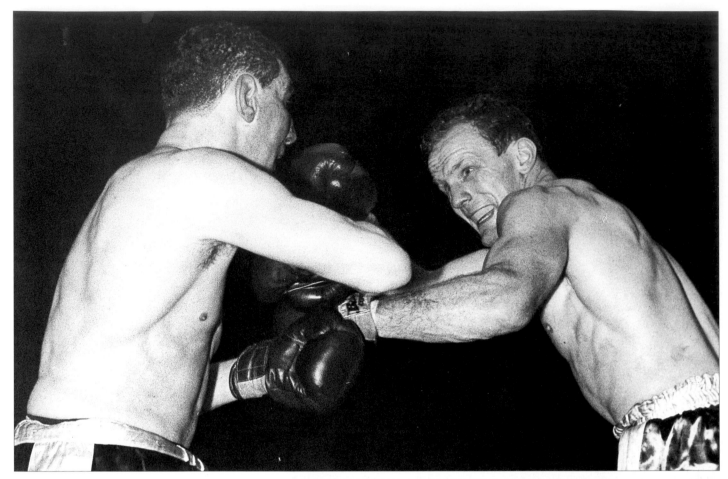

Cooper stops Erskine to retain British crown

Above: Former British and Empire heavyweight champion Joe Erskine (left) successfully blocks an attack from current title-holder Henry Cooper, during their fight at the Empire Pool, Wembley, March 21, 1961. Cooper retained the crown when Erskine retired with badly cut eyes at the end of the fifth round.

Right: Top American contender Eddie Machen (right) proved too strong for Britain's Brian London when the two met at Wembley, October 17, 1961. London's face was badly cut when he retired after five rounds.

Opposite: Rocky Marciano inspects the facial damage to his protégé, Tony Hughes, after the latter had been forced to quit at the end of the fifth round of his fight with Henry Cooper. The contest took place at Olympia Circus, January 1962.

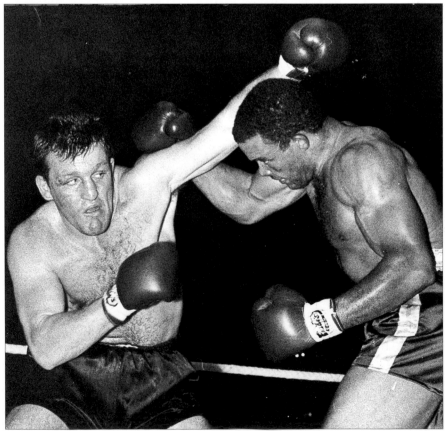

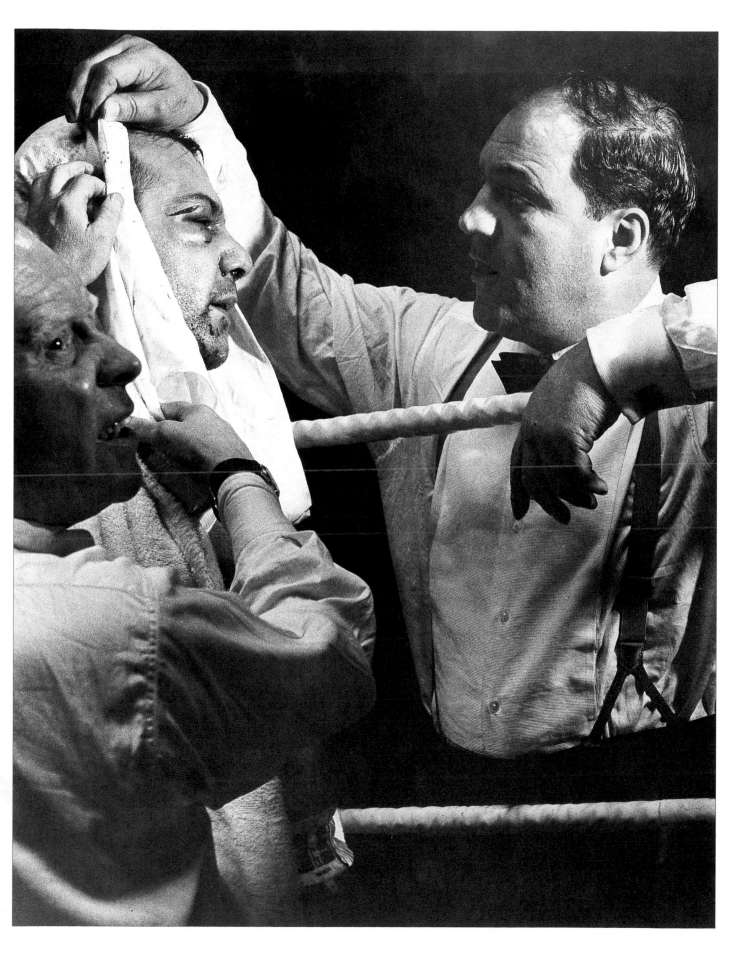

Another KO sets Liston up for title challenge

Right: Philadelphia, December 4, 1961. Germany's champion Albert Westphal is spread-eagled on the canvas just 1min. 58sec. into his contest with the most feared man in boxing, Sonny Liston. World champion Floyd Patterson had studiously avoided Liston for two years. Now the match was inevitable.

Below: Henry Cooper (left) in action against Tony Hughes at Olympia, January 1962.

Cooper stops Hughes in five
Hughes is slumped on the canvas and looks in difficulty against Cooper. He recovered from this knockdown, only to be stopped after five rounds with a badly cut eye.

Clay breaks the mould for heavyweight boxers

Above: The self-proclaimed greatest and prettiest. Most people thought Sonny Liston would shut the ultra-confident young upstart Cassius Clay's mouth. When he failed so spectacularly, everyone knew they were witnessing something very different and very special.

Opposite: March 1962. West Ham's Billy Walker notches his first professional win, stopping Belgium's Jose Peyre in the fifth round of their fight at the Empire Pool, Wembley.

About to shake up the world

Above: Never the shy, retiring type, the Louisville Lip lost no opportunity to inform the world of his talent. At first, some doubted Clay's ability to back up his claims in the ring. In particular, few thought he would be able to mix it with the ferocious Sonny Liston.

Opposite: Clay and promoter Jack Solomons take a stroll in London prior to the Cooper fight in June 1963. Clay came into this contest on the back of a tough points win over Doug Jones. The forthcoming fight would raise further questions about Clay's ability at the highest level.

Liston's two-year wait ends in two-minute victory

Below: Chicago, September 25, 1962. After two years waiting in the wings as the No. 1 contender, Sonny Liston takes just 2 min. 6 sec. to relieve Floyd Patterson of the heavyweight title. After connecting with some powerful jabs and body shots, Liston finished off Patterson with a huge left hook.

Opposite: Liston stands over the vanquished champion, looking every inch the meanest fighter on the planet, which was how he was regarded. Despite being the challenger, he had gone into the fight as the odds-on favourite.

Left: Helsinki, August 1962. World featherweight champion Davy Moore leaves the ring triumphantly after retaining his title against Finland's Olli Maki. The following year, Moore collapsed into a coma after losing his title to Cuba's Sugar Ramos. He never regained consciousness.

Sonny Liston

World Heavyweight Champion: 1962-1964

Legend has it that Charles "Sonny" Liston was a brute of a man, a bully and a thug. There is more than a degree of truth in this. Liston was so fearsomely intimidating that many an opponent was beaten before a punch was thrown. The icy stare was indeed extremely scary.

Two points ought to be made in mitigation of the man. Firstly, his family and close friends told a very different story. They spoke of a much warmer person, someone who was a considerate husband, good with children and polite to the elderly. In fact, he was quite the gentle giant - as long as he didn't feel threatened or pressurised. Secondly, if Liston was brutal - and at times he certainly was - it should be remembered that he was brutalised by his upbringing.

Violent father

He was born into a poor farming family in Arkansas in the early 1930s. There is some doubt about the exact year, though 1932 is often quoted. What is certain is that he was the 24th of the 25 children his father had by two wives. Liston senior was a violent man, and Sonny suffered some terrible beatings as he was growing up. At the age of 13 he ran away to St Louis, and was drawn into a world where you had to be streetwise and tough in order to survive. It was petty crime at first, but it was only a matter of time before things escalated and Liston landed himself in jail. The inevitable happened at the age of 18, when he was given five years for armed robbery.

Liston was saved from almost certain self-destruction by the attentions of Father Alois Stevens, a priest in charge of the prison sporting programme. He encouraged Liston to take up boxing, and his protégé was soon showing a remarkable aptitude for knocking over his opponents, this time in a more structured environment.

Laughter causes broken jaw

With Stevens's help he was released early and put into the care of people who would develop his boxing career and keep him on the straight and narrow. He progressed through the amateur ranks at a dizzying speed. In 1953 he won the Golden Gloves to become the USA's amateur heavyweight champion. He then turned professional, and the victories kept coming. His only reverse came in 1954, against a man named Marty Marshall. Marshall liked to clown around in the ring, and it is said that Liston was so amused that he became slack-jawed. Marshall seized his chance and broke Liston's jaw. Liston boxed on with the injury for several rounds, but Marshall got the decision. Liston vowed never to show humour in the ring again.

By 1960, he was the undisputed number one challenger for the heavyweight crown. He had beaten the likes of Zora Folley and Cleveland Williams, men whom Floyd Patterson had been accused of avoiding. Finally, Patterson agreed to the match. He craved acceptance and respect as a worthy champion. Perhaps he thought his lightning speed and superior technique would get the better of Liston's raw power and clubbing fists. If so, few agreed. Incredibly, when the two met in Chicago in September 1962, the challenger found himself a 7-1 on favourite to take the title.

Patterson beaten twice in four minutes

The bookmakers' odds were vindicated barely two minutes into the fight. Patterson was finally nailed with a left hook, and he beat a hasty retreat from the venue under heavy disguise. In July 1963, Patterson came back for more, and that's exactly what he got. Liston took four seconds longer this time, but the result was just the same.

Patterson was still not done for. He continued to be involved in title fights as late as 1968, but he would be a contender, not a champion. The more immediate concern was that he hadn't managed to do what almost everyone

across the social and political spectrum wanted: beat Liston in the ring. Even the leaders of the black movement were horrified; they didn't relish the prospect of having an illiterate ex-convict with links to mobsters as a role model.

No hero's welcome

Liston thought the title would change public opinion. He wanted to put the past behind him and be a worthy champion. He soon learned that people saw him as a leopard who was incapable of changing his spots. When he arrived home in Philadelphia as the new champion, he expected a hero's welcome. Nobody came.

Unlike the general populace, boxing aficionados judged Liston solely on his performances. They weren't interested in whether he was the kind of person you would invite to tea or like to have as a neighbour. They studied his destructive punching and near-perfect record and acclaimed him as one of the all-time greats.

His next opponent was a brash young upstart by the name of Cassius Clay. The 1960 Olympic light-heavyweight champion lost no time in telling the world that he was the greatest and the prettiest. There wasn't much doubt that he was prettier than the champion, but nobody gave him a prayer against Liston in the ring. Liston thought this Fancy Dan "ought to be locked up for impersonating a fighter". Clay might have been young and quick, but Liston planned to nail him and it would be sooner rather than later. He expected a short fight and trained accordingly. It was a huge mistake.

Sonny Liston

Born:	St. Francis, Arkansas USA May 8 1932		
Died:	December 1970		
Height:	6' 1"	Weight:	218lbs
World Heavyweight Champion:	1962-1964		
Record:	Won 50 (39 KOs) Lost 4		

Beaten Patterson slips away by back door

Below: Referee Frank Sikora gives beaten champion Floyd Patterson a helping hand after his first-round KO by Sonny Liston. Patterson left the Comiskey Park arena by the back door in heavy disguise, lending weight to the theory that he expected to lose.

Opposite: Sonny Liston's victory over Floyd Patterson put him third on the all-time list of fastest knockouts in heavyweight history, behind Tommy Burns and Joe Louis.

Jones takes Clay the distance

Above: Madison Square Garden, March 13, 1963. Cassius Clay sends beads of perspiration flying as he rocks Doug Jones with a right to the jaw. Jones was a rugged pro and a top contender, and gave Clay a lot to think about. Clay won a close decision over 10 rounds, and took another step towards a title fight against Liston.

Opposite: Clay opened up a bad cut over Henry Cooper's eye during the third round of their Wembley Stadium encounter in June 1963. Thinking the result was inevitable, he began his usual antics, dropping his hands and jutting out his jaw. Cooper welcomed the clowning, feeling that it would create an opening for him.

Right: Cooper used all his experience against Clay in the in-fighting. It wasn't flashy but it was effective, and Clay had to step up a gear to get on top of the British champion.

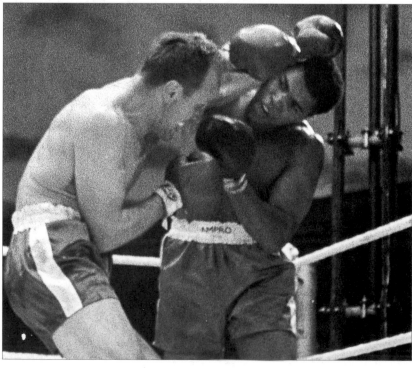

Was Clay saved by the bell?

Opposite below: So near and yet so far. Cassius Clay is on the canvas and disorientated after being hit with the hardest shot he has ever taken in his life. He gets to his feet groggily at a count of four, but the bell prevents Cooper from capitalising on his fourth-round knockdown.

Opposite above: Cooper's face is a picture of determination, while Clay looks somewhat apprehensive in the early stages of the fight. Cooper won both opening rounds, but was half-blinded by the cut to his left eye in the third.

Above: A panoramic view of Wembley Stadium, where a crowd of more than 40,000 witnessed the memorable encounter between Cassius Clay and Henry Cooper in June 1963.

Cooper takes the fight to Clay in the early exchanges, holding his own against a man who was seven years younger and 19lbs heavier. By the start of the third, Clay's prediction that he would win in five was looking distinctly optimistic. But Clay opened up with some dazzling combinations in that round, and the fight ended exactly when he had said it would.

"Eye injury cost me victory," says Cooper

Henry Cooper continues to press forward, despite the terrible eye injury sustained in the third round. Cooper later said he had no complaints about referee Tommy Little's decision to stop the fight in the fifth. "I couldn't see through the eye. But for the damage, I think I would have won. Clay developed quite a respect for me in those five rounds." As a mark of that respect - not to mention his own self-confidence - Clay immediately assured Cooper that he would give him a tilt at the world crown - when he had relieved Sonny Liston of the title. It was a promise he would keep three years later.

Henry Cooper

Nickname:	"Our Enery"
Born:	Bellingham England May 3 1934
Weight:	185 lbs.
European Heavyweight Champion:	1964 1967-1971
British and Commonwealth Heavyweight Champion:	1969-1971
British and British Empire Heavyweight Champion:	1958-1964 1965 1967-1969
Record:	Won 40 (27 KOs) Lost 14 Drawn 1

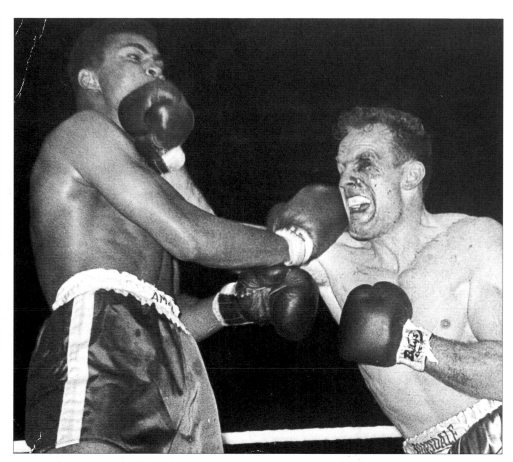

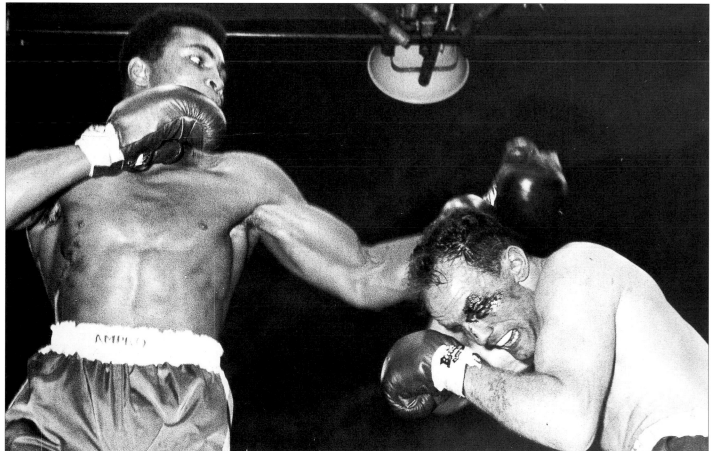

Game performance earns Cooper rapturous reception

Above: A disappointed Cooper gets a rapturous reception from the partisan crowd for his gallant performance against Clay. By contrast, there was booing for Clay as he held up five fingers, reminding the spectators that his prediction had been fulfilled. The hostility was short-lived. Clay praised Cooper's display in the post-fight comments, and British fans soon became some of the future champion's most ardent followers.

Opposite: The blood pumping from cuts above and below Cooper's left eye forces referee Tommy Little to end the fight after 1 min. 15 sec. of the fifth round.

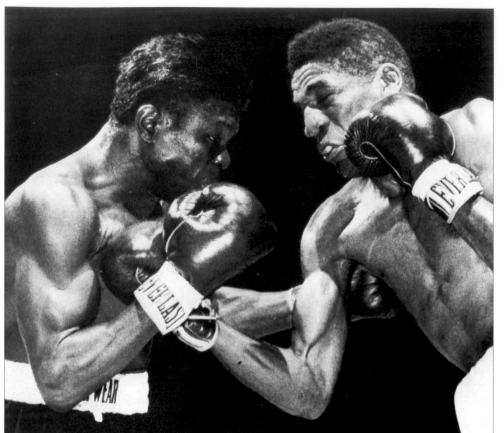

Liston KOs Patterson in one again

Opposite: Las Vegas, July 22, 1963. Floyd Patterson goes down for the third and final time in his rematch against Sonny Liston. The fight lasted 2 min. 10 sec., just four seconds longer than their first encounter the previous year.

Below: Patterson's attempt to overcome odds of 5-1 against him and regain the title for the second time ended in ignominious defeat. He landed just one decent punch in the brief duration of the fight, and Liston hardly blinked. By contrast, the champion caught Patterson with a flurry of devastating punches, and with a 21lbs weight advantage the result was never in doubt.

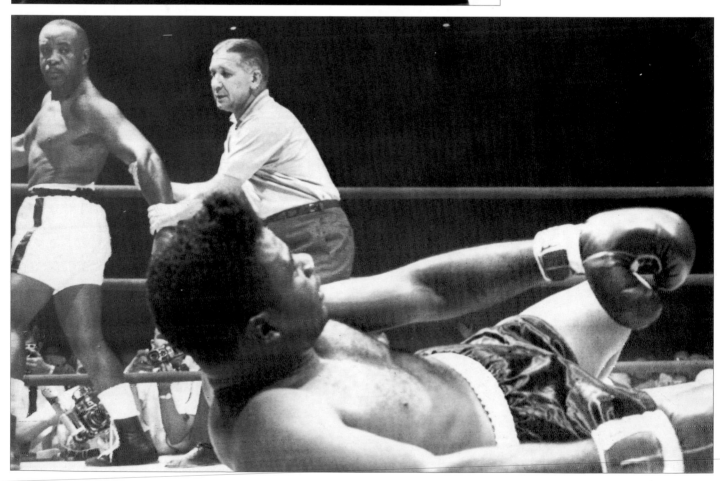

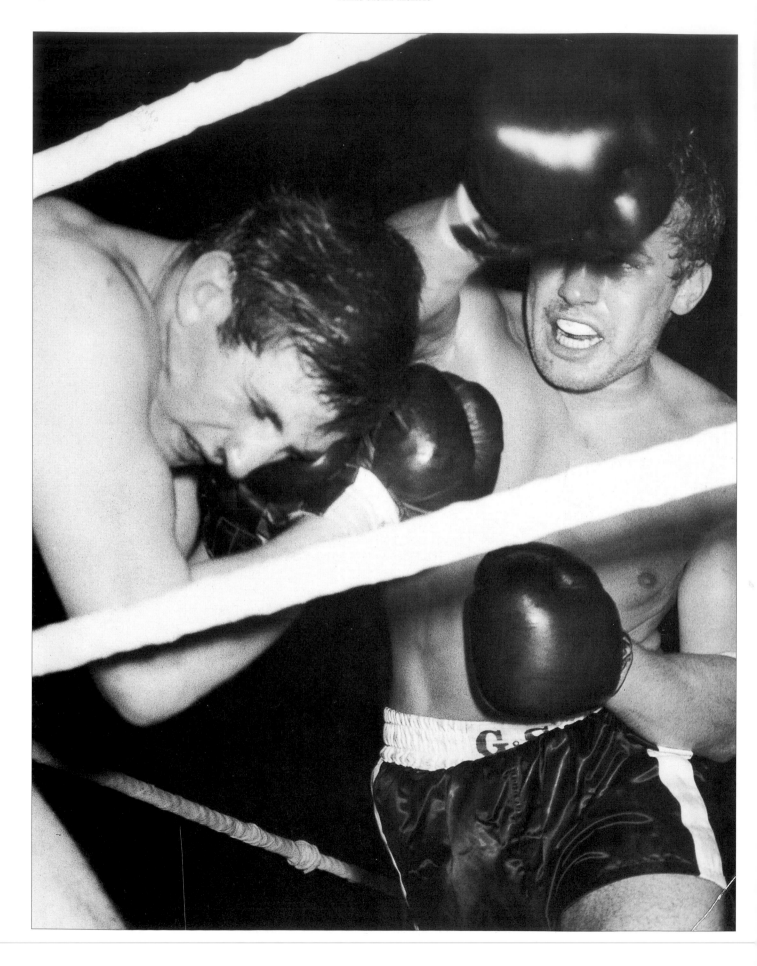

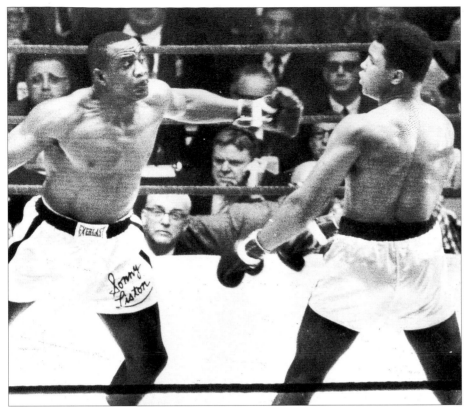

Clay blows away Liston's "invincible" tag

Below: Miami, February 25, 1964. Cassius Clay uses his quicksilver feet to stay well clear of Sonny Liston's raking left jab. His own punches were sharp and incisive, making his performance a masterclass of both attack and defence. It was the kind of display which encapsulated the Clay philosophy: "Float like a butterfly, sting like a bee".

Left: Liston attacks with a huge, swinging left, but Clay is unperturbed, ready to sidestep and counter. Liston was used to intimidating his opponents with his sheer ferocity; Clay made it clear he was utterly disdainful of his opponent's punching power.

Opposite: November 1963. Billy Walker drives Johnny Prescott onto the ropes during their fight at the Empire Pool, Wembley. Prescott recovered to win the contest on points.

Cassius Clay

Cassius Marcellus Clay broke the mould for heavyweight boxers. It wasn't simply his cocksure manner; many before him had displayed the arrogance of untested youth. But the poems, the predictions, and, in particular, the fighting style: this was all new. Old stagers must have been scratching their heads at the way he dropped his hands and presented his chin to his opponents. Some even managed to catch him with a solid punch. But the outcome was always the same. Clay danced and punched and put his man away, invariably in the prescribed round. He was a phenomenon.The phenomenon had taken up boxing in his home town of Louisville, Kentucky, at the age of 12. The young Clay had had his bicycle stolen and vowed to catch up with the perpetrator and "whup him", even though he had never had a boxing lesson in his life. He duly headed off to the gym, where he soon found that he could indeed "whup" all-comers. At 17 he became Golden Gloves champion. A year later, in 1960, he won the light-heavyweight title at the Rome Olympics. His first professional fight came in October that year, against Tunney Hunsaker. Clay gave a dazzling display in a unanimous points decision. Over the next two-and-a-half years he took a string of scalps and started to earn himself a big reputation. He was getting ever closer to being the number one challenger to Sonny Liston.

Clay faces Cooper in eliminator

On 18 June 1963 he took another step towards the top when he faced Britain's top heavyweight, Henry Cooper. This title eliminator has gone down in boxing folklore. Cooper was a rugged, experienced pro and landed some good punches early on. Clay went up a gear in the third and picked off his man with some sparkling combination punching. Cooper was cut badly; it looked all over. A momentary lapse by Clay towards the end of the fourth very nearly turned the fight on its head. Cooper saw his chance and connected perfectly with a bludgeoning left hook. Clay went down, his eyes rolling. It wasn't a knockout punch, but Cooper must have fancied his chances of finishing the job when Clay scrambled groggily to his feet. The bell intervened to deny him the chance, and this has remained in the realms of speculation ever since.

Cooper's chance disappears

What did happen next is that Clay recovered in a break that was extended because of a split glove. Cooper's chance had gone. Clay came out all guns blazing in the fifth, beating Cooper's face to a pulp until the referee stepped in. As usual, it was the round Clay had predicted. Many observers noted what had happened to Clay in the fourth

round. If Cooper could do that, what would Liston do to the flashy upstart? If it wasn't quite a minority of one who gave Clay a prayer against the champion, then you certainly wouldn't have needed many hands to count them. Liston was his usual intimidating self. The stare was as icy as ever, and when they stepped into the ring he did his usual trick of putting towels under his robe to make himself look even more gargantuan than he was.

"Too ugly to be champion"

The challenger was unperturbed. "He's too ugly to be world champion," Clay had said. Most people still thought that once the bell rang, Clay would suffer for the "big ugly bear" jibes he had dispensed so liberally in the run-up to the fight.Unknown to the fans, however, the balance of power had already shifted in Clay's favour, for a number of reasons. Liston was confused and concerned by Clay's near-hysterical ranting before the fight. He could cope with hard men, but madmen were a different proposition. The champion also found himself cast in an unfamiliar role. Even as champion he was still regarded as the "bad-ass nigger", the bogeyman of the white middle classes. Everything changed when Clay joined the Nation of Islam. Liston accepted his lot in a white man's world; Clay didn't. He rejected the values of a society which had subjugated the black population. He was articulate in espousing the "black is beautiful" mantra. He associated with the likes of Malcolm X. All this was far more worrying to the white population than anything Liston had done. The latter thus found himself championing the cause of those who wanted to preserve the status quo. That simply added to the confusion for the illiterate titleholder. If all this weren't enough to seal Liston's fate, he also underestimated Clay as a fighter. He had trained as though it would all be over in double-quick time. When the two faced each other in Miami on 25 February 1964, it was Liston who looked overawed. He found himself staring up at a magnificent physical specimen who exuded the confidence of a man destined to succeed.

Clay blinded

In the early stages, Clay took a few good shots, but he gave better than he got. A volley of punches at the start of the third opened a cut under Liston's left eye. At the end of the round, his corner men staunched the wound with some kind of ointment. No problem there, but the champion's gloves also became smeared with the substance, sparking a controversy which would exercise commentators and pundits for years. By the end of round four, Clay's eyes were smarting, his vision badly impaired. Liston had been accused of putting a caustic substance on his gloves before, against Zora Folley and Eddie Machen. Whether it was deliberate or not, this time it did him no good. Clay used his brilliant footwork to good effect in the fifth, dancing clear of trouble while his eyes watered and cleared. In the sixth round he came back with a vengeance. By now Liston was sluggish and tiring visibly. The fact that he had fought only two rounds in three years began to tell. He sat down at the end of the sixth and didn't come out for the next. The reason given was that he had sustained a shoulder injury.

Liston quits in his chair

Many have cast doubt on this claim. Liston was clearly shattered, while the younger, fitter man was champing at the bit to get at him. Did Liston simply see the writing on the wall? It was only the second time that a heavyweight champion had quit in his chair. Clay wasn't bothered about that. His post-fight comment was short and to the point: "I shook up the world!" The following day, the champion renounced Cassius Clay as a slave name. He was no longer a slave, and would henceforth be known as Muhammad Ali. The two men met again in Lewiston, Maine, in May 1965. If the first fight had had its controversial moments, they were as nothing compared with the rematch. A minute into the opening round, Ali caught Liston with a short right to the jaw. It was just about the first decent punch he had connected with, but it was no knockout blow. That's exactly what it turned out to be, though. There was total chaos as the referee - ex-champion Jersey Joe Walcott - struggled to get Ali to a neutral corner before he could start the count. An incensed Ali exhorted Liston to get up. Liston did eventually struggle to his feet, and Ali moved in while Walcott checked with the timekeeper to see how long Liston had been down. It was well beyond 10 seconds, and he declared Ali the winner.

Fastest knockout

Cries of "Fix!" accompanied the men on their way back to the dressing-room. It was all very unsatisfactory. Ali could shrug his shoulders, his title intact. Liston had to live with the fact that an innocuous punch had put him into the record books as the fastest recorded knockout victim in the championship's history. Floyd Patterson was next up for Ali. He had been overawed and overpowered by Liston. Against a boxer rather than a slugger, he quietly fancied his chances. Indeed, some say that Patterson had even quicker hands than Ali. They couldn't save him, however. Patterson injured his back early on and the champion exploited it mercilessly. The referee called a halt to the annihilation in the 12th. The Patterson fight took place on 22 November 1965. By 14 November 1966, Ali had fought and beaten five more men: a total of six fights in 51 weeks. Canada's rugged and durable heavyweight George Chuvalo took him the distance, though the result was never in doubt. Ali then

went on a European tour. Back in 1963 he had promised Henry Cooper a shot at the title when he became world champion. He was as good as his word. This time Ali steered well clear of "Henry's Hammer". He cut Cooper badly in the sixth and the referee stopped it a round later. Less than three months later Brian London proved to be less worthy opposition. A punch of similar magnitude to the one that floored Liston accounted for him in round three. It was a poor show. Germany's Karl Mildenberger was much more resilient and gave Ali a stiffer test. But the champion soon got the measure of his man and the fight was stopped in the 12th. Ali completed a whirlwind year of defences back on home soil.

Sheer poetry

His opponent, Cleveland Williams, was a difficult customer, someone Floyd Patterson had been accused of ducking during his reign. Although he was now past his best, nothing should detract from Ali's mesmerising performance that November night. His movement was sheer poetry, his artistry sublime, his punches devastating. Williams was finished in the third. In February 1967, Ali had what amounted to a unification fight against WBA champion Ernie Terrell. The WBA had stripped Ali of the crown for agreeing to a rematch with Liston in 1964. That organisation conducted its own tournament and Terrell emerged the victor. He had successfully retained the title against George Chuvalo and Doug Jones, and had beaten all the top men of the day - Ali excepted. Terrell made the mistake of deliberately calling the champion "Clay".

"What's my name?"

As had happened with Patterson, Ali wasn't just content to beat his man; he wanted ritual humiliation. He spun the

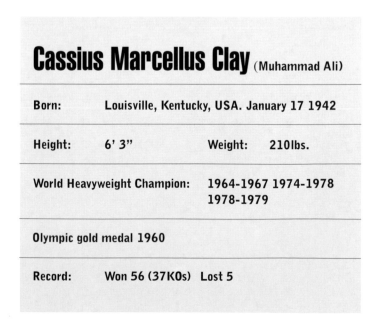

Cassius Marcellus Clay (Muhammad Ali)

Born:	Louisville, Kentucky, USA. January 17 1942		
Height:	6' 3"	Weight:	210lbs.
World Heavyweight Champion:		1964-1967 1974-1978 1978-1979	
Olympic gold medal 1960			
Record:	Won 56 (37KOs) Lost 5		

fight out for the full 15 rounds, toying with Terrell like a cat with a mouse. "What's my name?" Ali yelled as the blows pummelled his opponent. Six weeks later, Ali's ninth defence pitted him against veteran Zora Folley. Folley was a boxing stylist, but he was no match for Ali's new breed of artistry. Ali knocked him out in the seventh. Shortly afterwards, Ali's world came crashing round his ears when he was drafted into the US Army. The Vietnam war was raging and Ali's number came up. The champion was having none of it. "No Viet Cong ever called me nigger," he said as he refused to be inducted. The boxing authorities summarily stripped him of his title. He was sentenced to five years in prison and handed a $10,000 fine, but on appeal the Supreme Court decided that locking up a sporting legend was not a sensible course of action.

Ali rejects compromise

A compromise was sought, but Ali wouldn't play ball. He steadfastly refused to go along with any suggestion of a stage-managed solution. He wouldn't even allow himself to be photographed in uniform. He could have got himself off the hook quite painlessly, but he stuck to his principles. It was to cost him three-and-a-half years out of the profession he graced and loved. No American boxing commission would sanction any fight, and his passport was taken away, precluding the possibility of an overseas contest. This placed a severe financial burden on Ali, and he eked out a living by lecturing on the college circuit. More important as far as boxing fans were concerned, this shameful hiatus robbed them of seeing Ali at the absolute peak of his powers.

Were Liston's gloves smeared deliberately?

Opposite: A grimacing Sonny Liston ducks to try and avoid the pummelling fists of Cassius Clay in the fifth round of their title fight in Miami. This was the round in which Clay complained that his vision was considerably impaired, the result of a caustic subtance smeared on Liston's gloves getting into his eyes. If it was a deliberate ploy, it failed miserably.

Right: Having already opened up a cut under Liston's left eye, Clay goes to work on the right during the third round. Liston recovered well to keep the score fairly level going into the fourth.

Below: Liston takes more punishment before deciding to stay in his chair at the end of the sixth round. Some commentators felt that Liston's defeat was partly due to his frame of mind when he entered the ring. He was said to be dispirited and disillusioned by the way he had been treated as champion.

Clay taunts the doubters

Below: "Eat your words!" Clay shouts defiantly at the ringside critics who insisted that Liston was unbeatable.

Opposite: Clay is embraced by one of his corner men as referee Barney Felix declares that Liston is unable to continue. There would be many more victory embraces, but not by members of his entourage wearing shirts bearing the legend "Cassius Clay". The day after the fight, Clay renounced his "slave name" and said that henceforward he would be known as Muhammad Ali.

Left: Top of the world. Clay realised his boyhood dream at the age of 22 years 1 month, three months older than Floyd Patterson had been when he won the title.

"The Dodger" proves too elusive for Cooper

Above: November 1964. America's Roger Rischer (right) lives up to his nickname of "Roger the Dodger" as he outpoints British champion Henry Cooper at the Albert Hall. The Californian heavyweight proved too sprightly and elusive for Cooper, who hardly got the chance to use his famous left jab and hook.

Opposite: Cooper manages to get close to Rischer for once, something he didn't manage too often during their fight. Rischer, the world No 9 in the WBA rankings, was warned by referee Harry Gibbs at one point for being too negative, and the crowd showed their feelings by slow-handclapping the American.

"Walker hits harder than Ali"

Opposite: America's Charlie Powell manages to get to all fours but no further, and is counted out by referee Harry Gibbs. The man who put him down with a sledgehammer right is West Ham's Billy Walker. After the fight, which ended 2 min. 32 sec. into the second round, Powell paid tribute to his victor, saying that Walker's right was harder than Muhammad Ali's. The fight took place at Olympia, January 26, 1965.

Below: Royal Albert Hall, January 12, 1965: Henry Cooper defends against a raking left from New York's Dick Wipperman.

Left: Cooper digs a hard left into Wipperman's midriff. The British champion won by a TKO in the fifth, having twice floored the American earlier in the round.

Patterson ready to challenge Ali after win over Chuvalo

Opposite above: February 1965. Floyd Patterson (right) smashes a right to the jaw of Canadian champion George Chuvalo. Patterson outboxed and outpointed the tough Canadian champion, putting himself back into contention for yet another crack at the world title.

Above: Former champion Joe Louis reads the newspaper accounts of Muhammad Ali's hernia operation, which forced the rematch against Sonny Liston to be postponed.

Opposite below: Brian London (right) halts the progress of rising young star Billy Walker. London was a convincing points winner in the 10-round contest, which took place at the Empire Pool, Wembley, March 30, 1965.

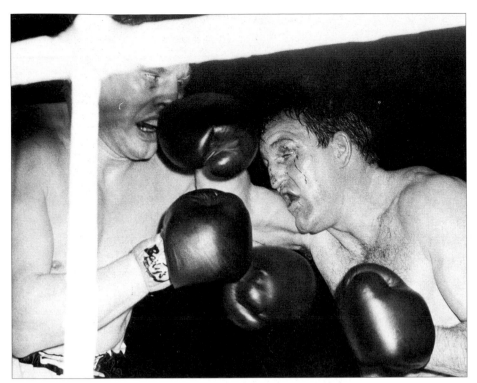

London wins battle of Britain's bulldozing heavyweights

Left: For the first eight rounds of their 10-round contest, Brian London (right) and Billy Walker went at each other like a pair of stags. Both men handed out and took a lot of punishment in a contest which thrilled the Wembley crowd. Only in the latter stages did the West Ham man begin to wilt, allowing London to press home his clear points advantage.

Opposite: Walker catches London with a solid right, but the veteran Blackpool heavyweight knew just a bit too much for the Blond Bomber.

Below: Walker manages a smile in defeat, while London puts a consoling arm around the West Ham heavyweight's shoulder.

Liston the fall-guy in boxing's most controversial KO

Above: Down and out. Liston makes a half-hearted attempt to get to his feet before slumping back to the canvas. This knockout has gone down as the most controversial in boxing history. Most observers - Ali included - felt that the punch which ended the fight should not have put a man of Liston's stature down for the count.

Opposite: The Ali camp is jubilant after their man's victory over Sonny Liston at Lewiston, Maine, May 25, 1965. Liston cuts an understandably forlorn figure in the background, while Ali himself hardly looks much happier. Far from being overjoyed at his 1 min. 42 sec. knockout, the champion had exhorted Liston to get up off the canvas and carry on the fight.

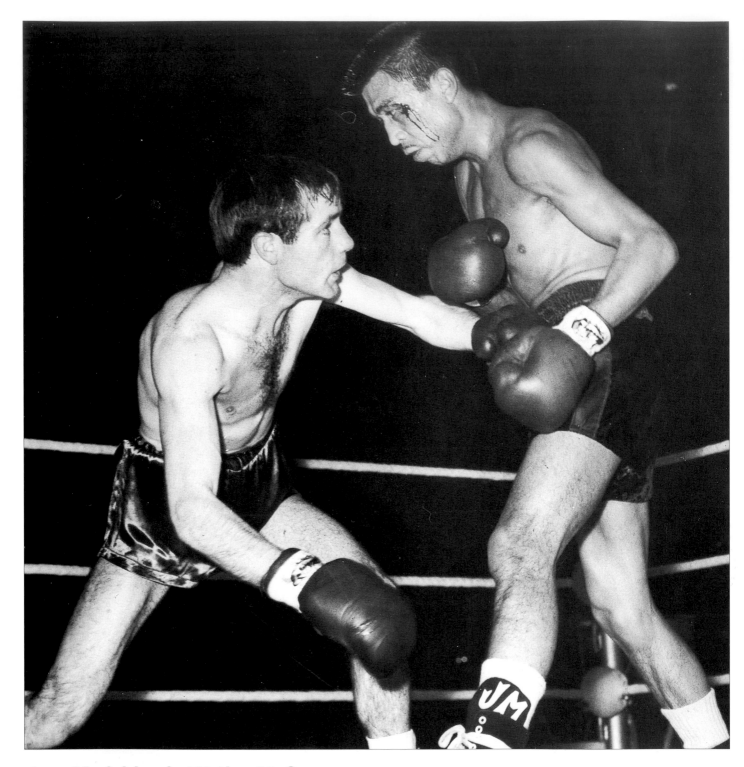

Jose Medel beats Walter McGowan

Above: Wembley, June 1, 1965. Mexico's bantamweight champion Jose Medel survived a badly cut by to score a TKO over Scotland's Walter McGowan in the sixth round. McGowan won the world flyweight title the following year to become Britain's first champion in that division since Terry Allen in the early 1950s.

Opposite: Earls Court, September 1965. Howard Winstone (back to camera) fails in his bid to take the world featherweight title from Mexico's Vicente Saldivar. The Welshman was beaten three times in all by the boxer who ruled the division in the mid-1960s and who was described as a "pocket-sized Marciano".

Game Prescott no match for Cooper

Above: British heavyweight champion Henry Cooper connects with a trademark left to the head of challenger Johnny Prescott. The two met at Birmingham City's football ground, June 1965, in front of 18,000 fans.

Opposite: Cooper quickly gets on top of his game opponent, and the fight turns into a one-sided affair. Prescott was finally put out of his misery when his manager, George Biddles, retired him at the end of the tenth round.

Right: 31-year-old Henry Cooper shows that he is still the man all British heavyweights have to beat, following his thorough demolition job on Johnny Prescott. It was Cooper's sixth successful defence of his British title.

London grinds to a halt as Ali comes to town

Opposite: What a difference three years makes. When Ali visited England in 1963 to take on Henry Cooper, he was little known outside boxing circles. Three years on, on his return to fight Cooper again, everyone wants to get a glimpse of The Greatest.

Above: Ohio's Amos Johnson keeps a wary eye on Henry Cooper's famous left jab during their encounter at Wembley, October 19, 1965. The American won the fight on points.

The Ali bandwagon takes to the road

Above: Ali waves to the fans as he arrives at the stage door of the Odeon, Leicester Square for the weigh-in prior to the rematch with Henry Cooper. This was the first of three European fights for Ali in the summer of 1966. He took to the road in response to the huge antipathy for him back home, following his outspoken comments about the Vietnam war.

Opposite: The British Boxing Board of Control's Dr Paul Saville examines Ali and declares him 100 per cent fit for the Highbury showdown with Cooper.

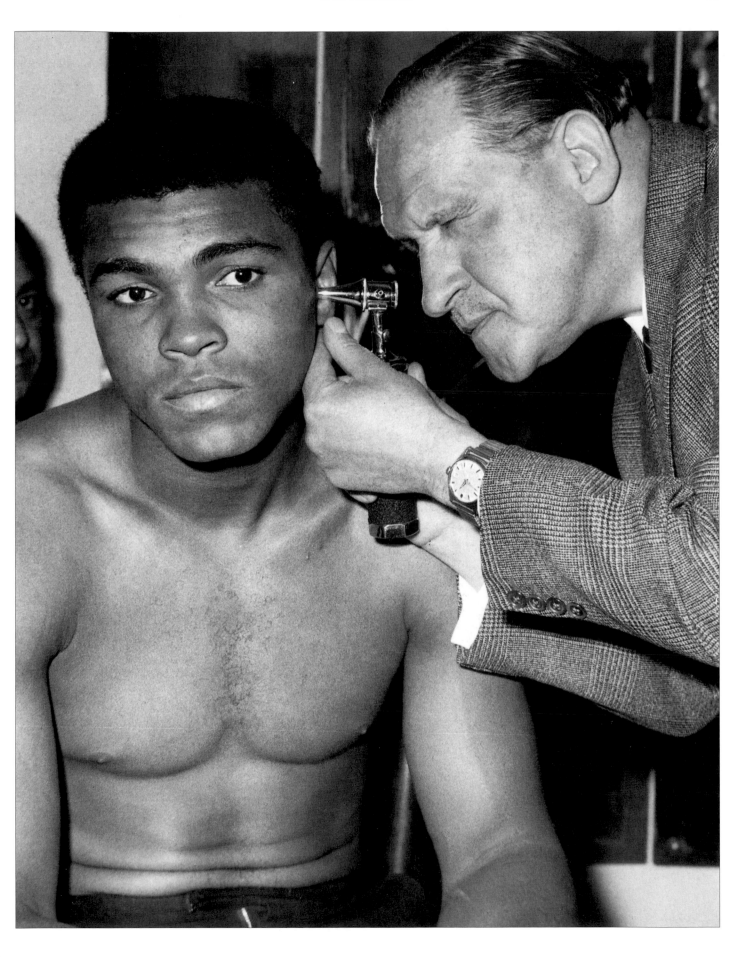

Above: Ali and his sparring partner, future champion Jimmy Ellis, take a breather during their early-morning run in Hyde Park. Note Ali's choice of footwear. He had incredible natural leg-speed, and such training methods would make him even more elusive for his opponents in the ring.
Opposite: Ali gears up for the Cooper fight at the Territorial Army gym in White City, London.

Ali shows Cooper respect

Round four of the Ali-Cooper clash, and the champion misses for once. Overall, Ali gave an accomplished performance, without the usual clowning. He showed Cooper respect, and certainly took no liberties whenever he was within range of the challenger's dangerous left.

Gashed eye ends Cooper's hopes again

It's round six, and nearly all over for Cooper. Ali throws a long right towards his face, which is already bleeding profusely, following a stinging punch earlier in the round. Ali implores the referee to stop the fight, and seconds later it's all over.

London offers little resistance

Opposite: August 6, 1966. Brian London (left) manages to stay clear of trouble in his fight with Ali - but not for long. Ali entertained the crowd for a couple of rounds, then knocked London out in the third.
Above: A thoughtful - and unmarked - Ali watches a re-run of the Cooper fight at a private showing in the West End. He said: "I have been overwhelmed with my reception in London. Everybody has been kindness itself. And Cooper! He's a real gentleman and a fine opponent."

Fans boo London's tame submission

Above: Brian London is totally outclassed by Ali in the brief duration of their fight. He landed just two punches, neither of any great quality. Ali entertained the crowd for the opening two rounds, then floored his man with a right to the jaw in the third.

Opposite: Ali waits to see if Brian London will beat the count. He doesn't, and the champion's reaction is similar to that at the end of his second fight with Liston: disbelief that the punch he has thrown should be good enough to finish the contest. The crowd agreed, and booed their countryman's lacklustre performance and tame submission.

Ali completes European hat-trick

Above: Frankfurt, September 10, 1966. Muhammad Ali completes a hat-trick of wins on his "European tour" by beating Karl Mildenberger. The German champion provided the stiffest opposition of the summer. An awkward and durable customer, Mildenberger lasted until the 12th round, when Ali dropped him to the canvas. He is seen struggling to recover, but referee Teddy Walthan has seen enough. It was Ali's sixth defence of the title.

Opposite: Wembley, September 20, 1966. A glassy-eyed Henry Cooper goes down in the third round of his scheduled 10-round contest against former world champion Floyd Patterson. The British champion survived just one more round.

Victory for Patterson thought to signal end for Cooper

Above: Henry Cooper is clinically dispatched by Floyd Patterson in the fourth round of their fight at Wembley, September 20, 1966. This defeat, coming hard on the heels of his six-round loss against Muhammad Ali in May, was thought to signal the end of 32-year-old Cooper's career. Patterson, meanwhile, was hoping to use this comprehensive victory as a springboard for another crack at Ali's world crown.

Opposite: A groggy Cooper is helped to his feet after being KOd by Patterson. His only consolation was that he was just a few weeks away from having held the British heavyweight title for seven years ten months, an all-time record.

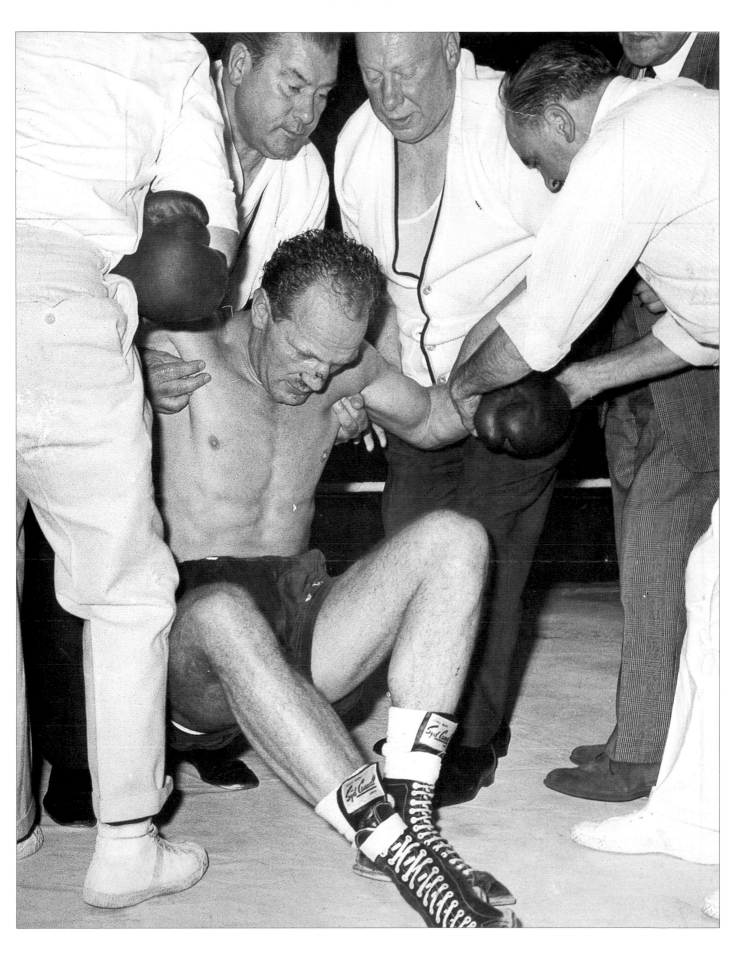

Big cat tamed

Opposite: Houston, November 14, 1966. A bird's-eye view of the ring shows 6ft 5in Cleveland Williams - the man nicknamed "The Big Cat" - stretched out on the canvas in the third round of his clash with Muhammad Ali. It was the fourth knockdown in total, and Ali is already celebrating his victory. Referee Harry Kessler soon made it official, awarding the fight to the champion on a TKO.

Left: Williams is on his way down for the fourth and final time, just 1 min 8 sec into the third round. Williams was a veteran class and a dangerous opponent. Ali made him look like a complete novice.

Below: Ali lays himself wide open for Ernie Terrell to try and land a punch, but the latter still prefers to cover up. Ali chose to torment Terrell mercilessly for the full 15 rounds instead of knocking him out. This was payback time, for Terrell had infuriated the champion by calling him "Clay" prior to the fight.

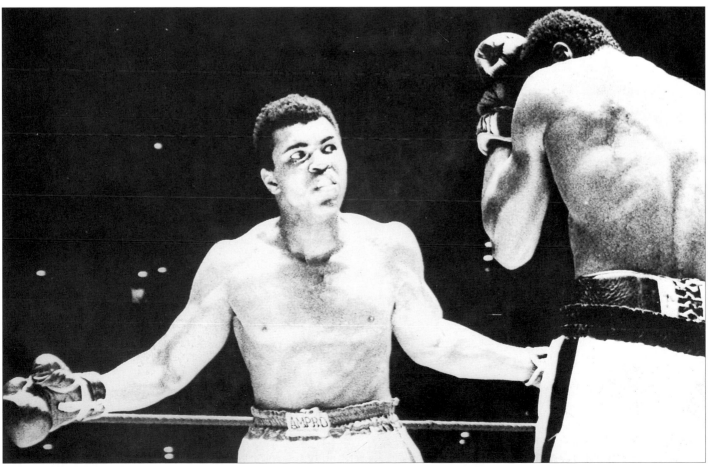

Walker's European dream in tatters

Wembley, March 1967. Billy Walker's dream of winning the European title ends after seven and a half rounds of bloody punishment at the hands of the reigning champion, Germany's Karl Mildenberger. Mildenberger, who had himself been stopped by Ali in 12 rounds the previous September, won every round comprehensively. Walker was left to count his money, and his blessings - for a victory would have set in motion plans for a meeting with Ali.

Frazier's rise continues with win over Chuvalo

Below: Joe Frazier takes the fight to George Chuvalo in the first round of their clash in New York, July 20, 1967. Frazier won by a TKO in the fourth round, becoming the first man to stop the rugged Canadian in his career.

Right: Leicester, January 1967. Jack Bodell makes hard work of a points win over lowly ranked American Sonny Moore. His failure to impress left observers feeling he was still a long way from being a credible contender for the British title.

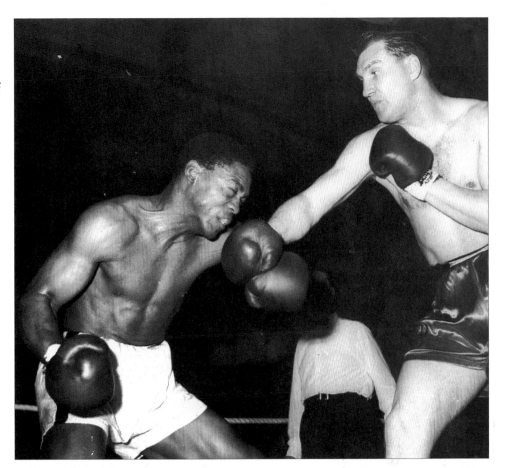

Quarry wins through to WBA "Final"

Above: Los Angeles, October 28, 1967. Jerry Quarry drops Floyd Patterson to the canvas with a hard right in the second round of their WBA title eliminator. Patterson beat the count but lost the fight on a split decision.

Left: Quarry's win over Patterson was somewhat controversial, many observers believing the former champion was hard done by. Quarry went on to contest the "final" against Jimmy Ellis, though all boxing fans still regarded Ali as the true champion.

Opposite below: Henry Cooper's trusty left does plenty of damage to Billy Walker when the two contest the British heavyweight title at the Empire Pool, November 7, 1967.

Opposite above: Referee George Smith stops the fight in the sixth, Walker having sustained a bad cut to the eye. Cooper thus retained his title, and also became the first man to win three championship belts outright.

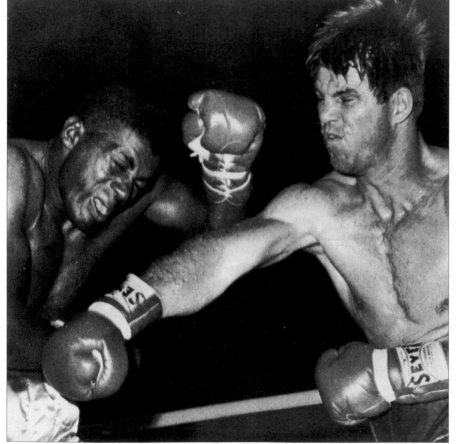

Above: George Smith leads a disappointed Billy Walker to his corner after stopping the fight for the British championship in Henry Cooper's favour.

Opposite above: Britain's Alan Rudkin in action against Ronnie Jones at the Royal Albert Hall in December 1967.

Opposite below: Royal Albert Hall, January 1968. Japan's Mitsunori Seki takes evasive action as Welshman Howard Winstone throws a left jab. Winstone, the British featherweight champion, took the vacant WBC world title by stopping Seki in the ninth round.

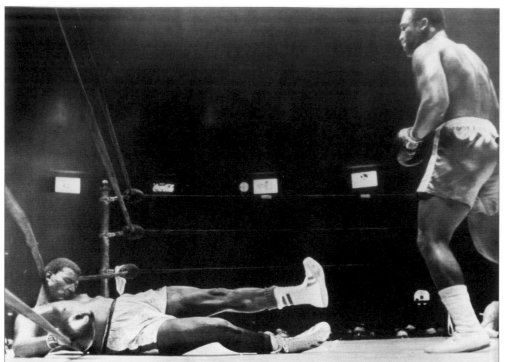

Frazier takes WBC crown

Left: New York, March 4, 1968. Buster Mathis lies in a crumpled heap in the eleventh round of his fight against Joe Frazier to decide the WBC championship. It was a sweet victory for Frazier, since Mathis had beaten him during their amateur days, the only stain on his boxing career.

Rudkin beats McGowan

Opposite below: Belle Vue, May 1968. Alan Rudkin shows off his Lonsdale Belt after beating Scotland's Walter McGowan to win the British flyweight championship. McGowan had won the world title in June 1966 with a win over Salvatore Burruni but his reign only lasted until December that year, when the Scot was stopped by Thailand's Chartchai Chionoi.

Above: National Sporting Club, June 1968. Ken Buchanan (right) swings and misses while his opponent, Ivan Whiter, scores a hit to the Scot's face. Buchanan, who had won the British lightweight title four months earlier, quit boxing soon after this contest, frustrated at the lack of money and opportunity to fight for the world title. The retirement was short lived, however, and he came back to win the WBA world crown in 1970.

Joe Frazier
World Heavyweight Champion: 1970-1973

Joe Frazier was unfortunate in that his career spanned those of two of boxing's greatest champions: Muhammad Ali and George Foreman. They were the only two men to get the better of him in a professional career lasting more than 10 years, and there was no disgrace in that. Frazier is rightly regarded as a fine champion in his own right. Had he fought in a less distinguished era, for example, between Tunney and Louis, or in the post-Marciano 1950s, he would almost certainly have been held in higher esteem.

Like his two great contemporaries, Frazier crowned a fine amateur career by taking Olympic gold. That was at Tokyo 1964, in the superheavyweight division. He wasn't a first choice for the team, however. He was drafted in after Buster Mathis sustained an injury and was forced to withdraw. Mathis was the man who stood between Frazier and a perfect amateur record, having twice outpointed Smokin' Joe. But it was Frazier who went on to greater glory in the professional ranks, and that was to include an avenging win over Mathis in a crunch title showdown. More of that later.

Frazier was a man in a hurry after he turned professional in 1965. His first three fights lasted less than five rounds in total. In 1966 he fought no less than nine times, and only the rugged Argentinian Oscar Bonavena took him the distance. Six more opponents were dispatched in 1967, including Doug Jones and George Chuvalo.

Revenge on Mathis

No one could accuse Frazier of ducking the best heavyweights around at the time. There was the small matter of Muhammad Ali, of course. Frazier was undoubtedly punching his way to a showdown with Ali when the latter was stripped of his title. At that point, different boxing organisations staged their own competitions to find a successor, something which has become an all too familiar sight over the past 30 years. Frazier entered the WBC's New York-based tournament, where he faced his old adversary Buster Mathis. He finally got his revenge on Mathis for those two defeats in their amateur days by stopping him in the 11th.

Frazier defended his WBC crown four times between June 1968 and June 1969, including a second points victory over Bonavena. Another of his victims was Jerry Quarry, the tough Irish-American who had lost to Jimmy Ellis for the WBA version of the title. The scene was set for a Frazier-Ellis showdown.

The two met at Madison Square Garden, on 16 February 1970. Ellis was a quality opponent and started well. But in the third Frazier hit back, connecting with some big shots. A round later he put Ellis down. Ellis's corner saw the writing on the wall and threw in the towel.

Boxing history is littered with light-heavyweights attempting to step up a division and try for the greatest prize. Bob Foster was the latest to do just that. Foster was a class act, and against a lesser heavyweight he may well have come out on top. But his best shots simply bounced off Frazier. The champion was brutally efficient, finishing the job inside two rounds.

Fight of the century

The world clamoured to see Frazier and Ali, the two undefeated titans of the ring, go head-to-head. They got their wish on 8 March 1971. Ali had had just two fights since regaining his licence the previous August. He couldn't wait any longer to get into the ring with the man who had his title. The fans couldn't either. New York was gripped by fight fever. Long gone were the days when promoters scoffed at the viability of two black heavyweights fighting for the crown. This was huge. Frazier and Ali shared $5 million for their 45 minutes' work, making it the fight of the century in financial as well as boxing terms.

The contest had another interesting dimension. While Ali embraced black consciousness and renounced his "slave name", Frazier studiously avoided the race issue. Ironically, he had known much greater hardship than Ali in his younger days. At the age of six he was helping his father eke out a living from farming. He had also been on the receiving end of considerable discrimination and bigotry. Yet when he became a top fighter and had money and a platform, unlike Ali, he wasn't interested in pursuing political ends.

Joe Frazier

Nickname:	Smokin		
Born:	Beaufort, South Carolina, USA. January 12 1944		
Height:	6' 3"	**Weight:**	205lbs.
World Heavyweight Champion:	1968-1973		
Olympic gold medal 1964 (first for a USA Heavyweight)			
Record:	Won 32 (27 KOs) Lost 4 Drawn 1		

Lay-off takes its toll

The two men fought out a bloody, bruising, attritional battle that went the full 15 rounds. Both men doled out and took heavy punishment. That Ali should find his man with stinging punches was no surprise. What was more remarkable was the fact that Ali's long lay-off had affected his famed leg speed, and as a result Frazier landed a lot of blows too. And Frazier's punches had a lot behind them. In round 11 he caught Ali with a terrific left hook to the jaw which nearly put him down. In the final round, Frazier connected with the same punch, an absolute peach. Ali looked down and gone, but miraculously managed to beat the count. It didn't much matter. Seconds later the fight was over and all three judges had Frazier the clear winner.

After such a brutal contest, perhaps Frazier could be forgiven for taking things a little easier, and that is precisely what he did. In 1972 he fought just twice, against journeymen boxers Terry Daniels and Ron Stander. Both were dispatched inside four rounds. Meanwhile, Ali remained in the background, seething and taunting. Frazier ignored him. For his next defence he decided to take on a rising star by the name of George Foreman.

Easy first defence for Frazier

New York, June 24, 1968. Joe Frazier makes short work of Manuel Ramos in his first fight as WBC champion. Referee Art Mercante has seen enough in the second round, and ends the contest on a TKO. It would be nearly two years before Frazier would face WBA titleholder Jimmy Ellis for the undisputed crown.

Ellis benefits from "worst-ever decision"

Opposite above: Stockholm, September 14, 1968. After losing out to Quarry in the tournament to produce a new WBA champion Floyd Patterson challenged Jimmy Ellis, the man who had won the WBC version of the title. Patterson (left) took Ellis the distance but lost the decision.

Opposite below: Patterson smiles ruefully as Jimmy Ellis gives a victory salute. The former champion broke Ellis's nose, put him down and generally gave the younger man a boxing lesson. Some observers have called this the worst decision in the sport's history.

Above: Wembley Stadium, September 18, 1968. Germany's Karl Mildenberger takes a compulsory count after being floored by Henry Cooper during their European heavyweight title fight. Cooper won the contest after Mildenberger, the defending champion, was disqualified in the eighth round.

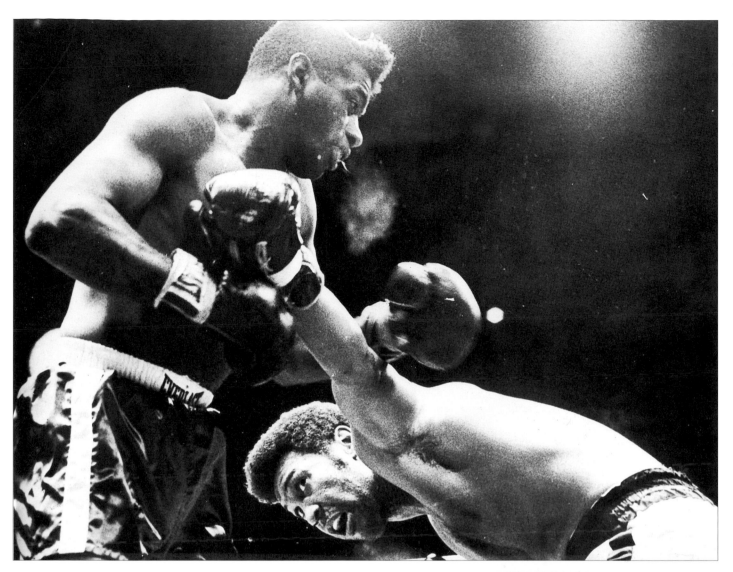

Bugner on the march

Above: Royal Albert Hall, October 1969. 19-year-old Joe Bugner gives another quality performance in beating America's Phil Smith inside two rounds. The young heavyweight from St. Ives, Huntingdonshire, needed just 4 min. 20 sec. to finish the job, referee Harry Gibbs intervening after two quick-fire knockdowns left Smith unable to defend himself.

Opposite: Bugner gives the best display of his career so far as he bludgeons veteran Johnny Prescott to a comprehensive defeat at the Royal Albert Hall, January 1970.

Joe Bugner

Born:	**Hungary, March 13 1950**	
European Heavyweight Champion:		**1971 1972-1984**
British and Commonwealth Heavyweight Champion:		**1971 1975-1987**
Record:	**Won 69 (41 KOs) Lost 13 Drawn 1**	

Frazier the undisputed champion - Ali excepted

Opposite: Madison Square Garden, February 16, 1970. Jimmy Ellis is left reeling on the canvas, following a brute of a left hook from Joe Frazier. It was the fourth round of the clash between the WBA and WBC champions.

Above: Ellis is sent sprawling for the second time in quick succession. Referee Tony Perez ushers Frazier away but it is academic. The bell for the end of the fourth round saves Ellis from being counted out, but he failed to come out for the fifth.

Right: Frazier celebrates becoming the undisputed champion, though Muhammad Ali will soon have something to say about that when he regains his licence and returns to the scene.

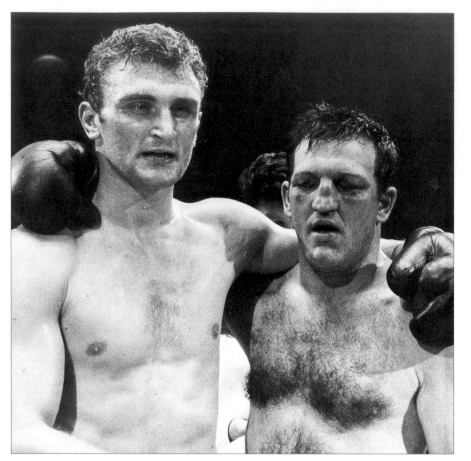

Ali back in action

Opposite: Return of The Greatest. Ali regains his licence in August 1970, and resumes his career with a fight against tough Irish-American Jerry Quarry in Atlanta, October 26.

Ali stops Quarry in the third round with a cut eye. There were flashes of the old Ali magic during the fight, but after a long lay-off there was inevitably an element of ring-rustiness.

Left: Joe Bugner (left) embraces battle-scarred Brian London after pounding him to defeat at the Empire Pool, Wembley, May 12, 1970. The referee stopped the fight in the fifth round to prevent the veteran former British champion from taking further punishment.

Below: Royal Albert Hall, April 21, 1970. Bugner notches yet another creditable victory, this time over New York's Ray Patterson. Bugner won the fight on points.

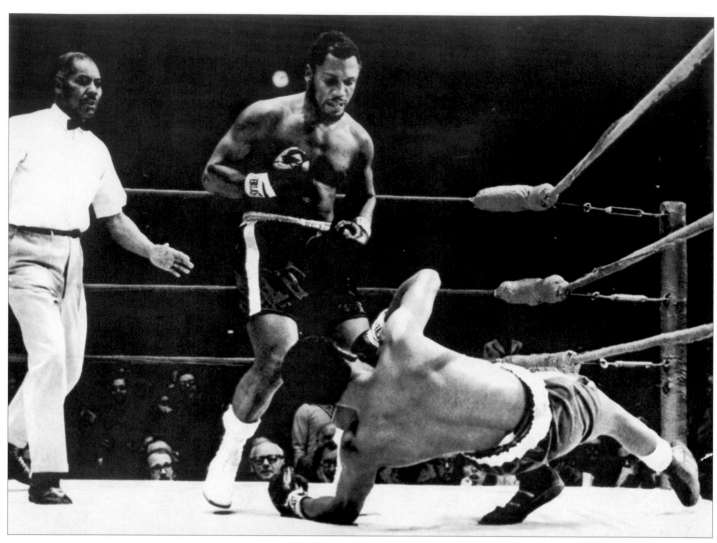

Clamour increases for Frazier-Ali showdown

Opposite and right: Detroit, November 18, 1970. Nine months after uniting the WBA and WBC titles by beating Jimmy Ellis, Joe Frazier takes on the brilliant light-heavyweight champion Bob Foster. Foster survived just one round and 49 seconds, when he stopped a pulverising left hook from Smokin' Joe. With Muhammad Ali back on the scene, the boxing world now clamoured for the two unbeaten champions to face each other.

Below: Wembley, November 20, 1970. Henry Cooper regains the European heavyweight title by stopping Spain's Jose Urtain at the start of the ninth round. French referee Bernard Mascot tells Urtain that the severe damage to both eyes leaves him no alternative but to stop the fight.

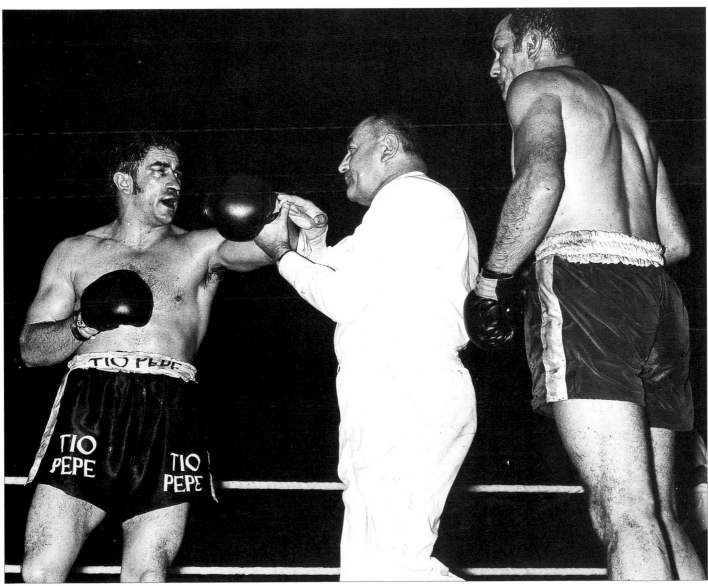

Frazier wins "fight of the century"

Below: Madison Square Garden, March 8, 1971. Ali and Frazier meet for the first of their three titanic encounters. Frazier scored the only knockdown of this bruising contest, connecting with a superb left hook to Ali's jaw in the 15th round. Although Ali recovered to finish the fight on his feet, Frazier had done enough to win a unanimous points decision.

Opposite: Ali squares up to British and Empire champion Jack Bodell at a dinner given by the World Sporting Club in London, October 18, 1971.

Left: Left: Madison Square Garden, June 26, 1972. Referee Johnny Lobianco pulls Roberto Duran off Ken Buchanan as the Scot sinks to the canvas in the 13th round. Buchanan, who had been on the receiving end of some roughhouse tactics from the 21-year-old Panamanian, was unable to continue. Duran walked away with the world lightweight title and refused to give Buchanan a rematch.

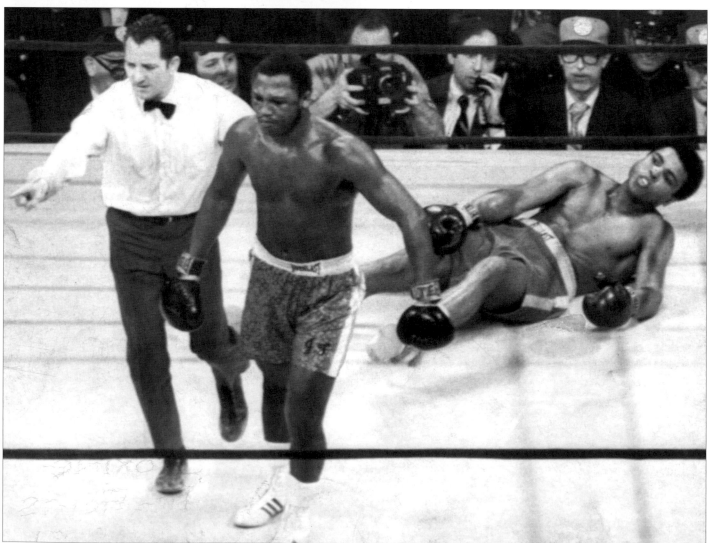

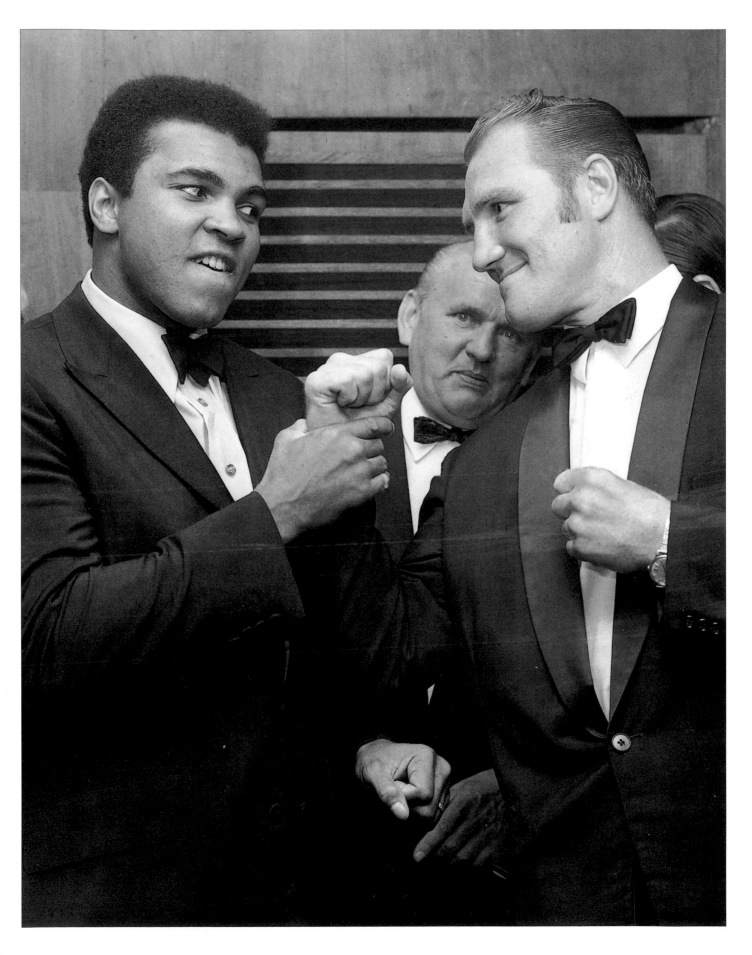

George Foreman

World Heavyweight Champion: 1973-74

The record books show that George Foreman held the heavyweight title for less than two years, and made just two successful defences. These bald statistics don't do him justice. When fans play the "all-time greatest" game, he would certainly rank above many who have worn the crown for longer and fought off many more challenges.

One of seven children born to a railroad construction worker, Foreman was a high school drop-out and a delinquent until serendipity took him into boxing. His good fortune came when he joined the Job Corps at the age of 17. This organisation took kids from the ghettoes who were in danger of going seriously off the rails and gave them some marketable skills, in Foreman's case bricklaying and carpentry.

"Hell of a fighter"

It was there that he came to the attention of Nick "Doc" Broadus, who took one look at Foreman's 6ft 3in muscular physique and decided that he would make a hell of a fighter. He was right.

A perfect amateur record culminated in Olympic gold at Mexico '68, and he turned professional the following year. From then until his meeting with Frazier in January 1973, Foreman had 37 straight wins, 34 of them inside the distance. Some of his opponents were second-raters but there were some quality scalps in there too. Besides, he could do no more than knock over whoever was put up in front of him.

Foreman climbed into the ring with Frazier in Kingston, Jamaica, on 22 January 1973. The day before the fight Foreman had celebrated his 25th birthday. It had been a significant day for Frazier too, for he had agreed terms for an eagerly-awaited rematch with Muhammad Ali.

Frazier's reputation destroyed

Foreman was to reduce that clash from a title fight to an eliminator in four-and-a-half devastating minutes. In that time he made a mockery of Frazier's reputation as the iron man of the ring. He clubbed Smokin' Joe to the canvas no less than six times, confirming to those who had any lingering doubts about his awesome punching power in both fists. He did to Frazier what Frazier had done to so many: shrugged off whatever his opponent threw at him and kept going forward. By the end, Frazier was wobbling around the ring like a frail old man.

While others immediately began mapping out future contests, Foreman simply wanted to let the magnitude of his achievement sink in. A bullish Frazier said he'd got his tactics all wrong. He would be back to reclaim his title with a better game plan. Representatives from Ali's camp said that Frazier had been beaten in the 17th round, not the second. They maintained that Frazier had not fully recovered from the gruelling 15-round battle with their man. In other words, Foreman had Ali to thank for softening Frazier up in their titanic battle almost two years earlier. Undermining the new champion's performance in this way was grossly unfair.

Two quickfire defences followed over the next 14 months. Jose Roman was put away in the first round and Ken Norton lasted until the second.

Next up was Muhammad Ali. Ali had trained his sights on Foreman after avenging his defeat by Frazier in January 1974. Ali-Foreman was set for October of that year. Fresh in the mind was the champion's demolition job on Frazier and Norton, both of whom had beaten Ali. Added to that, when the two men climbed into the ring Ali would have turned 32. Surely there was no way he could get the better of Foreman in the Rumble in the Jungle. Could he?

GEORGE FOREMAN

Born:	Marshall, Texas, USA. January 10 1949	
Height:	6' 3"	Weight: 224lbs
World Heavyweight Champion:	1973-74 1994-97	
Olympic gold medal 1968		
Record:	Won 76 (68 KOs) Lost 5	

In November 1994 Foreman won the WBA and IBF versions of the heavyweight title.

Underdog Foreman rocks Frazier

George Foreman astonished the boxing world and overturned odds of 3-1 when he took the world title from Joe Frazier in January 1973. The fight was meant to be a routine defence for Smokin' Joe, prior to another meeting with Ali. But in less than two rounds boxing had a new heavyweight champion.

Two months after winning the heavyweight crown, Foreman holds court at the Hertford Club, London. He shows off the weapons which dumped Frazier on the canvas six times and brought him the title.

Ali gunning for revenge and the title

Ali tunes up for his fight against British champion Joe Bugner, on February 14, 1973. He wanted it to be a stepping stone towards a rematch with Frazier for the world crown. Frazier's defeat by Foreman meant that he now had two men in his sights: one for revenge, the other for the title.

Opposite: Foreman prepares to fly home after his first visit to London as world champion. Despite the smiles, Foreman was mean and menacing, a fighter out of the Liston mould. Years later, he would find religion and become the archetypal gentle giant.

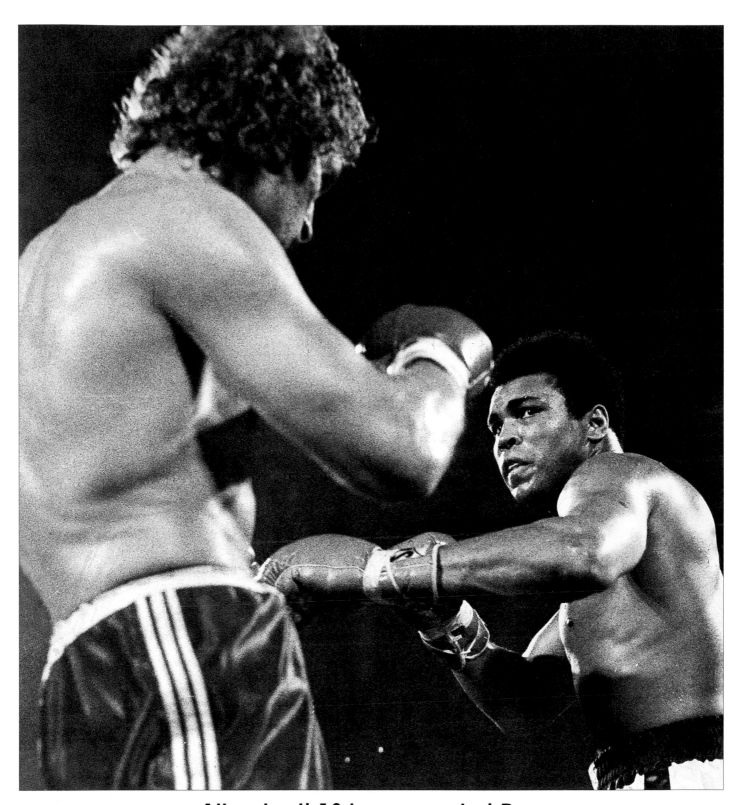

Ali makes it 10 in a row against Bugner

Ali was the wrong side of 30 when he faced Britain's Joe Bugner in Las Vegas, February 14, 1973. In training he looked rather lacklustre, but he was still too good for Bugner, whom he outboxed over 15 rounds.

Ali's points win over Bugner made it 10 victories in a row since the defeat by Frazier in 1971. Ken Norton was expected to be victim number 11 a couple of months later, but Ali's plans to regain his title were to hit the buffers in that fight.

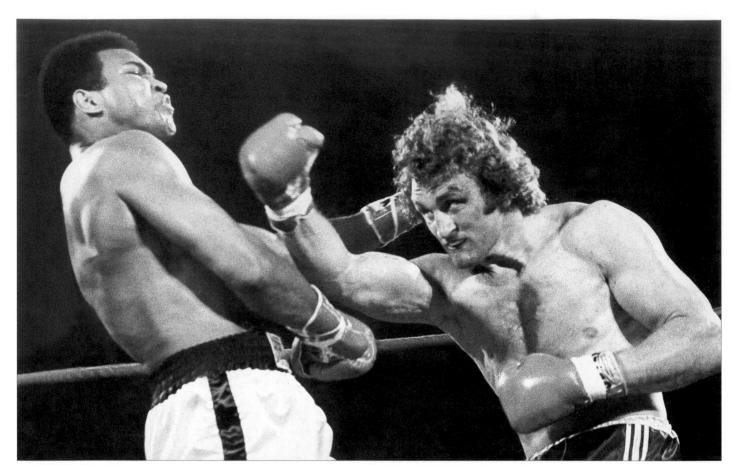

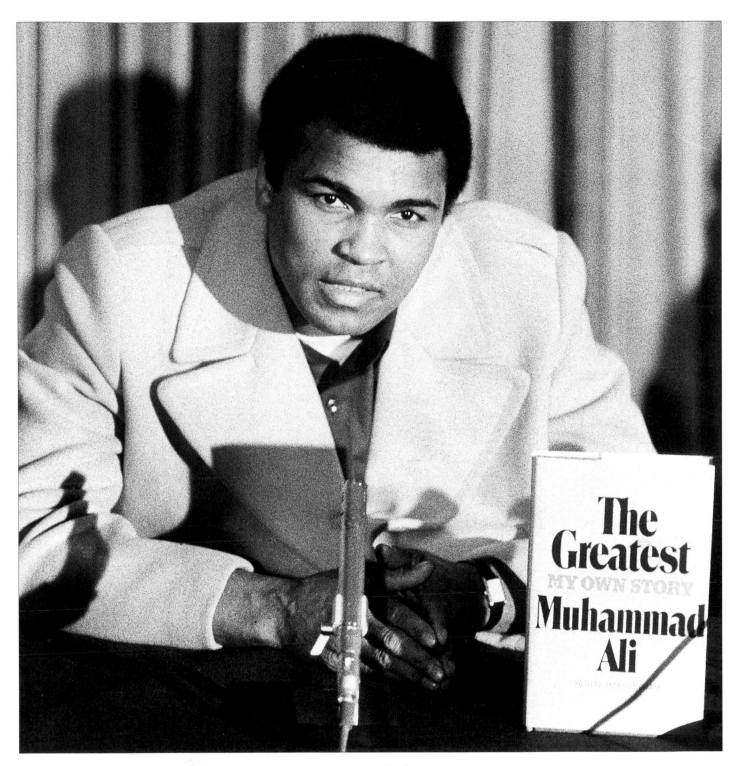

Bugner takes Frazier all the way

Opposite above: Joe Bugner goes on the attack against Muhammad Ali. Although Ali was a clear winner on points, the British champion's performance made a mockery of the 8-1 odds.
Opposite below: Bugner follows up his creditable performance against Ali by taking Joe Frazier the distance in July 1973. Frazier was on the rehabilitation trail, following his defeat by Foreman. He put Bugner down but couldn't finish him off, and had to settle for a points victory.
Above: What else could the title of Muhammad Ali's autobiography have been? Ali begins a whistle-stop promotional tour of the country with a Press launch at London's Savoy Hotel.

Muhammad Ali

World Heavyweight Champion: 1974-1978

Muhammad Ali was sidelined for three-and-a-half long years. His rehabilitation into the boxing fold began in August 1970, when Georgia, of all places, broke ranks and granted him a licence. Two months later, on 26 October, Ali stepped into the ring with Jerry Quarry for his first competitive fight since knocking out Zora Folley in March 1967.

Quarry had been a top contender during Ali's enforced absence. He had taken the WBA champion Jimmy Ellis the distance, and he had lasted seven rounds with the WBC title holder, Joe Frazier. It wasn't quite a vintage performance - it would have been amazing if it had been - but in the three rounds the fight lasted, Ali showed glimpses that the old verve, panache and silky skills were still there. Naturally, there was ring-rustiness to be shaken off, and the only cure for that was more fights.

He waited just six weeks to give himself another test, and a stiff examination it was, too. His opponent was Argentina's Oscar Bonavena, a very tough customer who had met Joe Frazier twice and given him plenty to think about. Bonavena lost both fights against Smokin' Joe on points, but he was certainly durable - and dangerous.

Ali cuts loose

Ali was scoring freely and comfortably ahead on points, but he couldn't put his man down, let alone out. There was no great shame in that, since nobody else had managed it either. Then, in an explosive 15th round, Ali cut loose and floored Bonavena three times in rapid succession. The Argentine got up each time, but under New York rules the third knockdown of the round brought the fight to an end.

The Bonavena fight was an enormous fillip for Ali and his supporters. He had proved he could go the distance if required, and he had put Bonavena on the seat of his pants, something the current champion, Joe Frazier, had failed to do. So it was that just two months and two fights into his comeback, Ali already had Frazier in his sights.

Murderous fight

The script was written for Ali's triumphant return, for him to assume the mantle that had merely been on loan to his opponent. It didn't work out that way, though. Frazier, like Ali, was an undefeated champion. Ali himself was gracious enough to recognise that his opponent was no usurper; Joe was a worthy title holder in his own right.

It was a murderous encounter, widely regarded as one of the most thrilling in the sport's history. Ultimately, it proved a step too far for the former champion. Frazier put him down with a brute of a left hook in the final round, but that was academic. All three judges had Frazier ahead when the bell sounded for the end of the contest, one of them by as much as an 11-4 margin.

Ali went off to hospital with a suspected broken jaw. Still dazed and disorientated, he muttered: "Must have been a helluva fight, I'm so tired". Those who subscribe to the "they never come back" school of thought must have believed he was also being carted off into boxing oblivion. He wasn't far short of his 30th birthday, and his famed leg speed, one of his most important attributes in the ring, seemed to have deserted him.

Doubters proved wrong

How wrong they were. When the dust had settled, Ali and his army of fans looked to the positive. After a long enforced absence he had taken the best in the business (himself excluded!) all the way; he had got up from a left hook that would have finished just about anybody else; and while he was having his jaw checked, Frazier was also on his way to hospital. Ali picked up the cudgels and started knocking over all the top contenders of the day, including Jimmy Ellis, Buster Mathis and Bob Foster. He praised Britain's Joe Bugner after the latter took him the distance. By contrast, Frazier was taking things easy. In 1972 he had just two uninspiring fights, against Terry Daniels and Ron Stander, both of whom were stopped in the fourth. Ali cranked up the pressure, taking every opportunity to taunt and belittle the champion. The world wanted to see Frazier v Ali 2.

Events overtook all thoughts of a rematch, however. In January 1973, Frazier lost his crown to George Foreman in four-and-a-half brutal minutes in Kingston, Jamaica. Ali turned his guns on the new champion, only to suffer an unexpected reverse himself.

Broken jaw

Nine weeks after Foreman's defeat of Frazier, Ali took on Ken Norton. He had already agreed a deal worth £1.4 million to fight Foreman in Houston that September. That unravelled in a single punch, when Norton broke Ali's jaw early in the contest. Ali again showed all his resilience and durability by taking the fight the distance, although defeat was inevitable. Joe Bugner watched the fight and professed himself hugely disappointed with Ali's performance - until he learned of the injury. Then he was full of praise, for he had first-hand experience of how painful and debilitating a broken jaw was.

Once again the sporting obituary writers were out in force. Ali was nearly 32; surely there was no way back this time.

As usual, Ali proved all the doubters wrong. After a period of recuperation and a couple of warm-up fights - including avenging the defeat by Norton - Ali was ready for the long- awaited rematch with Joe Frazier. It wasn't a title fight this time, but as an eliminator for the right to face Foreman it had just as much of an edge. Since the 1971 encounter, both men had tasted defeat; whoever was vanquished at Madison Square Garden in January 1974 would surely be staring retirement in the face.

It was a fight of high drama, arguably even better than the previous clash. In the third, seventh and eighth rounds Frazier hit Ali with some blows which fell just short of being decisive. Ali later said he was out on his feet a couple of times, and any other fighter would have succumbed.

Refereeing blunder

Ali's best moment came in the second, when he sent Frazier reeling with a chopping right. He was prevented from following it up, and maybe finishing the fight, by an amazing refereeing blunder. Believing he'd heard the bell, Tony Perez parted the two men some 10 seconds early. Had Ali not gone on to win a comfortable points decision, this incident would have gone down as one of the most controversial in the sport's history.

Ali had only one thing in mind after his victory. "If George Foreman wants to fight, we can get at it. I think he will meet me because his people want him to be number one and nobody can be that if he doesn't fight me. He's got the title, but I'm the people's champion." The Madison Square Garden crowd confirmed this latter point by booing Foreman when he was introduced before the Ali-Frazier fight. They didn't appreciate the fact that in his 12 months as champion he had fought just once, against a nobody.

"Rumble in the Jungle"

The Foreman-Ali fight took place in Kinshasa, Zaire on 30 October 1974. It was the first time that a heavyweight title bout had been staged in Africa, and what a spectacle it was for the 65,000 people ringside. The Rumble in the Jungle has acquired legendary status in the annals of boxing. At 32, Ali was seven years older than the champion. More tellingly, he had lost to both Frazier and Norton, men whom Foreman had brushed aside disdainfully. Ali remained supremely confident, however. "I shall be the matador, Foreman the bull."

The image was apposite. Ali knew that even he could no longer dance his way out of trouble for the duration of the fight, so he didn't try. Instead, he drew Foreman onto him, smothering, spoiling or simply absorbing Foreman's heavy artillery. He backed onto the ropes and into corners, inviting the champion to do his worst. Foreman pounded Ali's gloves and forearms; his wild swings often missed completely. Barely one punch in ten got through.

Flashing combination

When Ali had had enough of this, he launched devastating counter-attacks, picking off his man with volleys of jabs and hooks. By the eighth round, Ali had connected with 65 head shots. It was yet another flashing combination in that round which provided the denouement. The savage right which toppled the champion - in both senses of the word - left him a forlorn, bewildered figure on the canvas. He had never been off his feet before, and he looked helplessly at his corner as he tried to deal with this new and totally unexpected situation. There was no answer, however; the student had to give way to the master.

Joe Frazier was present at the fight, eager to throw down the gauntlet to the victor. Quite understandably, Ali chose three somewhat easier warm-up fights before agreeing to the one everybody wanted to see. His wins over Chuck Wepner and Joe Bugner were dull affairs. Ron Lyle gave a good account of himself before succumbing to an onslaught in the 11th.

Out on their feet

And so to Ali v Frazier 3 - the Thriller in Manila - on 1st October 1975. This was a punishing encounter. In the early stages, Ali had too much speed and too many tricks for his opponent. By round six he was comfortably ahead on points. Then Frazier started to find his target, landing some heavy blows to Ali's body and head. Both men were almost out on their feet by the end of the 14th. Frazier's face was a total mess, his eyes just about closed. His corner decided that another three minutes was simply too much to ask, too great a risk. Ali, too, had come perilously close to calling it a day, but in the event he wasn't required to front up for the 15th.

Once again Ali could have left the stage with his head held high; once again he declined to do so. He won six more fights in the next two years. Belgium's Jean-Pierre Coopman and England's Richard Dunn were easily dispatched, both in the fifth.

Declining force

The other four challengers all took him the distance. No one doubted the decision over Alfredo Evangelista. The other three fights, against Jimmy Young, Ken Norton and Earnie Shavers - were all mighty close. Ali was now a declining force, only occasionally showing flashes of his brilliance.

On 18 February 1978, Ali's luck ran out. His opponent was Leon Spinks, a novice pro who had taken Olympic light-heavyweight gold at Montreal in 1976, the same title that Cassius Clay had won 16 years earlier. Ali took his man lightly and undertrained. It was to cost him the title and bring his second reign as champion to an end. It would only be the end of another chapter, though; Ali wasn't finished yet.

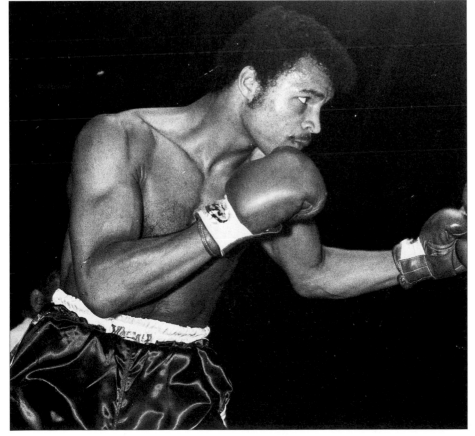

Ali v Bugner 2

Opposite and above: Kuala Lumpur, July 1, 1975. Ali and Joe Bugner go head-to-head again, this time in the enervating heat and humidity of Malaysia. The conditions quickly sapped both men, and it degenerated into a fairly dull contest. Once again, Bugner acquitted himself well by taking Ali the full 15 rounds. On the other hand, the champion never looked in trouble and won the fight comfortably on points.

Left: Following Bob Foster's retirement in September 1974, John Conteh and Argentina's Jorge Ahumada met at Wembley for the WBC light-heavyweight title. Conteh won on points to become the first Briton to hold the title since Freddie Mills in 1950.

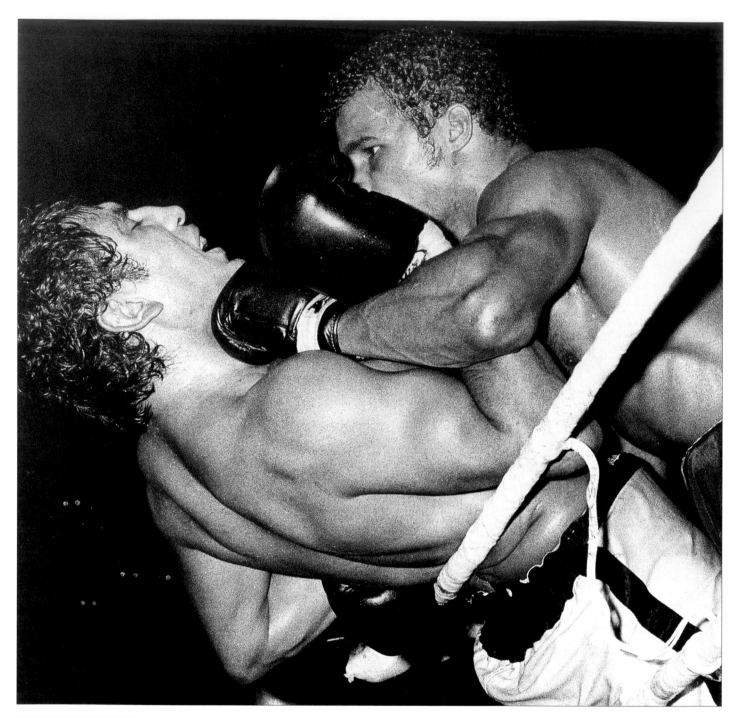

John Conteh

Born:	May 27 1951

World Light-Heavyweight Boxing Champion: 1974-1977

**British, Commonwealth and
European Light-Heavyweight Champion:**   **1973-undefeated**

Record:	Won 34 (23 KOs) Lost 4 Drawn 1

Wembley, October 1, 1974. John Conteh and Jorge Ahumada tangle on the ropes during their contest for the WBC light-heavyweight title vacated by Bob Foster. Conteh proved too strong and skilful for the Argentine over 15 rounds and gave British boxing its greatest night since Randolph Turpin's victory over Sugar Ray Robinson 23 years earlier.

Power struggle costs Conteh title

Above and right: John Conteh enjoyed a two-and-a-half-year reign as the WBC's light-heavyweight champion, He was stripped of the title in May 1977 for failing to defend it against Mexico's Miguel Cuello. The authorities wanted the fight to be staged in Monte Carlo, where live broadcast rights could be obtained. Conteh insisted that it take place in England, but the British Boxing Board wouldn't sanction a live telecast. The Liverpudlian pulled out of the fight at the last minute, and the WBC responded by stripping him of the title. He made three attempts to regain his crown over the following three years, all unsuccessful.

Dunn is Ali's last ko victim

Opposite: Muhammad Ali drops in on British and European champion Richard Dunn as the latter prepares for his fight with West Germany's Bernd August. Dunn went on to win that fight, then prepared to take on Ali himself.

Above: The Ali-Dunn fight took place in Munich, May 24, 1976. Ali quickly adapted to Dunn's southpaw style and after a string of knockdowns, the referee counted Dunn out on his feet. It was to be Ali's last KO in the ring.

Right: Las Vegas, February 15, 1978. Leon Spinks is a picture of unconfined joy as he discovers he has taken the world crown from the sport's greatest exponent. Spinks won on a split decision, both judges scoring the fight in his favour, while referee Art Lurie gave it to Ali.

Leon Spinks

Born:	St Louis, Missouri, USA. July 11 1953
World Heavyweight Champion:	1978
NABF Cruiserweight Champion:	1982
Olympic Gold Medal 1976	
Record:	Won 26 (14 KOs) Lost 17 Drawn 3

Record-breaking brothers

The Spinks brothers Leon (left) and Michael have the distinction of being the only siblings to win the world heavyweight crown. They are also both Olympic champions. Leon took the light-heavyweight title in Montreal in 1976, with younger brother Michael winning the middleweight division the same year. *Opposite*: Ali covers up during his 15-round fight with Leon Spinks in Las Vegas, February 15, 1978. Spinks had only turned professional the year before, and was unbeaten in seven fights in that time. Ali noted his opponent's lack of experience and made the mistake of training accordingly.

Leon Spinks

World Heavyweight Champion: 1978

In February 1978, Leon Spinks joined a very exclusive club. It had just two other members, Joe Frazier and Ken Norton. The entry test was specific and very stiff: you had to have beaten the great Muhammad Ali in the ring. Spinks had the good fortune of making his entry bid when Ali was 36 year old and a declining force. Nevertheless, the boxing world was still stunned when he took his opportunity and claimed the greatest prize in sport.

Spinks was born on July 11, 1953. One of seven children, he grew up in straitened circumstances in a St Louis ghetto. Lack of money and opportunity spurred him on to make a career for himself in the ring; and once he embarked on the road, the early privations gave him a fierce drive to succeed. First he scaled the heights of the amateur world by taking the light-heavyweight gold medal at the Montreal Olympic Games in 1976. It was the same title that his hero, Muhammad Ali, had won 16 years earlier. Spinks used his Olympic success to launch his professional career, which began in January 1977. In the next 13 months he had seven fights, including four first-round knockouts. Then, at the age of 24, he was given a shot at the world title.

Spinks wins split decision

Ali didn't rate Spinks. Always ready to undermine his opponents with a disdainful soubriquet, Ali cranked up the pre-fight hype by calling Spinks "Goofy". The bookmakers agreed with the assessment, if not the way it was expressed. Spinks was a 10-1 shot to depose the champion. They were the kind of outsider's odds that the young Cassius Clay had faced when he stepped into the ring against the "invincible" Sonny Liston 15 years earlier. An undertrained Ali tried to rope-a-dope the young pretender, but Spinks was young and strong and didn't tire as the champion expected. It was Spinks who landed the better punches, and he got the benefit of a split decision. Referee Art Lurie scored the fight in Ali's favour, with both judges giving it to Spinks. There was some dissent from those ringside, who felt that Ali was robbed. Ali was dignified in defeat, however. He conceded that it was a fair decision, and immediately disappointed those who wanted to see him retire by vowing to fight on.

While Ali was left to lick his wounds, the new champion had the world at his feet. His purse for the title fight had been £150,000. Now there was the prospect of getting a lot nearer the £1.75 million that Ali had been paid. It didn't work out as planned, however. The WBC ordered Spinks to meet Ken Norton in his first defence. Spinks demurred, preferring to line up a lucrative return with Ali. The WBC duly stripped Spinks of their title,

installing Ken Norton - the conqueror of Jimmy Young - as champion. Arrangements for the Spinks-Ali return continued regardless. The fact that only the WBA crown was now at stake didn't dent the interest that it generated. The fight took place in New Orleans, on September 15, 1978. This one also went the distance, but the decision was more clear-cut. Ali gave an outstanding performance, the last of his glittering career. He made Spinks look like a novice, and in the process gave him an unwanted place in the record books: his seven-months tenure as heavyweight champion was the shortest in ring history.

Steady decline

Still only 25, there should have been plenty of time for Spinks to bounce back. But Neon Leon had already reached his pinnacle; now there was a steady decline. After losing his crown, Spinks was knocked out in barely two minutes by Gerrie Coetzee. He recovered from that reversal to win his next four fights and earn himself a crack at Larry Holmes for the WBC title. That fight took place in Detroit, on June 12, 1981. Holmes destroyed the former champion in three rounds. Spinks continued to ply his trade, stepping down to the cruiserweight and junior-heavyweight divisions. There would be no more glory days, however. Nor was there much inner peace. Spinks was a man who often seemed to be at war with himself. He was also certainly ill-used by some of those around him, whose interest quickly waned when he became a loser. Spinks was no great boxer and certainly not a distinguished champion. But the record books show that he is up there in very illustrious company as someone who scaled the heights of the amateur boxing world, then repeated the achievement in the professional ranks.

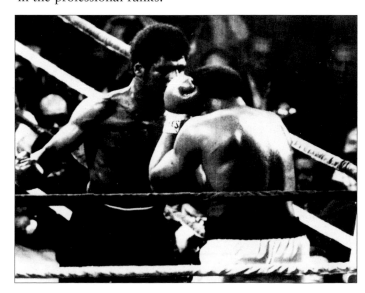

Spinks defies WBC and loses crown

Above: Leon Spinks reflects on what it's like to be king of the hill at 24. Understandably, interest centered on the identity of the first challenger to his title. The WBC soon weighed in with their own answer, insisting that Spinks should fight Ken Norton.

Left: Ali shakes the new world champion warmly by the throat as the two sign for their September 1978 rematch. The decision to opt for a lucrative second fight with Ali instead of Norton saw Spinks stripped of the WBC crown.

Opposite: A gap-toothed grin from "Neon Leon" prior to the big fight with Ali.

Muhammad Ali

Having lost his title to Leon Spinks in February 1978, Muhammad Ali could have walked away from the sport and nobody would have had anything but the highest regard for the man and his achievements. Indeed, many fervently hoped the 36-year-old legend would call it a day. But there were two stumbling-blocks. One was financial. He had earned a fortune from boxing - £1.75 million from the Spinks fight alone - but he was not that well off. There were two ex-wives and several children to support; there was a huge entourage and the inevitable hangers-on; there were some ill-judged investments; there was his natural generosity; and of course, there was Uncle Sam's cut to be taken care of. But the second reason for Ali's determination to fight on was probably the more pivotal. That was all about ego, professional pride and the burning desire to prove that he was still the best, even when others began to doubt it. Floyd Patterson had come back to win the title for a second time. So had Ali. But no one had won it three times, and that was motivation enough for the ebullient, ever-confident Ali.

Showdown with Spinks

Ali took Spinks far more seriously in New Orleans, on September 15, 1978. It wasn't the most exciting of contests, but Ali gave a masterly performance. There was no sitting back on the ropes inviting Spinks on to him. Ali jabbed and moved, holding the centre of the ring as much as possible. It was Spinks who was under-prepared this time, and the result was a unanimous points decision. Ali had rewritten the record books once again.

The victory over Spinks also meant that he had avenged each of the three defeats which blotted his ring career. To the relief of many fight fans, Ali then decided to hang up his gloves. It left the way clear for Larry Holmes, the outstanding heavyweight of the day. Holmes had beaten Ken Norton, the man the WBC had installed as champion following Spinks' refusal to meet him. There was a problem though. Holmes was declared champion when Spinks was still the rightful holder of the title, and the Easton Assassin's claim was rendered even more dubious when Ali triumphed over Spinks in the return. Holmes was to get his chance to silence all the critics and cement his grip on the title. For on October 2, 1980, Ali couldn't resist another tilt at the crown. Not content with three stints as champion, he wanted to put himself out of sight as far as the record books were concerned by winning it for a fourth time.

Larry Holmes paid homage to the master by holding something back, yet he still handed Ali a terrible beating in the 10 rounds that the fight lasted. The old spark failed to flicker even briefly that day in Las Vegas. Ali's failure to answer the bell for the 11th was one of the saddest moments in the history of sport, let alone boxing. A once mighty warrior, a superbly honed athlete, remained slumped in his chair and looked like a frail geriatric. It was Angelo Dundee who called time. Better to end the contest sitting on a stool than laid flat out on the canvas, Ali's mentor over 20 years and 65 fights pointed out. Even that wasn't enough for Ali. He came back one more time, in Nassau, December 1981, when he was outpointed by Trevor Berbick, a Jamaican based in Canada. Ali was a month short of his 40th birthday when the curtain finally rang down for good.

The passage of time soon erased the stain of those final two humiliating defeats. The world wanted to remember Ali at the peak of his powers. They wanted to pay homage to the man who had been a colossus of the sport for nearly two decades, gracing it with some of the most sublime skills ever seen in the ring. The onset of Parkinson's syndrome endeared him still further to a world that loved him already. The image of his unsteady hand lighting the Olympic flame at the 1996 Games in Atlanta will live long in the memory. He is still revered, still beautiful. And still The Greatest.

Ali relaxes with wife Veronica, prior to the return with Spinks. Losing to a fighter of his calibre had been the most painful episode of Ali's career. He trained hard for the rematch, determined to avenge the defeat, just as he had done with the other two men who had beaten him, Frazier and Norton.

Ageing Ali determined to avenge Spinks defeat

Above: Still pretty, but the years and the punishment are beginning to take their toll on Muhammad Ali. By now he was unable to fight without shots of Novocaine.

Alan Minter

Born:	Crawley, England August 17 1951
World Middleweight Champion:	1980
European Middleweight Champion:	1977 1978-1981
British Middleweight Champion:	1975-1981
Record:	Won 39 (23 KOs) Lost 9

Outright Lonsdale Belt winner
at Middleweight.
Undisputed World Middleweight
Champion 1980.

Awarded the WBA belt
29th April 2000 at Wembley Arena.

World titles at five weights

The great Sugar Ray Leonard. In a career spanning 20 years, Leonard won world titles at five weight divisions, a feat matched only by Thomas "The Hit Man" Hearns. *Opposite below*: Alan Minter was the world's only undisputed champion when he stepped into the ring with Marvin Hagler at Wembley Arena on September 27, 1990. A bad gash to Minter's eye caused the referee to stop the fight in the third round, and the crown passed to Marvelous Marvin.

Opposite above left: Marvin Hagler was regarded as a Jekyll and Hyde character: smiling and friendly outside the ring but a ruthless beast inside it.

Opposite above right: The bet's on and the hair's off. Marvin Hagler's attorney, Stephen Wainwright, keeps his promise to replicate Marvelous Marvin's tonsorial style if he succeeded in taking the world title from Alan Minter.

Sugar Ray Leonard

Nickname:	**"Sugar"**
Born:	**Wilmington, North Carolina, USA. May 17 1956**
Height:	**5' 9"**
World Welterweight Champion:	**1979-1980 1980-1982 1987-1991**
World Light Middleweight Champion:	**1981**
Record:	**Won 36 (25 KOs) Lost 3 Drawn 1**
Olympic gold medal 1976	

Larry Holmes

World Heavyweight Champion: 1979-1985

When Leon Spinks upset the odds by beating Muhammad Ali, it sparked yet another round of political in-fighting, which culminated in Larry Holmes taking the world crown. The WBC demanded that Spinks face top contender Ken Norton after Neon Leon's victory over Ali. The Spinks camp demurred, favouring a return bout with Ali. The WBC promptly stripped Spinks of his title and installed Norton as their heavyweight champion. Holmes would be his first challenger.

Holmes had spent four years as Ali's sparring partner in the mid-1970s, and had only recently broken out of the legend's shadow to make a name for himself in his own right. He felt that his victory over Roy Williams in 1976 was a turning point. Williams was a big man and a big hitter. Few relished the prospect of facing him, including Holmes. But it was business, it was what Holmes did, and he just got on with the job. He had been providing for himself since the age of 13, when he left school. A father at 17, he had always supported his family. Yet he was acutely aware that if it weren't for boxing, his seventh-grade education was unlikely to open many other doors. This was the mentality of the man who faced, and beat, Roy Williams.

Victory over Norton

Two years later, on 10 June 1978, Holmes took his 27-fight unbeaten record into the ring against Ken Norton. Both men emerged with immense credit in what was one of the great contests in the sport's history. Holmes took the fight to Norton from the start, clearly winning four of the first five rounds. Norton came back strongly in the middle part of the fight, but Holmes finished the stronger. The challenger looked the superior boxer throughout and won on a split Decision, none of the three judges having more than a point in it. Holmes was slumped in his corner, utterly exhausted, when the announcement was made.

After two comprehensive victories, over Alfredo Evangelista and Osvaldo Ocasio, Holmes faced Los Angeles heavyweight Mike Weaver, who was just breaking into the WBC's top ten. Holmes stopped him in the 12th.

On 28 September, 1979, just three months after the Weaver fight, Holmes made his fourth defence, against Earnie Shavers. It was to have been Ken Norton, but Shavers had demolished Norton inside a round on the same card as the Holmes-Ocasio fight. "Now we'll see if Holmes can take my punches," Shavers said after effectively ending Norton's career.

Holmes had easily outpointed the rough, tough Shavers a year earlier. He won again in September 1979, but not without a scare or two. In round seven Shavers unleashed a right that landed with such power that Holmes later said he thought his head had exploded. Shavers was almost celebrating becoming champion, but Holmes somehow made it to his feet and went on to stop his man in the 11th.

Holmes fights his idol

Boxing fans had entertained the hope that Holmes might take on his mentor, hero and former employer Muhammad Ali. It looked as if that would never materialise after Ali announced his retirement at the end of 1978. An ill-advised comeback by The Greatest two years later meant that master and pupil would indeed face each other in the ring. It was to be a sad spectacle.

More immediately, Holmes was denied his rightful place as the undisputed heavyweight champion. After Ali's retirement, the WBA was not about to bestow its title automatically on Holmes. Instead, the organisation sanctioned its own tournament. In October 1979, a month after the Holmes-Shavers fight, John Tate beat South Africa's Gerry Coetzee and was duly declared holder of the WBA's version of the title. Events then took a farcical turn when Tate was knocked out by Mike Weaver, in March 1980. Holmes's earlier victory over Weaver should have settled the issue, but the WBA wouldn't concede. Holmes had to be content with moral supremacy if not the actual unified title.

After three more quick-fire wins in 1980, Holmes finally got the fight he would rather not have had. His idol, Muhammad Ali, couldn't resist the lure of another big payday and the chance to enhance his status even further by taking the title for a fourth time. "What I'm about to do is considered impossible by a human being," Ali declared. "People think Holmes will whup me. I'm going to come back and wipe out Holmes. I trained him. He is my little boy. I'll eat him up."

38-year-old Ali was past backing up his words in the ring. It was a travesty and a mismatch. Ali covered up and barely threw a punch. Holmes paid his dues by refusing to go in for the kill, something he could have done with ease. Ali's corner finally called it a day after ten rounds. Holmes shed a tear for his vanquished opponent.

Holmes was finally taken the distance by his next challenger, Canada's Trevor Berbick. A mere points victory might have spoiled his record, but it meant that the Holmes juggernaut rolled on. By now he should have won over the fans. But for all his ruthless efficiency he lacked charisma. That, together with his defeat of the revered Ali, meant that the fans couldn't quite take Holmes to their hearts.

Revenge over Leon Spinks

His next defence saw him stop former champion Leon Spinks in three brutal rounds. Normally, boxing was just business with Holmes; there was nothing personal. The exception was Spinks, who had made some disrespectful comments about the champion and his family. Holmes exacted swift revenge.

The following year, 1982, Holmes came up against the Irish-American Gerry Cooney. Publicists talked up the race factor: the Great White Hope taking on the black champion. It was redolent of the Willard-Johnson clash of 1915. Holmes let the media get on with it, but there was no extra edge to the fight as far as he was concerned. The two actually got on rather well. As far as the fight itself was concerned, it quickly became clear that Cooney was out of his depth against a man of Holmes' class. It was all over in the 13th.

After four more victories, Holmes agreed to fight Marvis Frazier, Joe's son, in a fight not sanctioned by the WBC. Holmes went ahead anyway, took Frazier Junior out in one, and handed back the WBC belt.

He took over the newly-formed International Boxing Federation's version of the title. This left the WBC, like the WBA, scrambling around for a champion. These two titles passed through the hands of several boxers. But Holmes had either beaten the incumbents, or beaten men who had themselves scored victories against these so-called champions. Anyone analysing the situation dispassionately had to conclude that Holmes was the true champion.

Shaken by "Bonecrusher"

Holmes made harder work than anyone expected of his first IBF defence, in November 1984. James "Bonecrusher" Smith, who had dented Frank Bruno's progress the previous May, had Holmes in trouble on a couple of occasions, but each time fell a punch short of capitalising on his good work. "He hit me hard, shook me up," Holmes admitted after the fight. He was somewhat fortunate that a severe cut to Smith's eye finally ended the challenger's chances in the 12th.

Some thought the tide had turned for Holmes, despite the fact that he had just won his 46th fight. There was talk of retirement, but not from Holmes, who now had his sights firmly on Rocky Marciano's record mark of 49 straight victories.

Wins over David Bey and Carl Williams in 1985 moved Holmes to within one fight of his target. These two victories couldn't disguise the fact that Holmes was undoubtedly a declining force. Even so, most pundits firmly believed that he would have no trouble reaching a goal which had now become an obsession for the champion. The reason was simple. His opponent was the light-heavyweight title-holder Michael Spinks, the latest boxer to attempt to step up and challenge for the greatest

prize. Holmes was dismissive of his opponent's chances. "How does that skinny boy think he's going to hurt me? Surely not with his fists?"

As so often with heavyweight champions, or any top sportsmen facing an underdog, unwise predictions all too easily became hostages to fortune.

Above: Larry Holmes. Holmes dominated the heavyweight boxing scene in the late 1970s and early 1980s. Although Holmes became WBC champion in 1978, purists didn't accept his claim to be world No.1 until he fought Ali.

Larry Holmes

Born:	Cuthbert, Georgia, USA. November 3 1949	
Height:	6' 3"	Weight: 211lbs.
World Heavyweight Champion:	1978-1984 (lost IBF title in 1985)	
Record:	Won 67 (43 KOs) Lost 6	

Marvin Hagler

Nickname:	**Marvelous**
Born:	Newark, USA. May 23 1952
Height:	5' 7³/₄"
World Middleweight Champion:	1980–1987
Record:	Won 62 (52 KOs) Lost 3 Drawn 2

Duran v. Hagler

Above left: Scranton, March 27, 1983. Larry Holmes on his way to yet another victory. On the receiving end this time is the French European champion Lucien Rodriguez. Holmes won the 12-round fight on points.

Above right and right: The ageing warrior Roberto Duran took Marvin Hagler the distance when the two met at Caesar's Palace on November 10, 1983. Hagler was a worthy points winner but, amazingly, the WBC stripped him of their title as the contest had been fought over 15 rounds, not the stipulated championship distance of 12.

Opposite above left: Marvin Hagler rejoices after taking the middleweight crown from Alan Minter. Disgraceful scenes followed as disgruntled Minter fans showered the ring with missiles and hurled racist abuse.

Opposite below: Tough New Yorker Gerry Cooney gave heavyweight champion Larry Holmes a thorough examination on June 12, 1982. Cooney survived until the 13th round when the referee stepped in to save him from further punishment.

Bruno is Britain's brightest hope

Left: November 1983. Britain's unbeaten young heavyweight and rising star, 22-year-old Frank Bruno, pictured with his trainer Terry Lawless.

Below: In 1984, Trevor Berbick (right) was Commonwealth champion and No. 6 in the world rankings. London-based Nigerian Funso Banjo (left), and Frank Bruno (centre) were still looking to make their mark on the heavyweight scene.

Opposite above left: Bruno shows how he dispatched Argentina's Juan Figueroa in just 67 seconds at Wembley, March 13, 1984.

Opposite above right: May 3, 1984. James "Bonecrusher" Smith arrives in London for his Wembley clash with Bruno on the 13th.

Opposite below left: A former guard at a maximum security prison in North Carolina, Smith didn't turn professional until he was 26. He lost his first fight, to the formidable James Broad, but had been unbeaten since.

Opposite below right: Smith's nickname lends itself to a predictable photo-opportunity.

"Bonecrusher" halts Bruno's progress

Above: Amiable eyeballing from two amiable heavyweights. Smith and Bruno's pre-fight encounter was a far cry from those involving the likes of Liston and Foreman, when menacing glares were the order of the day. Opposite below left: Bruno reflects on the punch to the jaw that won Smith the fight in the 10th and final round.

Opposite above left: Wembley, September 25, Bruno gets a hug from Terry Lawless after a four-and-a-half-minute KO of Canada's Ken Lakusta. The relief was palpable, following the defeat by Smith four months earlier.

Opposite above right: Bruno reduces America's Jeff Jordan to a bewildered wreck in just eight minutes.

Left: Bruno was regarded as the best British heavyweight hope for a generation. He didn't have Cooper's susceptibility to cuts, he wasn't as easy to hit as Walker, and he had a bigger fighting heart than Bugner.

Opposite below right: Six months after the Bruno fight, "Bonecrusher" Smith stepped into the ring with Larry Holmes for the IBF title. A bad cut to the left eye caused the fight to be stopped in the 12th round.

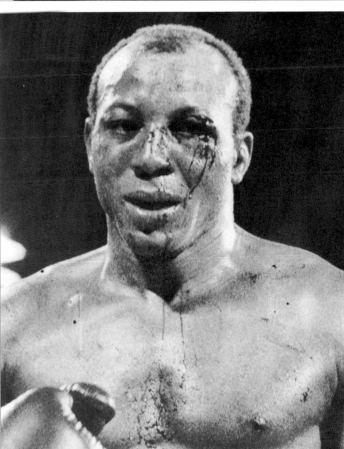

Michael Spinks

When Michael Spinks became Larry Holmes's twenty-first challenger in September 1985, history was very much against him. He was the latest in a long line of light-heavyweight champions seeking to step up and win the greatest prize in sport. All before had failed, including men of the stature of Georges Carpentier, Archie Moore and Bob Foster. Holmes felt that Spinks was a cast-iron certainty to join the roll of failure. "Don't forget, I've been punched in the head by monsters like Earnie Shavers, Ken Norton and Gerry Cooney, so taking punches from Spinks doesn't fill me with dread. When he receives my left jab in his face it will be like taking a solid right-hand punch from a light-heavyweight. I respect Michael in his own division, but this time he's taken on more than he can chew."

Spinks begged to differ. He studied film of his predecessors and noted in particular that none of the previous three light-heavyweight challengers had managed to go the distance. He was sure he could do better. Spinks himself had an impressive record since taking the middleweight title at the Montreal Olympic Games in 1976. Like so many illustrious fighters, he used this victory as the launchpad to a professional career, and in the nine years since, he had won all 27 of his fights - 19 inside the distance - and made ten successful defences of his light-heavyweight title.

Chasing the record books

Spinks was a 5-1 shot to beat Holmes, odds that were not quite as long as those his brother had faced against Muhammad Ali seven years earlier. Ali had been 8-1 on to beat Leon. If Michael could upset the odds, he could become one of the only pair of brothers to win the heavyweight crown. Holmes, meanwhile, needed to beat Spinks to equal Rocky Marciano's all-time record of 49 straight wins. In fact, there was doubt over one of Marciano's credited victories, so if Holmes could get the better of Spinks, he stood to put himself out there in front as the most successful heavyweight in history. Something had to give.

The fight went the full 15 rounds and ended in a hotly-disputed decision. Holmes had been a mere shell of his former self and couldn't nail the fast-moving Spinks, either with his right-hand or his famed left jab. Even so, two of the three judges scored the fight even going into the last round. Holmes was the aggressor in those final three minutes, Spinks boxing warily on the retreat. Nevertheless, the officials thought the challenger had done enough and he got the decision.

Holmes was incandescent. He launched a blistering attack on the judges, and even accused some of boxing's supremos of spiking his guns. In short, he felt he was robbed. When he had calmed down, Holmes accepted the decision philosophically, shrugged his shoulders and announced his retirement. That didn't last long, however, and a rematch was set for April the following year.

The second fight almost had a feeling of deja vu about it. Spinks was certainly negative in the early stages, waiting for 36-year-old Holmes to tire before he started opening up. As a result, he didn't really start scoring until the sixth. The champion did make up a lot of ground thereafter, but it was by no means one-way traffic in the second half of the fight. Holmes rocked the younger man in the ninth, 12th and 14th rounds. The latter was a terrific right which Spinks did well to recover from. Recover he did, and the two men fought a fairly even final round. Most observers thought it was close but that Holmes had done enough. Holmes himself had no doubt. "Michael boxed well but I beat the hell out of him." The judges saw it differently and gave Spinks the verdict. Holmes was left seething for the second time, once again espousing his conspiracy theories.

Superb athlete

Holmes's bitter railing should not be allowed to detract from Spinks's achievements. Unlike his brother Leon, who turned to drugs, Michael was a superb athlete and a worthy champion. He had bulked up to 14st 4lb for his fights against Holmes, 25lb over the light-heavyweight limit and a full two stones heavier than his last fight in the lower division.

After knocking out European champion Stefan Taangstaad, Spinks chose to fight Gerry Cooney. The contest was not sanctioned by the IBF, whose title Spinks had taken from Holmes. Like his brother before him, Michael was stripped of his crown.

In 1987, a new kid on the block by the name of Mike Tyson began hoovering up all the titles going. This included Spinks' IBF title, which he took away from Tony Tucker in August that year. The press hailed Tyson as undisputed champion; purists believed he had no right to call himself that until he met Michael Spinks. The issue was to be decided one way or the other on 27 June, 1988. And it was decided in dramatic fashion.

Tyson the man they all have to beat

Above right: By 1987 there was little doubt who was boxing's top dog. 20-year-old Mike Tyson sported his two belts as he paid a visit to London to see the Bruno-Tillis fight, adding a couple of quintessentially English accessories to mark his first trip to the country.

Right: Tillis congratulates Bruno on his fifth-round win. It was an important victory for Bruno, who needed to bounce back from defeat by Tim Witherspoon in his previous fight.

Above left: Las Vegas, April 19, 1986. Michael Spinks celebrates retaining his IBF title on a controversial split decision over former champion Larry Holmes. There was little applause from the crowd, who felt that Holmes had done enough to win the fight.

Michael Spinks

Born:	St. Louis, Missouri, USA. July 13 1956		
Height:	6' 2"	Weight:	200lbs
World Heavyweight Champion:		1985-1988	
World Light Heavyweight Champion:		1981-1985	
Olympic gold medal 1976			
Record:	Won 32 (21 KOs) Lost 1		

Tyson demolishes Holmes in four

Above left: Larry Holmes unwisely chose to come out of retirement to face Mike Tyson. The 38-year-old grandfather was smashed to the canvas in four brutal rounds.

Left: October 1987: Frank Bruno takes another step towards a world title fight with a comprehensive win over Joe Bugner at White Hart Lane.

Above: Rock star and fitness fanatic Sting joins Frank Bruno on a training run around London's Highgate Ponds. Bruno was gearing up for his Wembley showdown with Mike Tyson.

Opposite below: Royal Albert Hall, June 28, 1989: 23-year-old Lennox Lewis gets his professional career off to a blistering start with a second-round knockout of Al Malcolm. Lewis's proud mother, Violet, saw the fight and predicted that her son would be world champion one day.

Opposite above right: Roberto Duran enjoyed an extraordinary boxing career. He turned professional at the age of 16 and was still contesting title fights nearly 30 years later, in the mid-1990s. He won world titles in four different weight divisions.

Roberto Duran

Nickname: "Manos De Piedra" (Hands Of Stone)

Born: Guarare, Panama. June 16 1951

World Lightweight Champion: 1972-1979

World Welterweight Champion: 1980

World Light-middleweight Champion: 1983

World Middleweight Champion:1983-1984 1989

Record: Won 103 (69 KOs)   Lost 15

Duran won four titles at four weights.

Mike Tyson

World Heavyweight Champion: 1988-1990

The mid-1980s saw a concerted effort on the part of the various boxing authorities to unify the heavyweight title. Since Muhammad Ali's undisputed supremacy back in 1978, the title had been fragmented to a level verging on the farcical. It obviously wasn't in the sport's interest to have a string of boxers all laying claim to be world champion. A series of eliminators was proposed, with the object of establishing an undisputed top dog by the end of 1987. All the individual title holders were involved, together with the other top contenders of the day. One of those was Michael Spinks, the unbeaten IBF champion who had been stripped of his title for choosing to face Gerry Cooney instead of Tony Tucker. Another was Mike Tyson.

Brooklyn boyhood

Mike Tyson was the archetypal bad boy made good - almost. Cus D'Amato, the man who had guided Floyd Patterson to the top 30 years earlier, took the young Tyson under his wing and appeared to have saved him from himself. Tyson had drifted into petty crime and downright thuggery on the tough Brooklyn streets where he grew up. He was sent to reform school, and that could have set him on a path of repeated periods of incarceration in penal institutions, with every possibility of the felonies becoming increasingly serious as he moved into adulthood. D'Amato sought to rescue Tyson from all that. Not only did he set out to take Tyson to the top of the boxing world, but he became the troubled youngster's mentor, confidant and friend. He took Tyson into his home, giving him family stability and imbuing him with the kind of values which were to have kept him on the straight and narrow. For a time it worked to perfection. With D'Amato as both boxing tutor and father figure Tyson flourished both in and out of the ring. After turning professional in 1985 he made sensational progress. Between March of that year and September 1986 Tyson had no less than 27 fights. He won them all, which is impressive enough in itself, despite the fact that his opponents included a fair few journeymen. What is more noteworthy is the fact that these fights lasted just 74 rounds in total, and 15 of his opponents were put away inside the first three minutes.

Tyson's approach to boxing was simple and ruthlessly efficient. He flew at his opponents from the opening bell; not for him a tentative period of feeling out his man, assessing his strengths and weaknesses. He struck with scintillating speed and devastating power. He may have been just 5ft 11in, quite short in the modern era, yet the bull-necked 220lb Tyson was a fearsome fighting machine. His attacks were savage. If his man tried to protect his face,

Tyson sent piledrivers into the body. They couldn't run, they couldn't hide. They all went down sooner or later, and usually sooner.

November 1986 saw the start of a sensational 18-month period in which Tyson became the undisputed king of the ring. His first title was the WBC version, with Trevor Berbick the man on the receiving end of a two-round bludgeoning. Still only 20, Tyson had become the youngest man to hold a version of the heavyweight title. Unfortunately, Cus D'Amato didn't live to see his protege and pupil make it to the top. That was sad on a personal level; it would also have dangerous repercussions. Tyson still had the demons of an angry young man within him, and without D'Amato's guidance the potential for him to go off the rails was still there.

Four months later, Tyson added the WBA crown to his haul. His opponent was James "Bonecrusher" Smith, who had surprisingly wrested the WBA title from Tim Witherspoon three months earlier. The Tyson - Smith fight was poor fare, Smith concentrating on frustrating his opponent and surviving rather than winning the fight himself. He succeeded in that he took Tyson the distance, but the result was never in doubt.

Tyson wins IBF Crown

A comprehensive defence against Pinklon Thomas followed, Tyson finishing his man in the sixth with a devastating 18-punch salvo to which Thomas had no reply. He then took on Tony Tucker for the IBF title. The two met on 1 August 1987, in Las Vegas. The crowd expected Tucker to be the lamb, Tyson the man to slaughter him. They were disappointed. Tucker used his 10-inch reach advantage to land the odd blow, but for the most part they were innocuous cuffs and pats. Tyson kept coming forward and landing the heavier blows, though he couldn't find the big one to put Tucker away. The points margin ranged from 4 to 8 in Tyson's favour, reflecting his utter dominance of the fight.

Tyson's star was still rising, though some thought elevating him to the status of boxing legend was somewhat premature. Even so, the media now widely acclaimed Tyson as the undisputed champion, overlooking the fact that Michael Spinks had had his title taken off him out of the ring, not in it. There were three more fights before that clash, however. Tyrell Biggs was powerful and game but ran out of luck in the seventh, when Tyson hammered him into submission. In January 1988, Larry Holmes became the latest ex-champion to think he could roll back the years and regain his crown. The 38-year-old grandfather quickly discovered that although he could probably still mix it with a lot of heavyweights, Tyson was a different prospect altogether. The demolition job was reminiscent of Holmes's own comprehensive victory over an ageing Muhammad Ali eight years earlier. For the first three rounds Holmes used all his experience to keep out of trouble, and even connected with some decent shots of his own. Two of the three judges actually gave him round three. But Tyson shrugged that off, and in round four came forward like a battering ram to finish the job in brutal style. When Holmes hit the canvas, the referee wasn't about to allow him to make a fool of himself - or worse. "It's over, Larry," he said. "We don't want no tragedies, do we?"

"I'm the best in the world"

Michael Spinks was now touted as the only serious threat to Tyson. The champion was as dismissive of Spinks's chances as he had been of all the others. "I'm the best fighter in the world right now. I'll take on all-comers." Perhaps more pertinent was the comment of Larry Holmes after his comprehensive defeat. "Tyson is better than I thought. A lot better. People can talk about Spinks all they want; Tyson is the true champion."

Tyson versus Spinks was set for Atlantic City, 27 June, 1988. Tyson warmed up for the fight with a second-round knockout of Tony Tubbs in March. 30-year-old Tubbs was a former WBA champion and was chosen for his durability. He lasted just 5 minutes 54 seconds, when he ran into a savage left hook. It was victim No. 34 for Tyson. He had accounted for all of them in just 118 rounds.

First round victory over Spinks

Tyson lowered his rounds-per-fight average even further when he met Spinks. In just 91 seconds he removed every last shred of doubt that remained over his right to wear the crown. In his time as a pro Spinks had never been floored, let alone beaten, but the so-called "People's Champion" had no answer to the Tyson onslaught. He entered the record books in a way he would have preferred not to: as the man on the receiving end of the fourth fastest knockout in the history of the heavyweight championship.

Ringside that night were Frank Bruno and his manager Terry Lawless. Bruno had the dubious honour of being the next mandatory challenger for the world title. Interestingly, he had met Tyson years earlier, while training in the Catskills in America. Tyson was just a tough, starry-eyed kid at the time, but he told Frank that maybe the two of them would fight for the title one day. Those prophetic words were realised in Las Vegas, on 25 February, 1989.

Bruno came close to denting Tyson's aura of invincibility that night. One of the hallmarks of the champion was his explosiveness out of the blocks, but at the end of the first round it was he who was scrambling for survival. In the end, though, Bruno had to settle for glorious failure. Tyson recovered from that early setback and finished the contest with a ferocious barrage in the fifth.

Tyson's private turmoil

Tyson fought just once more that year, against Carl "The Truth" Williams. Instead of learning from those who had given Tyson a degree of trouble, Williams simply walked into a Tyson haymaker and went down in one. This fight merely reconfirmed Tyson's frightening reputation in the ring. His reputation out of it was also growing, but not for the right reasons. His private life was in turmoil. He mistrusted those who hung on to the shirt-tails of his success. It rankled that everyone wanted to know him now, while no one had given him the time of day before boxing brought him fame and fortune. Cus D'Amato was an exception, of course, but he was no longer around to exert a moderating, paternal influence. There were car crashes, brawls and a brief, stormy marriage to actress Robin Givens. It seemed that Tyson was spiralling out of control. The only area of stability and predictability was his performance in the ring, although even here the cracks were beginning to show. He seemed to have abandoned all the boxing skills he had learned from the master in favour of whirlwind assaults and attempting to finish his opponents off as quickly as possible. It was hardly classical or stylish, but it was uncompromisingly effective. Nobody, least of all the bookmakers, had any reason to think that James "Buster" Douglas would do anything other than become Iron Mike's 38th victim.

Mike Tyson

Michael Gerard Tyson

Born:	Brooklyn, New York, USA. June 30 1966
Height:	5' 11½"
Weight:	240lbs.
World Heavyweight Champion:	1986-1990, 1996
Record:	Won 49 (43 KOs) Lost 4 Drawn 0

Bruno stuns Tyson
but goes down in five

Above: Bruno has a close encounter with Iron Mike during their 1989 title fight. The British champion had his moments, notably when he stunned Tyson with a right in the first round. Tyson recovered to finish Frank in the fifth.

Right: Two of boxing's all-time greats, Sugar Ray Leonard (left) and Thomas "The Hit Man" Hearns pose for the cameras after signing for their June 1989 showdown in Las Vegas. Leonard's super-middleweight title was at stake in a contest that was dubbed "The War".

Opposite above right: Hearns floored Leonard twice during the fight, and most observers thought The Hit Man was hard done by when the officials ruled the fight a draw.

Opposite Below: Old adversaries Joe Frazier and George Foreman join Muhammad Ali in the ring one more time to promote the video Champions Forever, a montage of the greatest moments of Ali's career. Former rivalry was mostly cast aside for the occasion, although Frazier still harboured resentment for some of the comments Ali made about him in the run-up to their three titanic battles.

Above right: At 33, Sugar Ray Leonard (left) was a mere stripling compared to 38-year old Roberto Duran when the two met in December 1989. With one win apiece from their previous encounters, the public interest in the fight was huge. It was a largely disappointing affair, however, Leonard winning on points over 12 rounds.

Thomas Hearns

Nickname:	"Hitman"
Born:	Memphis, Tennessee, USA. October 18, 1958
Height:	6' 1"
World Welterweight Champion:	1980-1981 1982-1985
World Middleweight Champion:	1985-1987 1987-1988
World Light Heavyweight Champion:	1987 1991-1992
World Super Middleweight Champion:	1988-1991
Record:	Won 65 (46KOs) Lost 5 Drawn 1

James Douglas

World Heavyweight Champion: 1990

Every dog has its day, every person gets his or her 15 minutes in the spotlight, etc etc. Such sayings might have been conceived with James "Buster" Douglas in mind. He was a work-a-day heavyweight who did little prior to February 11, 1990, and not much after it. But on that day in Tokyo, everything conspired in his favour. Fortunately for him, it happened to be the day when he was fighting Mike Tyson for the heavyweight crown.

Douglas was born in Columbus, Ohio, on July 7, 1960. The son of a decent middle and light-heavyweight, Douglas had all the physical attributes of a top-class heavyweight. But he didn't have the boxing skills or mental strength to go with his magnificent physique. He was a solid professional, a decent contender, but nothing more. Even so, by 1987 he had notched up enough successes to earn himself a crack at Tony Tucker for the IBF heavyweight crown. He flopped badly and was knocked out in the 10th. Douglas also fought on the Tyson-Bruno undercard, against Trevor Berbick. It was a victory this time, but it was all dreary and uninspiring stuff.

42-1 outsider

Such was the background and calibre of the man lined up to fight Iron Mike in February 1990. Small wonder that few people gave him a prayer. As a measure of how seismic an upset this was, one only has to consider the bookmakers' odds. Douglas was a 42-1 shot, by far the longest odds in the championship's history. Tyson's behaviour was becoming increasingly wayward and unpredictable out of the ring, but no one believed that this volatility would have any bearing on his performance inside it. Besides, Douglas himself had had his own share of setbacks, albeit of a different kind. His mother had recently died, and his wife was seriously ill: personal blows which were hardly conducive to putting him in the frame of mind necessary to take on the most feared fighter on earth. Yet Douglas was in peak condition, both mentally and physically. Perhaps he gained inner strength from his loss, and was determined to dedicate the biggest fight of his career to his mother and his wife. Who knows? But the fact remains that Douglas frustrated Tyson, avoided all his best shots - with one notable exception - and emerged a glorious and wholly unlikely champion.

Tyson looked as though he had trained for the usual duration of his fights, in other words, a matter of minutes. When Plan A didn't work, the champion's aura of invincibility suddenly began to look like a rather thin veneer. He swung wild punches that Douglas easily evaded, and the challenger countered with good technique and plenty of solid blows which found their mark.

Saved by the bell

Finally, in round eight, Tyson connected with a meaty uppercut. All Douglas's good work could have been undone in an instant. What followed was an incident reminiscent of the famous "Long Count" of the Dempsey-Tunney fight more than 60 years earlier. Referee Octavio Mayran ushered Tyson to a neutral corner, delaying the start of the count by a few seconds. All well and good, but he then blundered by beginning the count himself instead of taking his cue from the timekeeper. Douglas took maximum advantage of the extra few seconds, staying down till nine, or rather the referee's version of that count. As he got to his feet the bell went, giving him even more time to recover. And recover he did. Douglas's crisis, and Tyson's one chance, ended at that point. Douglas meted out more punishment in the ninth round, and finished Tyson in the next with a barrage of heavy, accurate blows.

There followed a brief and undignified hiatus as Tyson and promoter Don King cried foul. They wanted the decision overturned because of the eighth round fiasco. Quite rightly, they were given short shrift by the authorities.

Douglas's reign lasted just eight months. In October 1990, his first defence pitted him against Evander Holyfield. Douglas couldn't reproduce the stunning form he showed against Tyson. In fact, he reverted to the style, or lack of it, that he had shown earlier in his career. His moment of glory had been and gone.

James Douglas

Nickname:	"Buster"
Born:	Columbus, Ohio, USA. April 7 1960
World Heavyweight Champion:	1990
Record:	Won 38 (25 KOs) Lost 6 Drawn 1

Opposite: It's all smiles from Mike Tyson and Frank Bruno in an off-duty moment. Things weren't so amicable on February 25, 1989, when the two stepped into the ring in Las Vegas.

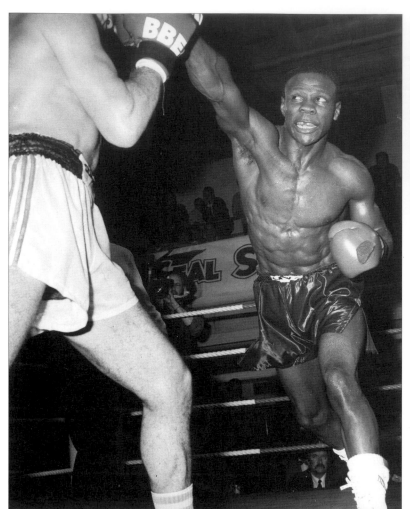

Eubank's challenge

Above left: Chris Eubank takes the fight to Argentina's Hugo Corti in their March 1990 clash. 23-year-old Eubank stopped Corti in the eighth round, and was seen as just one fight away from challenging for the world middleweight crown.

Above: June 1990. It's another victory for Lennox Lewis, but his 12th opponent, Puerto Rico's Osvaldo Ocasio, took him the full distance.

Left: Laying-on of hands. Terry Anderson becomes the latest man to fall victim to Reverend George Foreman. The 42-year-old former champion continued to rack up the wins during his comeback.

Opposite below left: Evander Holyfield brings down the curtain on "Buster" Douglas's reign in three one-sided rounds in Las Vegas, October 25, 1990.

Nigel Benn

Nickname: "Dark Destroyer"	
Born: Ilford, England. Jan 22 1964	
World Super Middleweight Champion: 1992-1995	
World Middleweight Champion: 1990	
Commonwealth Middleweight Champion: 1988-1989	
Record:	Won 42 (35 KOs) Lost 5 Drawn 1

Left: Chris Eubank looks on impassively as the Dark Destroyer tries out one of his most menacing stars.
Below right: Promoter Barry Hearn congratulates Eubank and Benn after their bruising encounter, which ended with a ninth-round stoppage in his man's favour. Eubank took Benn's WBO middleweight crown, which the Dark Destroyer had won seven months earlier.

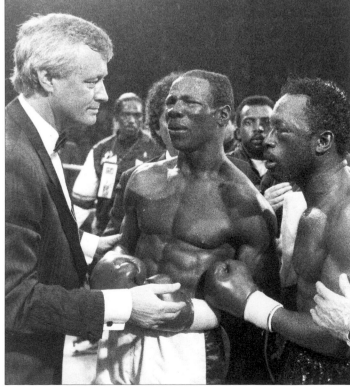

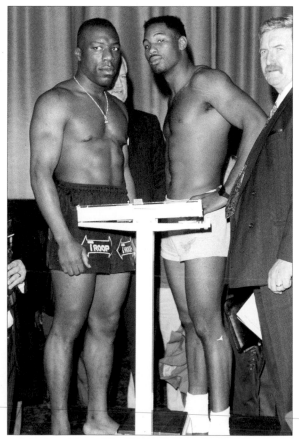

Lewis beats Mason

Opposite below right: Lennox Lewis (right) and Gary Mason at the weigh-in before their fight on March 6, 1991.

Below: Wembley Arena, March 6, 1991. Lennox Lewis and Gary Mason put on the best heavyweight show seen in Britain for 20 years. 28-year-old Mason made the early running. Lewis used his superior agility to stay clear of trouble and picked off his man with his ramrod left jab

Opposite below left: Having lost his world title, Mike Tyson hits the comeback trail by taking on Alex Stewart. It was back to business as usual, Tyson finishing the job inside a round.

Opposite above: Nigel Benn (left) on his way to losing his WBO crown to Chris Eubank.

Left: Marvin Hagler went one better than most boxers by changing his name to "Marvelous" Marvin by deed poll. It was an apposite nickname; Hagler reigned supreme in the middleweight division between 1980 and 1987.

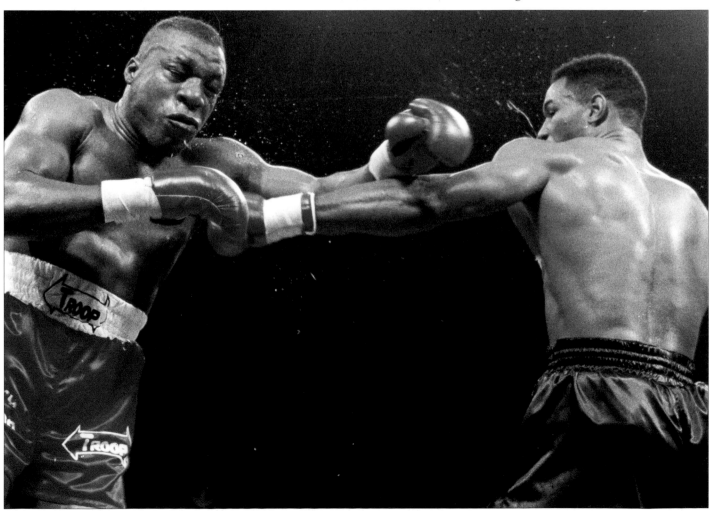

Lewis takes British title in style

Opposite: Wembley Arena, March 6, 1991. Lennox Lewis takes the British heavyweight championship belt with a clinical performance against Gary Mason. Mason, unbeaten in 35 fights, succumbed 44 seconds into the seventh round.

Left: Las Vegas, March 1991. Referee Richard Steele incurs the wrath of Razor Ruddock's camp by stopping their man in the seventh round of his fight against Mike Tyson. The ringside fans also made it clear that they felt the fight had been halted prematurely. A rematch was swiftly arranged.

Below: Tyson is no longer champion, but he remains the biggest draw in boxing - for now. Within a matter of weeks his popularity was to plummet when he found himself indicted on a rape charge.

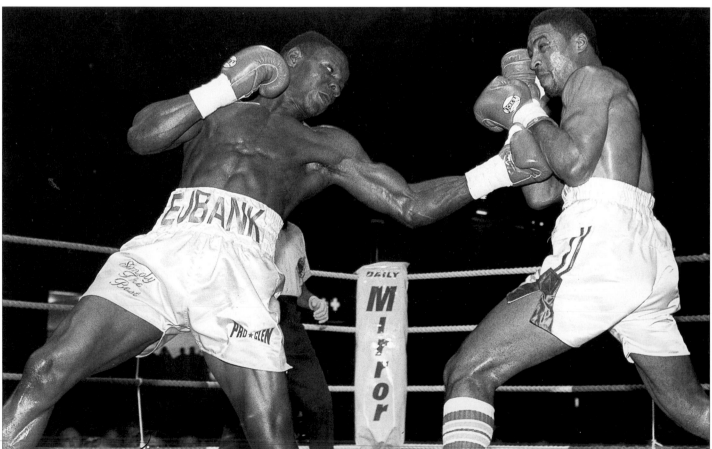

"Clones Cyclone"

Right: Barry McGuigan, the "Clones Cyclone", became the WBA featherweight champion in 1985, taking the title from the great Eusebio Pedroza. He held the title for a year, losing on points to Steve Cruz in June 1986.

Below: November 1991. Evander Holyfield gloves up with trainer George Benton for a gym workout.

Opposite above: Commonwealth champion Michael Watson (left) was the third man to challenge Chris Eubank for the WBO title. The two men met at Earls Court, June 22, 1991.

Opposite below: Eubank fails to get through with a left, but goes on to win a controversial decision over Michael Watson.

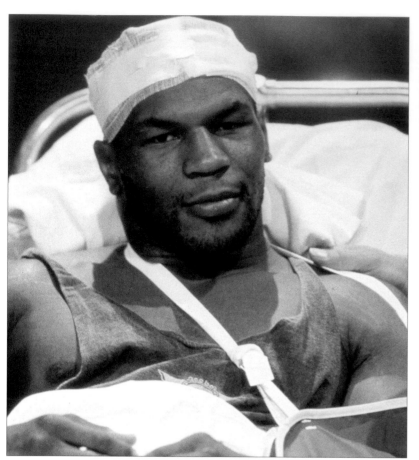

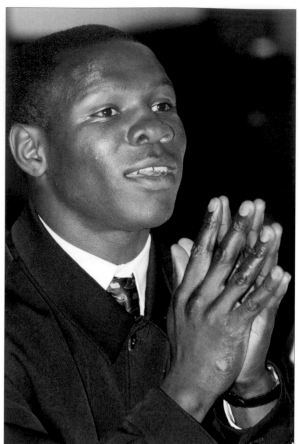

Don King's TV stunt

Opposite above left: Mike Tyson looked like one of his many ring victims when he arrived for a TV appearance in July 1991. It was all a charade. Tyson and promoter Don King staged the stunt to quash rumours of a rift between them.

Opposite below: Frank Bruno chases shadows at the Royal Oak gym in Canning Town.

Above: September 1991. Two years on from his defeat by Tyson, a pensive Bruno wonders if he will get another crack at a world title.

Opposite above right: Chris Eubank was perceived as arrogant and aloof, which didn't endear him to all boxing fans.

Right: White Hart Lane, September 21, 1991. Michael Watson in trouble against Chris Eubank as the two men vie for the vacant WBO super-middleweight title. Watson was well ahead on points going into the 12th and final round. The referee stopped the fight after an onslaught from Eubank.

McCrory has no answer to Lewis onslaught

Above and opposite above left: September 1991. Lennox Lewis has Glenn McCrory in trouble early in their clash at the Albert Hall. It took Lewis just 270 seconds to dispose of of McCrory and retain his British and European titles.

Opposite below: October 1991: With his chance of fighting Holyfield hanging in the balance, Mike Tyson takes his frustration out on his cheque book. He splashes out on four $85,000 BMWs, one for himself and the others for members of his entourage.

Opposite above right: Frank Bruno ponders his return to the ring for the first time since his defeat by Tyson.

Tyson put on hold

Opposite: Mike Tyson gears up for his Nov 1991 showdown with Evander Holyfield. Following the shock defeat by Douglas, Tyson had returned to winning ways against Henry Tillman, Alex Stewart and Razor Ruddock. He wanted his title back, and most neutrals thought the result of the Holyfield fight was a foregone conclusion. His subsequent incarceration meant that the fight would be put on hold for five years.
Above: Chris Eubank goes on the offensive in his WBO super-middleweight clash with Michael Watson. 26-year-old Watson collapsed into a coma after the fight, having suffered suffered a blood clot to the brain. An emergency operation saved his life, but he was confined to a wheelchair thereafter.

Tyson in race against time

Left: Tyson's smiles hide an ugly mood of frustration as a rib injury forces him to pull out of the November 8, 1991 clash with Evander Holyfield.

Below: Tyson cracked a rib doing sit-ups in early October. The camp hushed up the injury, hoping it would heal in time for the Holyfield fight a month later.

Opposite above: A bullish Don King (left) was still hopeful that Tyson would get to fight for the title before his court case began on January 27, 1992.

Evander Holyfield

Boxing history is littered with fighters from lower divisions attempting to step up and take the ultimate prize. The greater glory has been one motivating force; the huge purses up for grabs at the sport's top table is the other. Evander Holyfield is one of an elite group who have reached the top in one division, then beefed up to scale the heights of another.

Holyfield was born in Atmore, Alabama, on October 19, 1962. He rose to boxing prominence in 1984, when he won the Golden Gloves light-heavyweight title, then followed it up with a bronze at the Los Angeles Olympics. In the latter tournament he was denied a certain gold medal when he threw a punch after being told to break. He turned professional at the end of 1984, and for the next four years set about conquering the cruiserweight division.

Cruiserweight

Cruiserweight had entered boxing's vocabulary in 1979, when the WBC decided to institute a new division to sit between the 175lb light-heavyweights and the big boys. The cruiser limit was set at 190lb, which proved to be perfect for Holyfield. He took less than two years to capture his first world title, taking the WBA's version of the cruiserweight crown from Dwight Muhammad Qawi in July 1986. Qawi was a class opponent. He had held the WBC light-heavyweight crown, and had defended his cruiser title against former heavyweight champion Leon Spinks. Holyfield and Qawi fought an exciting 15-round contest in Atlanta, Holyfield winning on a split decision.

In May the following year, Holyfield added the IBF title by beating the incumbent, Rickey Parkey, in three rounds. Then, in April 1988, he established his total supremacy of the division by stopping the WBC title-holder, Carlos De Leon, in eight. In systematically mopping up all these titles, Holyfield was matching the performance of Mike Tyson in the heavyweights. The difference was that Holyfield was king of a much smaller hill. Almost immediately, he set his sights on Tyson's heavyweight crown, relinquishing his three hard-won cruiserweight titles so that he could strike for the greatest prize.

Holyfield's progress was swift. He took out James "Quick" Tillis in five, and followed it up with victories inside the distance over Pinklon Thomas and Michael Dokes. A couple of wins later, Holyfield put himself in line for a crack at Iron Mike himself. "Buster" Douglas's win over Tyson shook up the boxing world and changed Holyfield's plans. The "Real Deal" now had the new champion in his sights, and the two men duly met in Las Vegas on October 25, 1990. Most observers' verdict on Douglas that day could be summed up in a single word:

surrender. With $20 million dollars safely in the bank, Douglas saw little need to train hard or compromise his safety. He succumbed to a short right in the third, handing 28-year-old Holyfield the crown in one of the easiest fights of his career. The poor quality of the opposition left a question mark over the new champion. Matters weren't helped by the fact that his first defence was to be against 42-year-old George Foreman the following spring. Just when heavyweight boxing seemed to be edging towards a disrepute charge, Foreman stepped in to restore the faith. Not for him a quick capitulation and even quicker exit with a sackful of cash.

Holyfield beats gutsy Foreman

The former champion took Holyfield the full 10 rounds, and although he went down fairly and squarely on points, Foreman acquitted himself very well. So did Holyfield. He was now earning the respect he wanted, and being hailed as a talented and worthy champion. These were fine credentials, though many reserved judgment until he came up against Tyson.

Notwithstanding the defeat by Douglas, Tyson was still regarded as the greatest fighter of the day. If Holyfield aspired to true greatness and universal acclaim, he would have to step into the ring with Iron Mike Holyfield wanted the fight and plans were set in train. The match was made for October 1991, only to be deferred a month after Tyson injured a rib in training. Tyson was soon to be put out of commission for a much longer time. He had been indicted on a rape charge in September 1991. His subsequent conviction and six-year jail sentence meant that the world would have to wait for a Holyfield-Tyson clash.

The veteran Bert Cooper was called up as a replacement for Tyson. Holyfield won, but the challenger had him in trouble in the fourth, putting him down for the first time in his career. Those who still harboured doubts about Holyfield would have found much support to their view in this somewhat hollow victory. Next up for Holyfield was another 42-year-old ex-champion, Larry Holmes. Holmes fought on the retreat, using a cross-armed defence to survive - but lose - round after round. It was a poor spectacle, most notable for Holmes' post-fight comment. When asked if he should have done anything differently, Larry replied: "Yeah, I should have fought him in 1980."

Holyfield left Las Vegas with his title intact but his reputation further tarnished. If he wanted to restore any degree of credibility, he couldn't afford to take on another grandfather. In fact, there were three worthy contenders waiting in the wings: Riddick Bowe, "Razor" Ruddock and

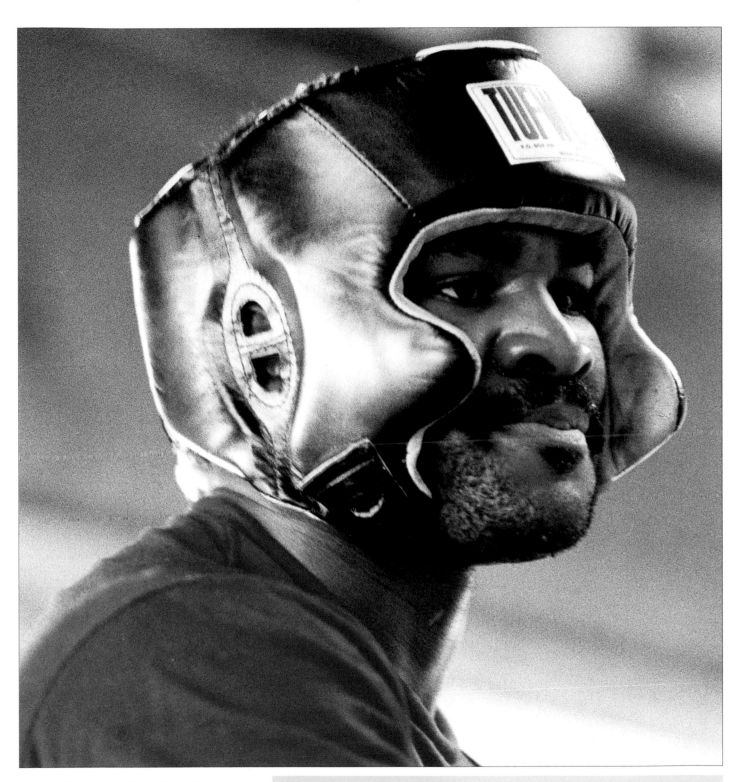

Lennox Lewis, the British and European champion. Holyfield agreed to take on Bowe, with the victor to meet the winner of the Ruddock-Lewis fight. The champion's critics were to feel vindicated on November 14, 1992. Up against the first quality opponent of his reign, Holyfield was finally found wanting.

Evander Holyfield

Born:	Atmore, Alabama USA October 19 1962	
Height:	6'2"	Weight: 235lbs.
World Heavyweight Champion: 1990-1992 1993-1994 1997-1999 2000-2001		
Record:	Won 37 Lost 5 Drawn 2 (25 KOs)	

"Smoking" Bert takes Tyson's place

All trained up and no one to fight. Evander Holyfield had to look elsewhere for an opponent after Tyson was forced to pull out of their title fight. The champion, who had just celebrated his 29th birthday, eventually took on "Smoking" Bert Cooper, who gave him plenty of problems. That provided even more ammunition for those who thought that the true champion was languishing in jail. Many of those critics would revise their opinion after some of Holyfield's performances later in his career.

Bruno's back

Left and opposite: Frank Bruno's long-awaited return to action in November 1991 was something of a damp squib. Dutch heavyweight John Emmen lasted less than a round, making it a frustrating day for the promoters and the ring-rusty Bruno. The fans who turned out at the Albert Hall didn't seem too bothered by the mismatch; they gave Bruno a tumultuous reception.

Above: Evander Holyfield , pictured in front of his own "wall of fame" at his Houston home.

Above and overleaf: Chris Eubank had to face a huge psychological hurdle when he stepped into the ring for the first time after the Michael Watson fight. He passed the test, beating Thulani "Sugar Boy" Malinga on points at Birmingham's Indoor Arena in February 1992.
Opposite: Back on the winnig trail. Referee Mickey Vann holds Bruno's arm aloft after his demolition job on John Emmen. The following week saw Frank back in the spotlight - in pantomime at Bristol.

Chris Eubank

Born:	Dulwich, London England August 8 1966	
World Super Middleweight Champion:		1991-1995
World Middleweight Champion:		1990-1991
Record:	Won 45 (23 KO's) Lost 5 Drawn 2	

Shock win earns Holmes title shot

Left: February 1992. 42-year-old grandfather Larry Holmes (left) rolls back the years and gains an unexpected decision over the Olympic gold medalist Ray Mercer, a man 12 years his junior. The victory put Holmes in line for a title fight against Holyfield.

Below: A superbly conditioned Frank Bruno in training for his April 1992 fight against Jose Ribalta.

Opposite above: Bruno goes on the offensive against the Cuban-born Ribalta, knocking him out in the second round with a terrific right hook.

Opposite below: Bruno milks the applause after the win over Ribalta. He regarded this as a crossroads fight. The quality of the performance breathed new life into his world title ambitions.

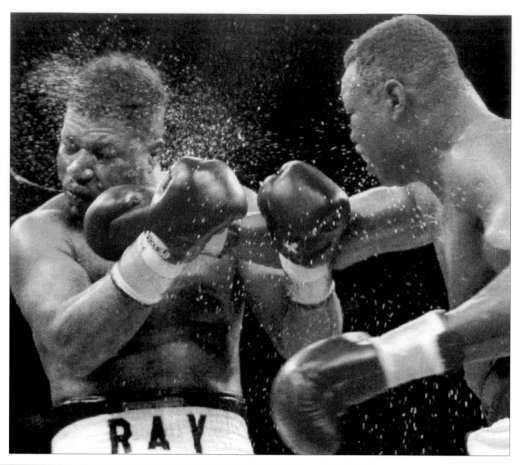

Frank Bruno MBE

Born:	Hammersmith, London, England. November 16 1961
Height:	6' 3"
Weight:	247 lbs.
World Heavyweight Champion:	1995-1996
European Heavyweight Champion:	1985
Record:	Won 40 (37 KOs) Lost 5

Triple crown for Lewis

Above and opposite above: Lennox Lewis adds the Commonwealth crown to his British and European titles with his victory over Derek Williams. He became the first man to hold all three titles since Joe Bugner in 1976. He also earned a Lonsdale belt outright. Evander Holyfield's manager, Shelley Finkel, was ringside for Lewis's latest impressive showing.

Opposite below: October 1992. South Africa's Pierre Coetzer winces as Frank Bruno lands another clean blow on his way to an eight-round victory. Despite the success, Bruno found himself behind Lennox Lewis, "Razor" Ruddock and Riddick Bowe in the pecking order for a shot at Holyfield's crown.

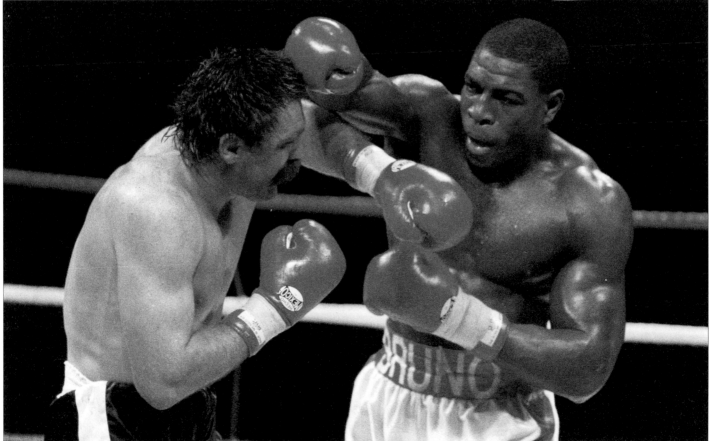

Lewis one step away from title glory

Earls Court, October 31, 1992. Lennox Lewis moves into the millionaire class with a paralysing right which disposes of "Razor" Ruddock in just 3min 46sec. Lewis earned £600,000 for his night's work, but that would be dwarfed by his next purse. He stood to make £5 million from his guaranteed title fight against the winner of the Holyfield-Bowe contest. Razor Ruddock had twice gone up against Mike Tyson. Although he lost on both occasions, Ruddock extended Iron Mike much further than the 3min 46sec he managed with Lewis.

Riddick Bowe

Not for nothing was Riddick Bowe called "Big Daddy". While undisputed champion Evander Holyfield was scientifically pumping himself up from the 190lb cruiserweight limit to turn himself into a 210lb heavyweight, Bowe was regularly tipping the scales at around the 240lb mark. He was also a dangerous opponent. He had represented the USA at the 1988 Seoul Olympics, where he lost to Lennox Lewis in the super-heavyweight division. Lewis took gold on that occasion, but four years later, Bowe was probably regarded as the bigger threat to Evander Holyfield's world crown.

While Holyfield busied himself with beating the likes of Larry Holmes and George Foreman - who were both over 40 - many observers thought he was deliberately putting off the day when he would have to face Bowe. Things came to a head in mid-1992, when Holyfield finally agreed to meet Bowe, with the winner to defend the title against either Lennox Lewis or Donovan "Razor" Ruddock. Bowe's 30lb weight advantage proved decisive in his fight against Holyfield. The champion's superb athleticism and fitness kept him on his feet, but the challenger was a clear winner on points. Bowe now held all three major belts, albeit briefly.

Stripped of the WBC title

He refused to honour the agreement to face Lennox Lewis - who had easily disposed of Ruddock - and was subsequently stripped of the WBC title. Bowe deposited the belt in question in a dustbin, then said exactly what he thought of that organisation and his own status within the sport: "I, the undisputed, undefeated, universally accepted heavyweight champion of the world reject, renounce, repudiate and totally dismiss the unfair, immoral, unethical and downright silly actions of the WBC and their president, Jose Sulaiman. Boxing titles are won and lost in the ring. In order to be a champion you must fight a champion and beat a champion. I did that, and now the ugly head of corrupt politics from an organisation who have become hated and disrespected around the world is threatening and challenging my right to be called the world champion. They are wrong and I will not be intimidated by them. I am the heavyweight champion of the world and today I withdraw my recognition of the WBC." Strong stuff indeed.

From a situation that was in danger of producing more heat than light, two inescapable facts remained: Bowe was the conqueror of Holyfield; and the WBC's action was unilateral, Bowe retaining the WBA and IBF belts. Bowe's first defence of his two titles took place on February 6, 1993 at Madison Square Garden. His opponent was former WBA champion Michael Dokes. Dokes weighed in at 244lb, a pound more than Bowe, making it a true heavyweight battle.

It was a short-lived battle, though, Bowe stopping his man inside a round. The champion's second defence, on May 22, 1993, hardly set the pulse racing any quicker, despite being staged in his home town of Washington DC. His opponent was Jesse Ferguson, a man who had no great pedigree and who didn't improve it this time out either, succumbing as he did in round two.

"Real Deal" wins rematch

The fans were restless for a worthier opponent. Re-enter Evander Holyfield, who had decided that announcing his retirement following the Bowe defeat had been premature. The two met in Las Vegas, on November 6, 1993. It was almost a year to the day since "Big Daddy" had taken the title from the "Real Deal". Many will remember the fight for the extraordinary sight of a paraglider dropping out of the sky to interrupt proceedings for nearly 30 minutes. Riddick Bowe would remember it as the first defeat in his 35-fight professional career.

Riddick Bowe

Nickname:	"Big Daddy"
Born:	Brooklyn, New York, USA. August 10 1967
World Heavyweight Champion:	1992-1993 1995-1997
Continental Americas Heavyweight Champion:	1994-1997
Olympic Super Heavyweight Silver Medal 1988	
Record:	Won 40 (32 KOs) Lost 1

Opposite: Riddick Bowe vents his spleen at a press conference after being stripped of the WBC title in December 1992.

McGuigan forms PBA

Right: The tragic consequences of the Watson-Eubank fight spurred Barry McGuigan on to form the Professional Boxers Association, effectively a trade union for fighters. McGuigan had personal reasons for wanting to improve safety measures and minimise risks. In 1982, McGuigan knocked out Nigerian fighter Young Ali, who collapsed into a coma and died five months later.

Opposite below and above left: Lennox Lewis shows off the WBC belt awarded to him up by default, following Riddick Bowe's refusal to meet him in the ring.

Opposite above right: "Big Daddy" Riddick Bowe, looking none too pleased at the WBC's decision to take away his title.

Below: Riddick Bowe (left) poses for the cameras with British heavyweight Herbie Hyde in February 1993.

Evander Holyfield

Many boxing fans would have noted Evander Holyfield's defeat by Riddick Bowe in November 1992 with an air of smug satisfaction. Here was a pumped-up cruiserweight whose rise to the top had been carefully orchestrated. His schooling had even included sessions with a 70-year-old ballet teacher, brought in to help improve his agility. His weight gain had been scientifically engineered. Then there was the question of his opponents. Douglas handed him the title on a plate; thereafter he struggled against second-rate opposition.

Worthy champion

The entire Holyfield package, far from being the "Real Deal", smacked of a cynical, manufactured marketing exercise. Fortune had conspired to sustain the illusion by putting Mike Tyson out of circulation at just the right moment from Holyfield's point of view. The murmurings could be clearly heard: "Just think what Iron Mike would have done to the likes of Burke Cooper, George Foreman and Larry Holmes." Such was the case for the prosecution.

The defence - quite naturally including Holyfield himself - saw things rather differently. He had beaten two ex-champions on his way to the title; he couldn't be held responsible for the condition Douglas chose to be in when he entered the ring, nor the less seemly side to Tyson's character which prevented their meeting. Prior to the Bowe fight, he had beaten all 28 men put up before him. If the jury was firmly out for the duration of Holyfield's first stint as champion, he proved himself a very worthy champion when he hit the comeback trail. That began just short of a year after the defeat by Bowe, when he stepped into the ring against the same man. Holyfield fought magnificently and scored a majority points win to reclaim the WBA and IBF titles. He couldn't claim to be the undisputed champion, though. The WBC had stripped Bowe of their title after the latter reneged on a deal to meet the winner of the Lewis-Ruddock fight. 1993 thus saw a return to the bad old days, with Lewis holding the WBC title, Holyfield the WBA and IBF versions. And then there was the recently formed WB0, whose champion was Michael Moorer. It was Moorer who spoked Holyfield's second coming. Moorer had renounced his WB0 title in 1993, setting his sights on the more established and prestigious versions of the crown. He targeted Holyfield's WBA and IBF titles, and in April 1994, proceeded to take them.

Opposite above right: "Big Daddy" towers over a British bobby, helmet and all. Bowe was on a visit to England in February 1993, having just successfully defended his WBA and IBF titles against Michael Dokes.

Left and above left: Evander Holyfield responded to losing his title by bringing in a new trainer, Emanuel Steward, widely regarded as one of the best in the business. 51 weeks after his defeat by Bowe, Holyfield gave an inspired performance to regain his title against the same man.

Opposite below: Frank Bruno prepares for his April 1993 fight against American veteran Carl "The Truth" Williams at Birmingham's NEC.

Lewis weighs in for Bruno

Left: Frank Bruno comes through his test against Carl Williams to set up an October showdown with Lennox Lewis for the WBC title.

Below left: Lennox Lewis's hangs on to his WBC belt after fending off a challenge from former IBF champion Tony Tucker. Lewis survived a stiff examination to win on points.

Below: Lennox Lewis in upbeat mood at the weigh-in for the Bruno fight in October 1993. Cardiff Castle forms the impressive backdrop.

Opposite: October 1, 1993. Cardiff Arms Park was the setting for the battle of British supremacy, as well as the small matter of the WBC crown. Bruno rocked the champion in the third, but couldn't follow it up.

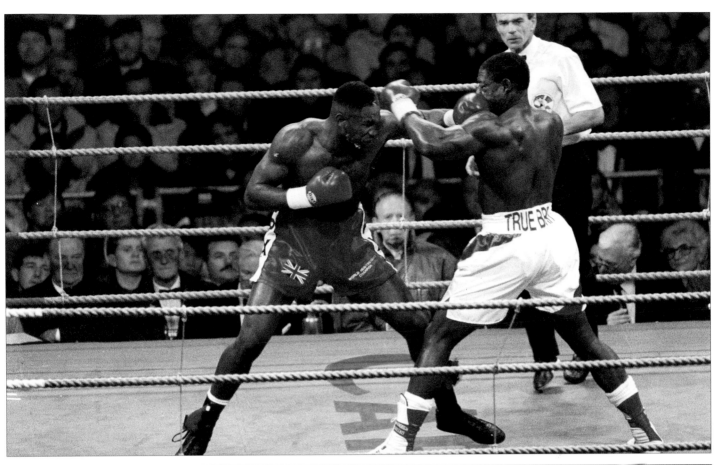

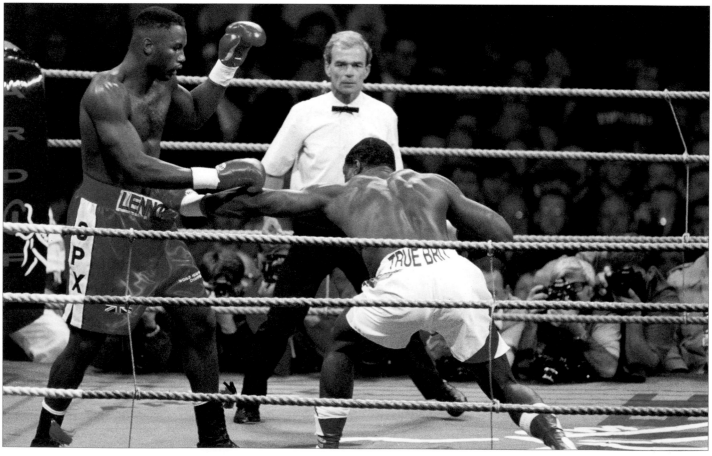

'Pretty average' Lewis

Lennox Lewis retains his WBC title by knocking out Frank Bruno in the seventh round. It wasn't a classic, nor a top-drawer display. Lewis himself described it as a "pretty average" performance. Lou Duva, who was preparing Evander Holyfield for the rematch with Riddick Bowe, wasn't impressed either. He commented that Bowe would have no trouble knocking Lewis out. As far as Bruno was concerned, it looked as if the game might be up. But events were to take a dramatic turn in the following two years, and his long-held dream of winning the world title was to be realized.

Michael Moorer

World Heavyweight Champion: 1994

Many boxers have made the step up from light-heavyweight, seeking the greater honours and bigger purses on offer in the heavyweight division. Michael Moorer did that, but he went one better: he also relinquished titles with one of the minor boxing organisations so that he could embark on the glory trail with one of the more prestigious bodies. Moorer became the newly-instituted World Boxing Organisation's first light-heavyweight champion in December 1988, when he stopped Ramzi Hassan.

Over the next three years he successfully defended the title eight times, then relinquished it so that he could compete at heavyweight level. Initially, he remained within the WBO fold. This organisation ignored the claims of the likes of Tyson and Holyfield, and the crown passed through the hands of a succession of second-rank heavyweights. Moorer became the WBO heavyweight champion in May 1992 with a fifth-round victory over Bert Cooper. However, he soon reached the conclusion that he was too big a fish swimming in too small a pool. In 1993, he gave that title up, too. His decision was vindicated in April the following year, when he was given the chance to win the WBA and IBF belts. Standing in his way was the incumbent, Evander Holyfield. After his inspired comeback

victory over Riddick Bowe, Holyfield gave a somewhat lacklustre performance that day in Las Vegas. The fight went the full 12 rounds, with Moorer getting a majority decision. Moorer had become the first southpaw heavyweight champion in history. Unfortunately for him, his reign was also to be one of the shortest. On November 5, 1994, less than seven months after his surprise win over Holyfield, Moorer himself was on the receiving end of a shock decision. His opponent was a 45-year-old preacher by the name of George Foreman.

Michael Moorer

Born: Brooklyn, New York, USA. November 12 1967

World Heavyweight Champion:1992-1994 1996-1997 (IBF)

World Light-Heavyweight Champion:1988-1991

Record: Won 39 (31 KOs)   Lost 2

McCall upset for Lewis

Lennox Lewis prepares for his fight with Oliver McCall at Wembley Arena, Sept 24, 1994. Having followed up the win over Bruno with an eighth-round stoppage of America's Phil Jackson, Lewis was confident that his fourth WBC defence would be relatively straightforward. 29-year-old McCall was best known as a sparring partner to Mike Tyson and had no great record. The scene was set for a major upset.

Bruno beats McCall

Above and right: After wresting the title from Lennox Lewis, Oliver McCall had made just one successful defence, against Larry Holmes, before taking on Bruno at Wembley Stadium, Sept 2, 1995 where Bruno won a 12-round decision.

Opposite above left: Nigel Benn (foreground) and Chris Eubank fight out a draw in their super-middleweight unification fight in October 1993.

Opposite above right: Former world bantamweight champion Juan Polo Perez became Prince Naseem Hamed's 19th victim.

Opposite below: Las Vegas, August 19, 1995. Mike Tyson is victorious over Peter McNeeley on his return to the ring after a four-year absence.

Right: September 1995. Built for power, not for speed, but Britain's new world champion, Frank Bruno, puts in some road work by taking part in the Great North Run. Keeping pace is model Heather Mills, who had lost a leg in a motorcycle accident.

Opposite below: March 12, 1996. Mike Tyson, pictured outside the Golden Gloves gym in Las Vegas four days before his title showdown with Frank Bruno. Tyson followed up his win over Peter McNeeley with a third round KO of Buster Mathis Junior the previous December.

Below: Mike Tyson hardly needed a world title to his name to cause a media scrum. But the glare of the spotlight was that much brighter after he regained his WBC crown in March 1996.

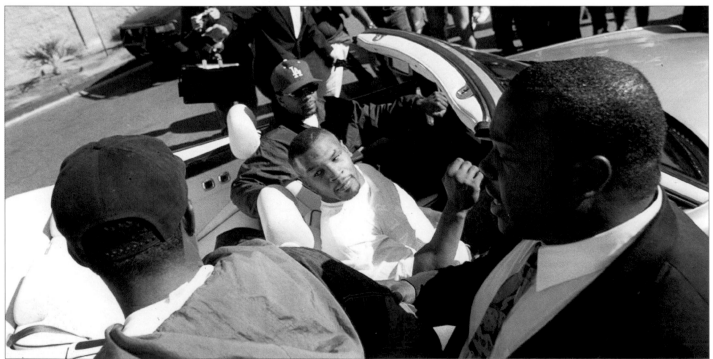

George Foreman

World Heavyweight Champion: 1994

In November 1994, George Foreman entered the champions' hall of fame for the second time. Others had managed that feat. Ali had won the title three times, and Holyfield would go on to do so too. But Foreman's two entries in the record books stand twenty years apart, a unique achievement that may never be beaten.

It was a much more genial George Foreman who hit the comeback trail in the late 1980s, after being out of action for the best part of a decade. His friendly demeanour couldn't disguise the fact that he was a flabby 40-year-old who had too great a weakness for hamburgers. Nevertheless, he knocked over 19 opponents in succession. Most were dismissed by commentators as third-rate, and many were just that. Not all, though. One of his victims was Bert Cooper, the man who was to pose Evander Holyfield plenty of problems during the latter's reign. Foreman swatted Cooper aside in three rounds. Foreman's run of success finally earned him a crack at Holyfield in 1991. There was

honour in defeat that day, for the champion couldn't put George away. Three years later, Foreman got another chance, against Holyfield's conqueror, Michael Moorer.

For Foreman it was a one-punch fight. He took a lot of punishment in the first nine rounds, then produced a gem of a straight right that connected with Moorer's jaw and sent him into oblivion. At 45, Foreman had become the oldest heavyweight champion in history. Foreman now possessed both the WBA and IBF belts. Within a year both had slipped through his fingers, though not from defeat in the ring. The WBA stripped him of their title for his refusal to face Bruce Seldon. The IBF followed suit shortly afterwards, when Foreman turned down a return match against Axel Schulz, whom he had narrowly outpointed in their first meeting. Genial George shrugged his shoulders and continued to fight on, merely for the love of the sport. Meanwhile, the WBA and IBF titles were now vacant and up for grabs.

Tyson back on the glory trail

Opposite above left: A focused Mike Tyson prepares to take on Frank Bruno.

Opposite above right: Tyson throws the final punch of the fight, a right uppercut in the third round. There was no coming back for Bruno.

Opposite below: The new champion exudes confidence and menace in equal measure as referee Mills Lane steps in to remove the gumshield from the vanquished Bruno's mouth.

Left: Referee Mills Lane gives Bruno some much-needed support after his defeat by Tyson. Observers said he entered the ring half-beaten and exited it totally pulverised.

Below: Back on the glory trail. Tyson shows off the WBA belt, and is soon targeting Bruce Seldon's WBA title.

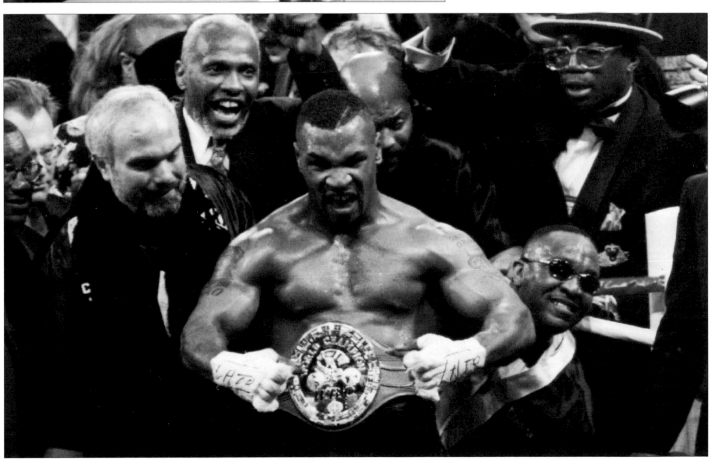

Prince Naseem retains WBO

Left: Newcastle, June 1996. Puerto Rico's Daniel Alicea becomes the first man to put Prince Naseem Hamed on the seat of his pants. The knockdown irritated Naz more than it hurt him, as Alicea discovered in the very next round.

Below: Prince Naseem Hamed performs his trademark celebration after flattening Alicea in the second round to retain his WBO world title.

Opposite: Lennox Lewis gets a few tee-time tips from Robert Forde. Lewis agreed to sponsor Forde, one of the few black golf professionals on the English circuit. The two men had come from similar backgrounds, and Lewis recalled his own early struggles when he started out in boxing.

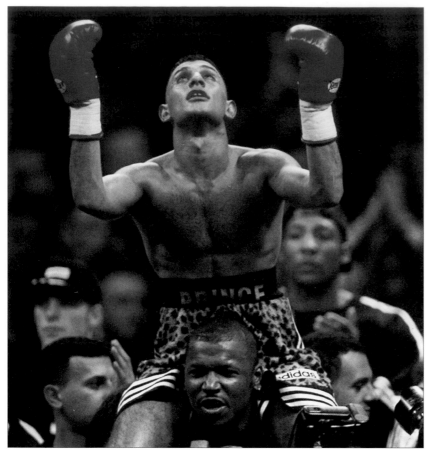

Shock defeat for Naz

Left: Prince Naseem Hamed is paraded round the ring after destroying Tom "Boom Boom" Johnson in eight rounds at London Arena, February 8, 1997. Hamed added Johnson's IBF featherweight title to his WBO crown.

Below and opposite: One of the great showmen of recent years, Naz has proved time and again that he has the talent to match the PR. The fanfare entrances to rap music and somersaults into the ring have been backed up with some sensational performances. The Sheffield southpaw set his sights on becoming a legend of the sport and winning world titles at five different weight divisions. He was on course to do just that, until a shock defeat by Marco Antonio Barrera.

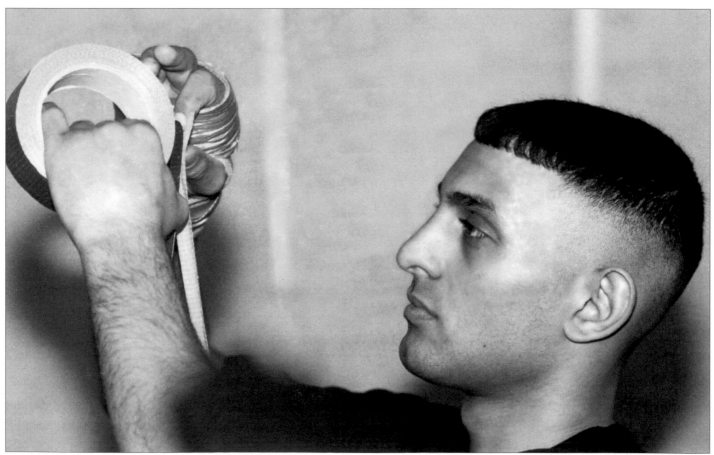

Naseem Hamed

Height:	5' 3"	**Weight:**	125 lbs.
World Featherweight Champion:	1995-2001		
Nickname "Prince"			
European Bantamweight Champion:	1994-1995		
Born: Sheffield, England. February 12 1974		**Record:** Won 35 (31 KOs) Lost 1

Evander Holyfield

World Heavyweight Champion: 1996-1999

Having won and lost the title twice, 32-year-old Evander Holyfield could have walked away from boxing with his head held high and a telephone-number bank balance. Indeed, that is what he seemed to have decided, announcing his retirement shortly after the defeat by Michael Moorer. But a year later, he was back in the ring, and some of his greatest moments still lay ahead of him. A third clash with Riddick Bowe didn't augur well for Holyfield. He dumped Bowe on the canvas in the sixth round with a tremendous left hook. But "Big Daddy" paid him back with interest, and the referee stopped the fight two rounds later. After that struggle, few gave Holyfield a prayer against Mike Tyson.

Released from jail and looking to make up for lost time, Tyson seemed intent on taking his enforced break out on his opponents. After quick-fire wins over Peter McNeeley and Buster Mathis Junior in 1995, he demolished WBC champion Frank Bruno in three rounds in March of the following year. The expectation was that Tyson would go on to hoover up all the titles, as he had done a decade earlier. He carried on in the same vein in his next fight, taking the WBA crown from Bruce Seldon inside two minutes. This was the daunting situation which faced Evander Holyfield in November 1996.

Holyfield beats Tyson

Five years after their planned meeting had been forestalled by the American judicial system, Holyfield and Tyson were finally able to show what they could do in the ring. Despite Holyfield's credentials as a two-time world champion, the bookmakers had him as a 22-1 rank outsider. They got it all wrong, and a host of so-called experts were soon called upon to consume large quantities of humble pie. In 10 rounds and 37 seconds of breathless action, Holyfield showed complete disdain for the aura of menace and invincibility that was supposed to surround Tyson. When referee Mitch Halpern stepped in to end the 11th round onslaught, it was Tyson he was protecting. The return match will be forever remembered for the infamous and despicable ear-biting incident. Tyson's third-round disqualification left his future in the sport hanging in the balance, while Holyfield had confirmed once again what a true champion he was, both in his performance and his demeanour.

Holyfield's Indian summer was completed with an eight-round win over Michael Moorer, the man who had deposed him in 1994. With that victory came Moorer's IBF belt. The only top-ranked fighter that Holyfield hadn't faced was Lennox Lewis, the reigning WBC champion. That was the obvious next match, and the one everyone wanted to see. They met at Madison Square Garden on

March 13, 1999. The much-hyped fight failed to deliver, and was most noteworthy for the controversy sparked by the scorers. One of the judges made Lewis the winner by three points, which many observers felt was about right. A second judge had them all-square, while the third - the American Eugenia Williams - provoked a storm of protest by awarding the fight to Holyfield. A drawn contest in such controversial circumstances meant that a rematch was inevitable. That fight took place eight months later, on November 13, 1999. It was to be the swansong for the heavyweight of the 1990s.

Below: Mike Tyson dragged boxing to a new low in his rematch with Evander Holyfield at the MGM Grand in Las Vegas, June 28, 1997. In the third round, Tyson was guilty of ear-biting on two occasions. The first incurred a warning and a two-point penalty, the second resulted in his disqualification.

Opposite above left: South Africa's Francois Botha is knocked out by Mike Tyson in the fifth round of their contest in Las Vegas, January 1999. Tyson had been out of action for 19 months following the infamous ear-biting incident, and it showed.

Opposite: Tyson in training for the Botha fight.

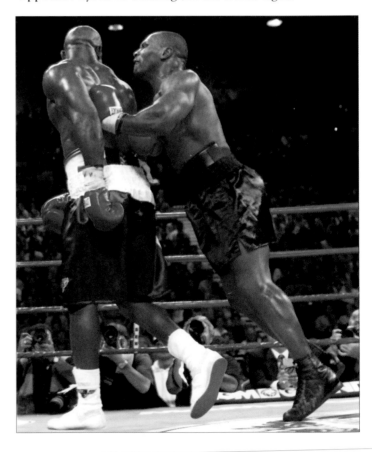

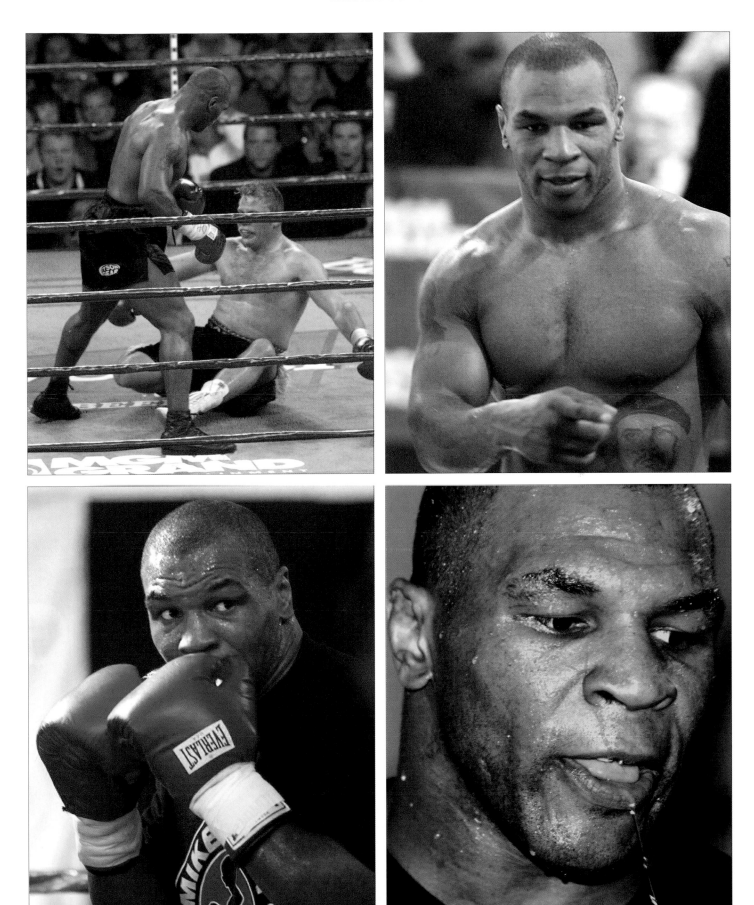

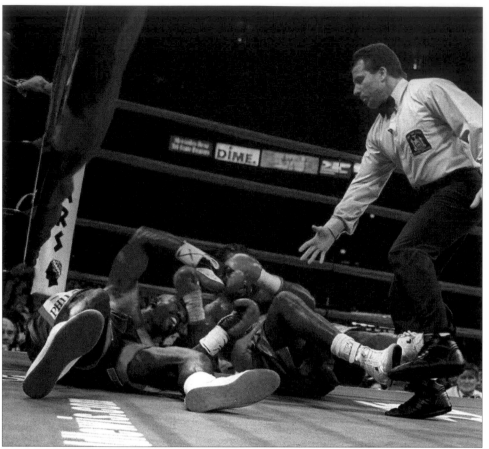

Lewis-Holyfield fight for unification

Following a period in which all three major belts had changed hands outside the ring, Lennox Lewis and Evander Holyfield met in 1999 to unify the heavyweight title for the first time in seven years. Lewis was the holder of the WBC crown, Holyfield the WBA and IBF champion. The two fought a controversial draw at Madison Square Garden on March 13, 1999, and had to do it all over again eight months later.

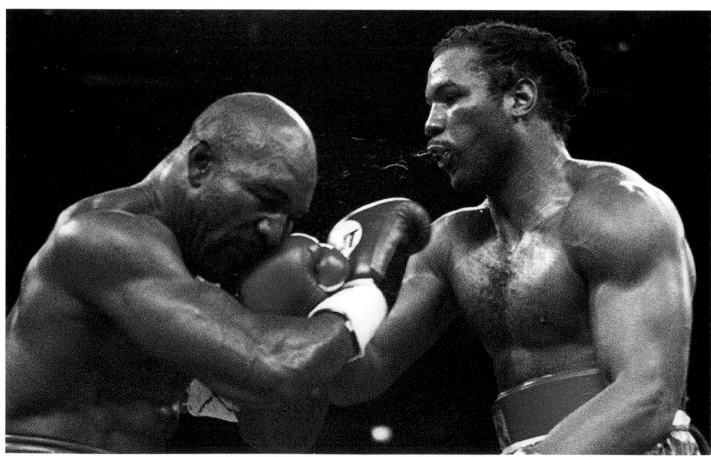

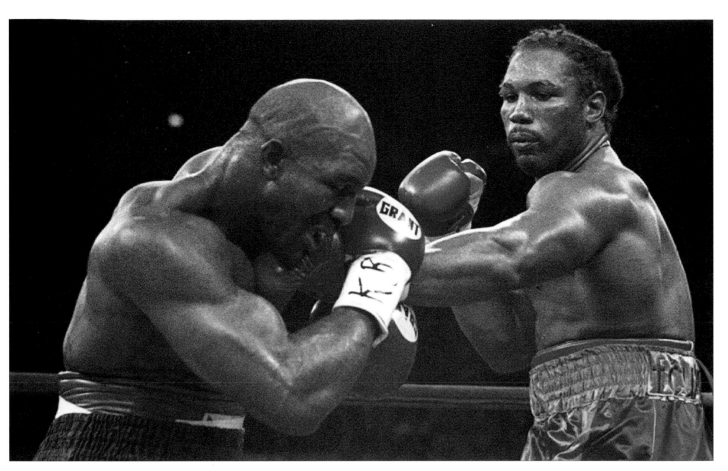

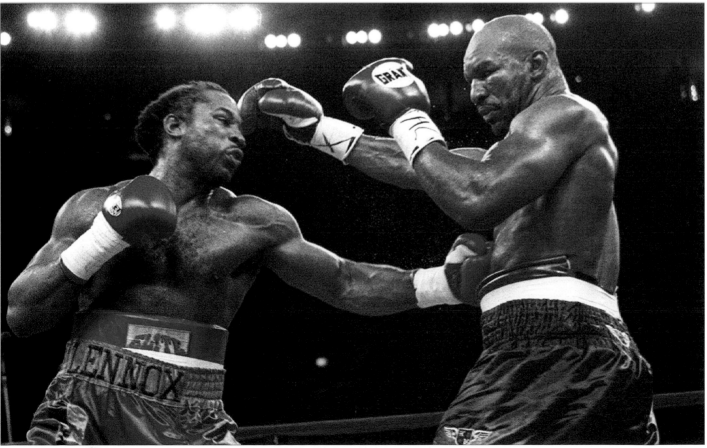

Lewis takes all crowns in rematch

Lewis-Holyfield One was a hugely controversial affair. It went the distance, with most impartial observers believing Lewis had done more than enough to get the decision. Only one of the three judges saw it that way, however. A second scored the fight even, while America's Eugenia Williams sparked an outcry by awarding the fight to Holyfield. The rematch eight months later laid the matter to rest, Lewis gaining a unanimous points decision.

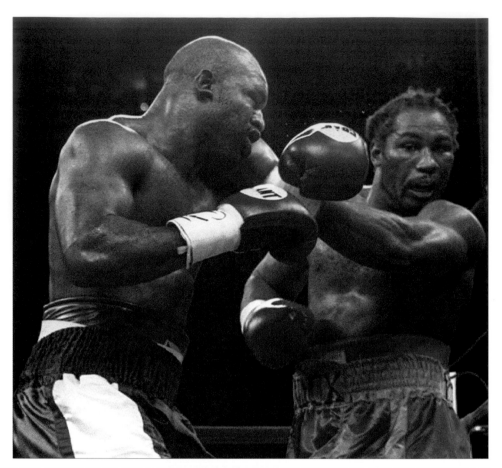

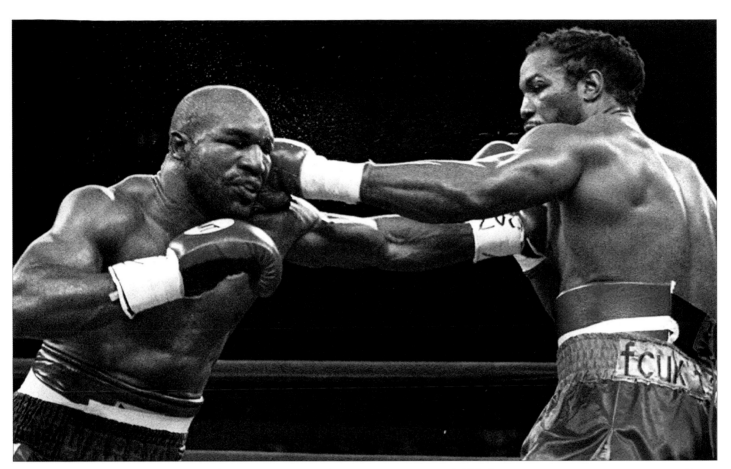

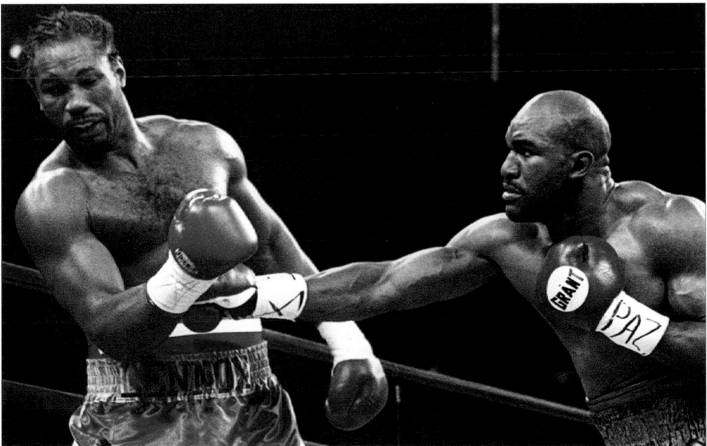

Lennox Lewis

World Heavyweight Champion: 1999-2001

While Frank Bruno was going down bravely in five rounds to Mike Tyson in 1989, 23-year-old Lennox Lewis was preparing to make his professional debut. Lewis had won Olympic gold in the super-heavyweight division in Seoul the previous year, and was marked out as the rising star of the British heavyweight scene. Ironically, he had also been boxing's golden boy in Canada, and had competed at the 1984 Olympics in Los Angeles for that country. Lewis was born in the East End of London but moved to Toronto with his mother, Violet, at the age of 12. It was there that he started taking boxing seriously. By the late 1980s, when he was living back in England and making a name for himself in the sport, Lewis was diplomatic about his dual nationality.

Popular appeal

He wanted his appeal to go far beyond both Britain and Canada; he aimed to attain popularity the world over as heavyweight champion. In March 1991, Lewis executed a brilliant seven-round demolition job on Gary Mason to take the British title, in what was only his 15th professional fight. A year later, he claimed his first world crown, in somewhat farcical circumstances.

Lewis was one of three top contenders for Evander Holyfield's title, along with Donovan "Razor" Ruddock and Riddick Bowe. A deal was done in which Lewis would fight Ruddock, with the winner to meet whoever came out on top in the Holyfield-Bowe contest. Lewis duly knocked Ruddock out in two rounds in London, on October 31, 1992. He then sat back and waited to see who he would face, the Holyfield-Bowe clash taking place two weeks later. Bowe won a unanimous points decision, then promptly reneged on the agreement and refused to fight Lewis. The WBC responded by stripping Bowe of their title, and Bowe famously showed what he thought of that decision by depositing the belt in question into a trash can in full view of the cameras. When it was salvaged from the rubbish, the WBC awarded it to Lewis. It was all very unsatisfactory: shades of Ernie Terrell in the 1960s and John Tate in the 1970s, both of whom were installed as champions by default, without throwing a punch.

Defeated by McCall

After successfully defending his title against Tony Tucker and Frank Bruno, Lewis suffered a surprising reverse against Oliver McCall. Lewis may have been disappointed by that September 1994 defeat, though some purists may have regarded the title as tainted goods anyway. Riddick Bowe certainly did. When he made his infamous dustbin gesture, he emphasised the view that championships could only be won and lost in the ring, not by political shenanigans involving men in suits. Lewis was the innocent party in all this. He wished for

nothing more than to be given a chance to fight for any title that was going. He was certainly keen to get into the ring with Frank Bruno, after the latter took the WBC crown from McCall. But Frank took one look at Lewis and another at Mike Tyson, and there was hardly a decision is to be made. A second meeting with a hungry Tyson on the comeback trail was where the big bucks lay, and Lewis's hopes were again thwarted. He finally got his chance to do battle for a coveted belt in February 1997. His opponent was once again Oliver McCall, and the prize at stake was once again the WBC title, which McCall had regained. This time Lewis made no mistake, with a fifth-round technical knockout.

Second reign

Lewis's second tenure as WBC champion thus had the stamp of approval that his first reign lacked. It was only one title, though. The other two major honours, and WBA and IBF titles, lay in the hands of a rejuvenated Evander Holyfield. The "Real Deal" had shocked everybody by halting Mike Tyson's comeback in its tracks, taking Iron Mike's WBA crown in the process. He followed that up with a revenge victory over IBF holder Michael Moorer.

By 1999, the world was desperate to see an undisputed champion for the first time since Holyfield's first reign of the early 1990s. The unification fight took place at Madison Square Garden on March 13, 1999. The fight went the full distance, and was something of a disappointment. Nevertheless, by common consent Lewis had done enough to get the decision. South African judge Stanley Christoudoulou was part of that consensus, scoring the fight 116-113 in Lewis's favour. England's Larry O'Connell had them level at 115 points-all. It was the scoring of the third judge, Eugenia Williams, which was met with utter incredulity. She had Holyfield the winner by 115-113. A split decision - particularly such a controversial one - meant that everything was on hold until Holyfield-Lewis 2 could take place. Eight months later, the two men duly stepped into the ring to do it all over again.

Unanimous verdict over Holyfield

If an injustice was done in the first encounter, amends were made second time round. Lewis won a unanimous points decision, and had thus added the WBA and IBF titles to his WBC crown. Holyfield had been the heavyweight of the 1990s, but his era was now effectively over. Lewis had the world at his feet. Three successful defences followed in 2000. Michael Grant was blown away in two rounds in April; Francois Botha lasted until the 11th in July; and David Tua took the champion all the way but went down on points in November. Lewis thus went into 2001 with three successful defences under his belt, yet he had still

managed to lose one of his titles. The WBA had gone to court to strip him of their crown in April 2000.When Lewis opened his 2001 campaign by taking on Hasim Rahman in April, only the WBC and IBF titles were at stake. That hardly mattered. Lewis was the undisputed champion, and "The Rock" knew that was the honour which was up for grabs. And grab it Rahman certainly did.

Lennox Lewis

Born: London, United Kingdom 2 September 1965
Height: 6'5" Weight: 245 lbs.
World Heavyweight Champion: 1992-1994 1997-1999 1999-2001 2001-
Record: Won 40 (31 KOs)   Lost 2   Drawn 1
Canadian Olympic gold medal 1988. Commonwealth gold medal 1986

Above: Lennox Lewis on his way to victory inside two rounds against South Africa's Francois Botha in July 2000.

Opposite above: Rahman and Lewis square up in a pre-fight press conference.

Opposite below: Frank Maloney and Lennox Lewis.

Right: Untroubled but untested. Tyson didn't have to break sweat to dispose of Lou Savarese after 38 seconds. The clamour for a showdown with Lewis soon became deafening.

Hasim Rahman

Nickname:	"The Rock"
Born:	Baltimore, USA November 7 1972
Height:	6' 2¹/₂"
Weight:	220 lbs.
World Heavyweight Champion:	2001
Record:	Won 35 (29 KOs) Lost 2 Drawn 0

Above: Lennox Lewis in training for the rematch with Hasim Rahman. Lewis blamed his April 2001 defeat on a lucky punch. Others said he underestimated his opponent and underprepared for the high-altitude conditions in South Africa

Opposite: Don King diplomatically raises the hands of both Rahman and Lewis as the two sign for the return contest. Both men were confident that their arm would be raised at the end of the fight, which was to take place in Las Vegas on November 17.

Hasim Rahman

World Heavyweight Champion: 2001

When it was announced that Lennox Lewis would open his 2001 campaign by fighting Hasim Rahman, most people's response was: Hasim who? Rahman was no household name, not even among boxing aficionados. The most prepossessing thing about this Baltimore heavyweight was his nickname: "The Rock". His ring record wasn't quite so impressive. Rahman had begun boxing at the age of 20, turning professional after stringing together 10 wins at amateur level.

Rahman was regarded as someone who would provide a good payday without posing a serious threat, a lucrative stop-off for Lewis en route to a showdown against Tyson. The Lewis-Rahman fight turned out to be anything but a routine defence. Johannesburg, April 21, 2001 produced boxing's biggest shock since "Buster" Douglas's win over Tyson a decade earlier. The 20-1 underdog landed a bomb in the fifth round, and the shock waves reverberated round the world - including the desks of sports journalists who hadn't thought the fight worth attending. Lewis was stunned. He glossed over the fact that he had undertrained, and that he had interrupted his preparation to take a cameo role in the film Ocean's Eleven. According to the now ex-champion, it was just a lucky punch which caught him off balance. He even thought the referee had

counted too quickly. While the recriminations started in earnest in the Lewis camp, Rahman celebrated his victory. There was no luck as far as he was concerned. The referee could have counted to 20 and it would have made no difference. The world now had to sit up and take notice of the new heavyweight champion. A month after his victory, Rahman signed up with Don King, and arrangements were made for a fight with David Izon in August. Lewis wasn't having any of that. He filed a lawsuit and won his right to a rematch. That cranked up the friction between the two men, as did a celebrated spat on television, when Lewis took exception to a comment by Rahman questioning his sexuality. Yes, this was all about hyping up the return and putting backsides on seats. But for Lewis the needle gave him added focus for their second meeting, on Nov 17. Rahman was talking another good fight. "Lewis is underestimating me again. I'll knock him out again." So confident was "The Rock" that he turned down a big-money contract before the Lewis fight, preferring to cut an even more lucrative deal for himself afterwards as a free agent - assuming he was still champion, of course. He warned viewers not to go to the bathroom or put the kettle on, as the fight would be explosive and could finish at any moment. He was right.

Lennox Lewis

World Heavyweight Champion: 2001-

What Lennox Lewis dismissed as a "lucky punch" by Hasim Rahman could have had catastrophic consequences for the man from West Ham. The problem certainly wasn't financial. Lewis had already earned more than £60 million, making him Britain's highest paid sportsmen. But in his mid-30s, Lewis knew that he was one more defeat from retirement.

Lewis, however, gave a top-notch display, dominating from the outset and capping it off with a scintillating left-right combination which laid "The Rock" out for the count in the fourth round. Rahman's reign had lasted 209 days, four days less than Leon Spinks. Lewis found himself in the exalted company of Muhammad Ali and Evander Holyfield as the only men to win the heavyweight crown three times.

Lewis's thoughts immediately turned to a proposed April 2002 meeting with Tyson. Lewis filed a suit claiming a mid-January fight between Tyson and Mercer wouldn't allow enough time to promote his clash with Iron Mike three months later. Lewis got his way, and Tyson was not best pleased at the champion's interference in his affairs. He pointed out that he had stood aside as the WBC's No 1 challenger to allow the second Lewis-Rahman fight to go ahead. This contre-temps ensured that the ill-feeling

between the two warriors was simmering nicely. It was soon in danger of boiling over when Tyson made some wildly intemperate remarks about what injuries he would like to inflict on Lewis, and some disgraceful ones involving the champion's family. No doubt this was partly down to the usual pre-fight hype that is now de rigeur. But there was also a tangible feeling that this time it was personal. The touch paper was lit. Everybody stood well back and waited for the fireworks.

Opposite: Las Vegas, November 17, 2001. Lennox Lewis lands a knockout blow to the jaw of Hasim Rahman in the fourth round to regain his WBC and IBF titles. Lewis was particularly pleased that he KOd Rahman one round earlier than "The Rock" had finished him seven months earlier.

Below: Two of only three heavyweights in history to win the world title on three occasions meet up at the BBC Sports Personality of the Year awards. The other member of the elite trio is Evander Holyfield.

Lewis and Tyson set date for showdown

Above and left: Mike Tyson works out with trainer Stacy McKinley in preparation for his fight with Lennox Lewis. After much speculation and controversy about the date and venue, the meeting of the two top heavyweights in the world was set to take place on 8 June in Memphis, Tennessee. Tyson was in belligerent and confident mood. 'I'm ready to get it on and crush this guy's skull.I want to show them who the real champion is, the best fighter in the era.'

Opposite above left and below: Lennox Lewis at a press conference for the fight as the big day draws near.

Opposite top right: Lewis relaxes by playing chess with local school children in Memphis.

Boxing's last "misfit"

Below and opposite below: Lennox Lewis, during training for his showdown with Tyson. Lewis says he is 'ready to rid boxing of its last misfit'.

Opposite top: Lennox Lewis, in training with Emanuel Steward.

Left: Mike Tyson, during a training session. Trainer McKinley was in confident mood about his man: 'This guy's going to give 100% of his body. Mike's going to fight entertainingly with everything he's got.' Because of fears that Tyson might go berserk as he did at their joint-press conference in January, the weigh-in was organised so that the fighters would not meet face to face. Lewis appeared at midday while Tyson weighed in at three pm.

Tyson humbled by Lewis

Opposite: Lewis weighed in one stone heavier than Tyson.

Left: Yellow-shirted security guards linked arms diagonally across the ring to keep the contestants apart all the way through the introductions and up to the first bell.

Below: Lewis triumphant. In the third minute of the eighth round a vicious right from Lewis put Tyson on the canvas. Tyson won only the first of the eight rounds, Lewis dominating the fight from then on. Lewis landed 193 blows on his way to victory; Tyson connected just 49 times. Tyson was uncharacteristically generous in defeat. 'I don't know how I could ever beat this man if he keeps fighting like this.'

Former heavyweight champion George Foreman went further: 'He's knocked out everybody. There has never been a heavyweight this good.' Lewis announced he would take a few weeks before deciding about his future. 'What else is there for me to prove? I've proved everything.'

World Heavyweight Champions

John L. Sullivan 1885-1892

James J. Corbett 1892-1897

Bob Fitzsimmons 1897-1899

James J Jeffries 1899-1905

Marvin Hart 1905-1906

Tommy Burns 1906-1908

Jack Johnson 1908-1915

Jess Willard 1915-1919

Jack Dempsey 1919-1926

Gene Tunney 1926-1928

Max Schmeling 1930-1932

Jack Sharkey 1932-1933

Primo Carnera 1933-1934

Max Baer 1934-1935

James J Braddock 1935-1937

Joe Louis 1937-1949

Ezzard Charles 1949-1951

Jersey Joe Walcott 1951-1952

Rocky Marciano 1952-1956

Floyd Patterson 1956-1959

Ingemar Johansson 1959-1960

Floyd Patterson 1960-1962

Sonny Liston 1962-1964

Muhammad Ali 1964-1970

Joe Frazier 1970-1973

George Foreman 1973-1974

Muhammad Ali 1974-1978

Leon Spinks 1978

Muhammad Ali 1978-1979

Larry Holmes 1979-1985

Michael Spinks 1985-1988

Mike Tyson 1988-1990

James "Buster" Douglas 1990

Evander Holyfield 1990-1992

Riddick Bowe 1992-1993

Evander Holyfield 1993-1994

Michael Moorer 1994

George Foreman 1994-1995

Evander Holyfield 1996-1999

Lennox Lewis 1999-2001

Hasim Rahman 2001

Lennox Lewis 2001-

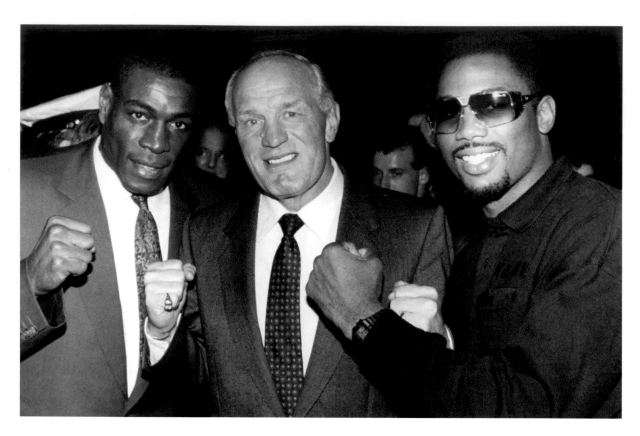

Best of British

Henry Cooper (centre) dominated British heavyweight boxing in the 1960s and will forever be remembered for the punch that flattened Cassius Clay in 1963.
Frank Bruno (left) proved he was more than just a great entertainer and decent contender by taking the WBC crown in 1995.
Lennox Lewis (right) secured his place in the record books with his victory over Hasim Rahman in November 2001, becoming only the third man in history to win the title on three separate occasions.